ULTIMATE BOOK OF
MODERN
Farmhouse Plans

CRE▲TIVE
HOMEOWNER®

Book content provided by Design America, Inc., St. Louis, MO.

Current Printing (last digit)
10 9 8 7 6 5 4 3 2 1

Printed in China

Ultimate Book of Modern Farmhouse Plans
ISBN-13: 978-1-58011-870-5

CREATIVE HOMEOWNER®
www.creativehomeowner.com

Creative Homeowner books are distributed by

Fox Chapel Publishing
903 Square Street
Mount Joy, PA 17552
www.FoxChapelPublishing.com

Library of Congress Control Number: 2022937282

Contents

Top to bottom: Plan #F11-139D-0090 on page 28; Plan #F11-101D-0144 on page 260; Plan #F11-123D-0056 on page 200; Plan #F11-101D-0149 on page 37; Plan #F11-051D-0977 on page 141; Plan #F11-155D-0070 on page 124.

3

Getting Started:

what's the right **plan** for you?

Choosing a house design is exciting, but can be a difficult task. Many factors play a role in what home plan is best for you and your family. To help you get started, we have pinpointed some of the major factors to consider when searching for your dream home. Take the time to evaluate your family's needs and you will have an easier time sorting through all of the house designs offered in this book.

Budget is the first thing to consider. Many items take part in this budget, from ordering the blueprints to the last doorknob purchased. When you find the perfect house plan, visit houseplansandmore.com and get a cost-to-build estimate to ensure that the finished home will be within your cost range. A cost-to-build report is a detailed summary that gives you the total cost to build a specific home in the zip code where you're wanting to build. It is interactive allowing you to adjust labor and material costs, and it's created on demand when ordered so all pricing is up-to-date. This valuable tool will help you know how much your dream home will cost before you buy plans (see page 282 for more information).

Make a list!

Experts in the field suggest that the best way to determine your needs is to begin by listing everything you like or dislike about your current home.

Family lifestyle After your budget is deciphered, you need to assess you and your family's lifestyle needs. Think about the stage of life you are in now, and what stages you will be going through in the future. Ask yourself questions to figure out how much room you need now and if you will need room for expansion. Are you married? Do you have children? How many children do you plan on having? Are you an empty-nester? How long do you plan to live in this home?

Incorporate into your planning any frequent guests you may have, including elderly parents, grandchildren or adult children who may live with you.

Does your family entertain a lot? If so, think about the rooms you will need to do so. Will you need both formal and informal spaces? Do you need a gourmet kitchen? Do you need a game room and/or a wet bar?

Floor plan layouts When looking through these home plans, imagine yourself walking through the house. Consider the flow from the entry to the living, sleeping and gathering areas. Does the layout ensure privacy for the master bedroom? Does the garage enter near the kitchen for easy unloading? Does the placement of the windows provide enough privacy from any neighboring properties? Do you plan on using furniture you already have? Will this furniture fit in the appropriate rooms? When you find a plan you want to purchase, be sure to picture yourself actually living in it.

Exterior spaces With many different Modern Farmhouse plans throughout, flip through these pages and find which Modern Farmhouse home design appeals to you the most and think about the neighborhood in which you plan to build. Also, think about how the house will fit on your site. Picture the landscaping you want to add to the lot. Using your imagination is key when choosing a home plan.

Choosing a house design can be an intimidating experience. Asking yourself these questions before you get started on the search will help you through the process. With our large selection of sizes and styles, we are certain you will find your dream home in this book.

10 steps to building
your dream home

1 talk to a lender

If you plan to obtain a loan in order to build your new home, then it's best to find out first how much you can get approved for before selecting a home design. Knowing the financial information before you start looking for land or a home will keep you from selecting something out of your budget and turning a great experience into a major disappointment. Financing the home you plan to build is somewhat different than financing the purchase of an existing house. You're going to need thousands of dollars for land, labor, and materials. Chances are, you're going to have to borrow most of it. Therefore, you will probably need to obtain a construction loan. This is a short-term loan to pay for building your house. When the house is completed, the loan is paid off in full, usually out of the proceeds from your long-term mortgage loan.

2 determine needs

Selecting the right home plan for your needs and lifestyle requires a lot of thought. Your new home is an investment, so you should consider not only your current needs, but also your future requirements. Versatility and the potential for converting certain areas to other uses could be an important factor later on. So, although a home office may seem unnecessary now, in years to come, the idea may seem ideal. Home plans that include flex spaces or bonus rooms can really adapt to your needs in the future.

3 choose a homesite

The site for your new home will have a definite impact on the design you select. It's a good idea to select a home that will complement your site. This will save you time and money when building. Or, you can then modify a design to specifically accommodate your site. However, it will most likely make your home construction more costly than selecting a home plan suited for your lot right from the start. For example, if your land slopes, a walk-out basement works perfectly. If it's wooded, or has a lake in the back, an atrium ranch home is a perfect style to take advantage of surrounding backyard views.

Some important criteria to consider when choosing a site:

- Improvements will have to be made including utilities, walks and driveways
- Convenience of the lot to work, school, shops, etc.
- Zoning requirements and property tax amounts
- Soil conditions at your future site
- Make sure the person or firm that sells you the land owns it free and clear

4 select a home plan

We've chosen the "best of the best" of the Modern Farmhouse plans found at houseplansandmore.com to be featured in this book. With over 18,000 home plans from the best architects and designers across the country, this book includes the best variety of styles and sizes to suit the needs and tastes of a broad spectrum of homeowners.

5 get the cost to build

If you feel you have found "the" home, then before taking the step of purchasing house plans, order an estimated cost-to-build report for the exact zip code where you plan to build. Requesting this custom cost report created specifically for you will help educate you on all costs associated with building your new home. Simply order this report and gain knowledge of the material and labor cost associated with the home you love. Not only does the report allow you to choose the quality of the materials, you can also select options in every aspect of the project from lot condition to contractor fees. This report will allow you to successfully manage your construction budget in all areas, clearly see where the majority of the costs lie, and save you money from start to finish.

A cost-to-build report will determine the overall cost of your new home including these 5 major expense categories:

- Land
- Foundation
- Materials
- General Contractor's fee - Some rules-of-thumb that you may find useful are: (a) the total labor cost will generally run a little higher than your total material cost, but it's not unusual for a builder or general contractor to charge 15-20% of the combined cost for managing the overall project.
- Site improvements - don't forget to add in the cost of your site improvements such as utilities, driveway, sidewalks, landscaping, etc.

6 hire a contractor

If you're inexperienced in construction, you'll probably want to hire a general contractor to manage the project. If you do not know a reputable general contractor, begin your search by contacting your local Home Builders Association to get references. Many states require building contractors to be licensed. If this is the case in your state, its licensing board is another referral source. Finding a reputable, quality-minded contractor is a key factor in ensuring that your new home is well constructed and is finished on time and within budget. It can be a smart decision to discuss the plan you like with your builder prior to ordering plans. They can guide you into choosing the right type of plan package option especially if you intend on doing some customizing to the design.

7 customizing

Sometimes your general contractor may want to be the one who makes the modifications you want to the home

you've selected. But, sometimes they want to receive the plans ready to build. That is why we offer home plan modification services. Please see page 285 for specific information on the customizing process and how to get a free quote on the changes you want to make to a home before you buy the plans.

8 order plans

If you've found the home and are ready to order blueprints, we recommend ordering the PDF file format, which offers the most flexibility. A PDF file format will be emailed to you when you order, and it includes a copyright release from the designer, meaning you have the legal right to make changes to the plan if necessary as well as print out as many

copies of the plan as you need for building the home one-time. You will be happy to have your blueprints saved electronically so they can easily be shared with your contractor, subcontractors, lender and local building officials. We do, however, offer several different types of plan package depending on your needs, so please refer to page 283 for all plan options available and choose the best one for your particular situation.

Another helpful component in the building process that is available for many of the house plans in this book is a material list. A material list includes not only a detailed list of materials, but it also indicates where various cuts of lumber and other building components are to be used. This will save your general contractor significant time and money since they won't have to create this list before building begins. If a material list is available for a home, it is shown on the home plan index on pages 276-279 in this book.

9 order materials

You can order materials yourself, or have your contractor do it. Nevertheless, in order to thoroughly enjoy your new home you will want to personally select many of the materials that go into its construction. Today, home improvement stores offer a wide variety of quality building products. Only you can decide what specific types of windows, cabinets, bath fixtures, etc. will make your new home yours. Spend time early on in the construction process looking at the materials and products available.

10 move in

With careful planning and organization, your new home will be built on schedule and ready for your move-in date. Be sure to have all of your important documents in place for the closing of your new home and then you'll be ready to move in and start living your dream.

Browse the pages of The Ultimate Book of Modern Farmhouse Plans and discover 350 popular and stylish Modern Farmhouse home designs offered in a wide range of sizes. Whether you love a more rustic or a sleek design, there is a Modern Farmhouse style here for everyone featuring all of the amenities homeowners want in a new home today. Start your search right now for the perfect Modern Farmhouse!

what is a **modern farmhouse**?

Gone are the days of the cookie-cutter ranch homes of the 1960s, today's homeowners are looking for a unique, uncluttered and simple approach to residential architecture that pairs down the floor plan to include only the bare necessities, and relies on texture rather than color to create its iconic style. These concepts are the heart and soul of the Modern Farmhouse.

Many architects and designers alike blame home and garden, and fixer upper television shows for the advent of this unique residential style, but no matter who you credit for its creation, the Modern Farmhouse is a sensation sweeping the nation, and everyone looking to build a new home is falling in love with its style and undeniable personality. But, before you just select a Modern Farmhouse plan, do you know what makes a Modern Farmhouse truly what it is? There are several key characteristics that make a Modern Farmhouse all its own.

Exterior

gables & roof pitches
Modern Farmhouse style uses a gable roof in a steeper pitch than a typical home built in the last two or three decades. Perhaps it's a popular feature because of its ability to create higher, more dramatic vaulted ceilings, in turn, opening up the interior spaces and making them feel larger. When steep gables aren't being used, then a flat roof is often added to the mix.

exterior finishes
Although simple in overall design, subtle texture really takes a prominent role in the look and feel of a Modern Farmhouse. Board and batten (also called clapboard siding), vertical and horizontal siding, a steel roof, and even a small amount of brick or stone combine to create a Modern Farmhouse that feels fresh and new, yet still feels like a modern-day version of its former timeless self.

color
Most often white is the color of choice for the exterior, but gray and other neutral colors are also popular for both interior and exterior. Black and natural wood also have a role in the finished look. Color takes a supporting role to all of the texture provided by the various siding styles being used.

unique exterior footprint
Farmhouses of the past were usually rectangular in shape and built simply in order to quickly create a dwelling for a family ready to work their land. Construction had to be done around the growing cycles, so the design was modest and straightforward. Today's Modern Farmhouses still have a common simplicity similar to their past counterparts, yet many have varied roof lines, an L-shape, or the look of multiple buildings, which promotes additional natural light in the interior because there is more exterior wall space for extra windows and doors.

large porches
Often referred to as "outdoor living spaces," large front and back covered porches are common and an important feature offering additional living space for dining, entertaining, or relaxing. Add a sleek porch swing, or updated rocking chair in black, or a vibrant color and these porches are less "Grandma's house," and more current with the time.

windows
As discussed, windows are an important design element. Typically, double-hung and seen with black framing that stands out against the stark white exterior and interior finishes, windows play an important role in keeping the home bright, friendly and open. Traditional double-hung style keep the design grounded to its original roots.

Interior

simple & minimal

A Modern Farmhouse has a laid-back personality that's bright and inviting, and promotes a simple lifestyle. Homeowners want their homes to be a refuge from the clutter in their daily lives. Between traffic, email, social media, and other constant distractions, a Modern Farmhouse is meant to be a peaceful, inviting retreat, somewhat like a sanctuary that shelters its owners from the outside noise. Even the floor plans are designed to maintain a sense of openness with generally very few walls. Large windows for added natural light, and large, open spaces for effortless daily living including even spacious mud and laundry rooms, which are quite popular. Think clean and functional.

color palette

Neutral by nature, the interior of the Modern Farmhouse mimics the exterior by sticking to a neutral color palette that's bright and airy. In addition to the most popular color, which is white; soft gray, beige and blue are often used to promote a sense of calmness.

architectural interest

With the popularity of using reclaimed wood and other architectural elements from buildings of the past, it makes perfect sense that Modern Farmhouse style incorporates these unique features. From rustic timber beams and rafters, to the current favorite wall paneling affectionately called, "Ship Lap," although the overall color palette may be white or neutral, rustic elements are added for architectural interest. Even steel and polished concrete have found a place in this style because of their industrial look and durability.

kitchen design

A Modern Farmhouse kitchen is the heart of the home. It is a place where family will eat, socialize and relax. Typically, these kitchens are open to the surrounding living spaces, have a neutral color palette, which of course is usually white. They incorporate several windows, Shaker-style cabinets, white marble or quartz countertops, subway tile, Industrial-style light fixtures, a large island for cooking and casual dining, and open shelving with almost-Utilitarian dishes and glassware. Think uncomplicated, and less "your grandmother's flowery china pattern."

home decor

Home accessories are not matching, more complementary, but with character. Modern Farmhouse décor uses carefully placed, thoughtful accessories that add personality to a space. The decor mixes sleek, modern accessories with timeless ones. Artwork may be the one thing that adds a special pop of color. The majority of the texture comes from throw rugs, and the fabrics used on the sofas and chairs. Bold light fixtures, and natural wood floors are a must, and if you're looking for a sleeker vibe, then steel, wrought iron, and other metals can be added to create a more Industrial feel.

barn doors

Besides being a stylish space-saving option, barn-style doors are a rustic addition when using natural wood, or paint them white and add black hardware for a cleaner look. Either way, "barn doors" are a staple in Modern Farmhouses and offer plenty of character while taking up less space.

If you're enthralled with Modern Farmhouse style, you are not alone. This style is the darling of residential architecture today and it's easy to see why. It combines so many wonderful features to create something so utterly simple and effortless. Thoughtful, subdued, smart, and functional have all met their match with the invention of the Modern Farmhouse, and we think it was about time.

Plan #F11-032D-1067

Dimensions: 66' W x 50' D
Heated Sq. Ft.: 3,599
Bedrooms: 3   **Bathrooms:** 3
Exterior Walls: 2" x 6"
Foundation: Crawl space standard; floating slab, monolithic slab or basement for an additional fee
See index for more information

Images provided by designer/architect

Special Features

- Symmetrically pleasing to the eye, this Modern Farmhouse design is truly a stunner
- The front entry has a large laundry room to the left and a quiet study/office/den to the right
- The vaulted dining and living rooms are open to one another with the kitchen just mere steps away
- The kitchen includes a large island and a walk-in pantry
- The second floor has a huge game room over the garage
- The master suite is special with a unique walk-in closet leading to a private bath and there's also a private second floor balcony only accessible from the master suite
- 1-car front entry garage

First Floor
1,747 sq. ft.

Second Floor
1,852 sq. ft.

Plan #F11-123D-0109

Dimensions:	56' W x 64' D
Heated Sq. Ft.:	2,810
Bedrooms: 3	**Bathrooms:** 2
Exterior Walls:	2" x 6"

Foundation: Slab standard; crawl space, basement or walk-out basement for an additional fee

See index for more information

Special Features

- A Modern Farmhouse home design that channels barn-style living in style
- Enter the vaulted great room and discover an open-concept kitchen, dining area and great room combination with a cathedral ceiling and loft with railing above
- A split bedroom floor plan promises extra privacy for the homeowner
- A private office near the front entry is a handy extra feature
- A mud room with a bench and lockers connects the garage with the dining area
- 1-car side entry garage, and a 2-car rear entry garage

© Copyright by designer/architect

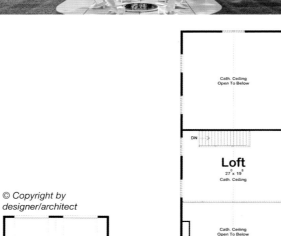

First Floor
2,297 sq. ft.

Second Floor
513 sq. ft.

Loft
27 x 19

Cath. Ceiling
Open To Below

Images provided by designer/architect

Plan #F11-011D-0657

Dimensions: 26' W x 34' D
Heated Sq. Ft.: 1,394
Bedrooms: 3   **Bathrooms:** 2½
Exterior Walls: 2" x 6"
Foundation: Crawl space or slab standard; basement for an additional fee

See index for more information

Special Features

- Stylish Modern Farmhouse design is a great size open floor plan, perfect for today's family
- The living room and dining area are open to one another as well as the kitchen with island
- All three bedrooms are on the second floor for convenience and privacy
- The laundry room is centrally located on the first floor

MASTER
13/0 X 12/8

6/4 X 5/2

LIN

DN

BR. 2
12/0 X 10/6 +/-

BR. 3
10/4 X 10/6

Second Floor
680 sq. ft.

© Copyright by designer/architect

PATIO

12/8 X 12/8 +/-
(9' CLG.)

DINING
9/6 X 10/6 +/-
(9' CLG.)

LIN

REF

STOR

D

W

PAN

LIVING
15/0 X 14/6 +/-
(9' CLG.)

UP

COVERED
PORCH
22/0 X 6/0

First Floor
714 sq. ft.

Plan #F11-139D-0106

Dimensions: 40' W x 65'6" D
Heated Sq. Ft.: 2,402
Bedrooms: 3 **Bathrooms:** 2½
Exterior Walls: 2" x 6"
Foundation: Slab standard; crawl space, basement, daylight basement or walk-out basement for an additional fee

See index for more information

Special Features

- This stunning Modern Farmhouse has tremendous curb appeal thanks to its large windows and multiple gables
- Enter the foyer and find a private home office on the right and straight ahead the vaulted family room and open kitchen
- The master suite is located on the first floor for convenience and features a large bath with a roomy walk-in closet
- The second floor has two spacious bedrooms and a full bath
- 2-car side entry garage

UNFINISHED
24'-3" x 10'-2"

OPT. ESPACE

LIN

BATH
8'-0" x 9'-5"

WIC

BEDROOM #3
11'-9" x 14'-11"

WIC

BEDROOM #2
12'-11" x 16'-4"

Second Floor
682 sq. ft.

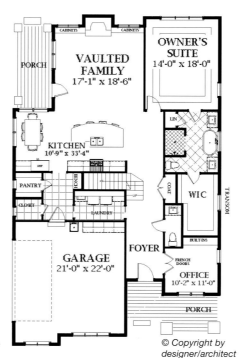

CABINETS   CABINETS

PORCH

VAULTED FAMILY
17'-1" x 18'-6"

OWNER'S SUITE
14'-0" x 18'-0"

LIN

KITCHEN
10'-9" x 33'-4"

COAT

WIC

TRANSOM

PANTRY

BENCH

UP

CLOSET

LAUNDRY

FOYER

BUILT-INS

GARAGE
21'-0" x 22'-0"

FRENCH DOORS

OFFICE
10'-2" x 11'-0"

PORCH

First Floor
1,720 sq. ft.

© Copyright by designer/architect

Images provided by designer/architect

Plan #F11-101D-0093

Dimensions:	76'9" W x 70'6" D
Heated Sq. Ft.:	2,615
Bonus Sq. Ft.:	2,274
Bedrooms: 2	**Bathrooms:** 2½
Exterior Walls:	2" x 6"
Foundation:	Basement

See index for more information

Special Features

- The great room and kitchen combine creating a central gathering place in this home
- Tucked away in the rear is a cozy hearth room for peace and quiet
- What an impressive master bedroom with covered deck access, a large walk-in closet and a bath with a corner freestanding tub, a separate shower and a double bowl vanity
- The optional lower level has an additional 2,274 square feet of living area and features a home theater, a Lego® room, a living room, billiards space, a wet bar, two bedrooms, two full baths, and a half bath
- 3-car front entry garage

© Copyright by designer/architect

First Floor
2,615 sq. ft.

Optional Lower Level
2,274 sq. ft.

Images provided by designer/architect

Plan #F11-028D-0097

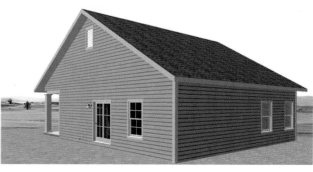

Dimensions:	60' W x 53' D
Heated Sq. Ft.:	1,908
Bedrooms: 3	**Bathrooms:** 2
Exterior Walls:	2" x 6"
Foundation:	Slab

See index for more information

Special Features

- This smartly sized farmhouse design has the bedrooms separated for privacy and a centrally located dining room, great when entertaining
- Enter and find two secondary bedrooms that share a bath
- The kitchen has a corner walk-in pantry, plenty of counterspace and cabinets for storage
- A vaulted dining room bridges the kitchen and great room
- The master bedroom is tucked in the back of the home offering peace and quiet
- 2-car front entry garage

Images provided by designer/architect

houseplansandmore.com

Plan #F11-091D-0535

Dimensions: 51' W x 59' D
Heated Sq. Ft.: 3,879
Bedrooms: 4   **Bathrooms:** 3½
Exterior Walls: 2" x 6"
Foundation: Basement standard; slab, crawl space or walk-out basement for an additional fee

See index for more information

Special Features

- Every so often a home comes around that truly distinguishes itself from the rest, and this is the one
- Step into the warm and inviting foyer and find a functional pocket office to the left
- The formal dining room connects to the kitchen via a stylish butler's pantry
- The vaulted and open kitchen enjoys a huge island that anchors the space and adds casual dining space that overlooks the great room's fireplace
- A sunny breakfast nook enjoys access to the screen porch, which has backyard views and an outdoor fireplace
- All of the bedrooms can be found on the second floor along with an open loft area, and a laundry room
- 2-car front entry garage

Second Floor
2,162 sq. ft.

© Copyright by designer/architect

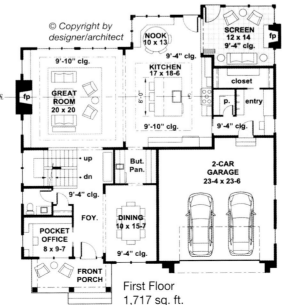

First Floor
1,717 sq. ft.

Images provided by designer/architect

Plan #F11-032D-1123

Dimensions: 44' W x 46'6" D
Heated Sq. Ft.: 2,496
Bonus Sq. Ft.: 1,126
Bedrooms: 4   **Bathrooms:** 2½
Exterior Walls: 2" x 6"
Foundation: Basement standard; crawl space, floating slab, monolithic slab or walk-out basement for an additional fee

See index for more information

Special Features

- The first floor has an open layout with a kitchen featuring an island and walk-in pantry
- An attractive and convenient mud room enjoys a built-in bench seat under a trio of windows
- The two-story living room has an open feel thanks to all of the windows
- The optional lower level has an additional 1,126 square feet of living area
- 2-car front entry garage

Second Floor
1,370 sq. ft.

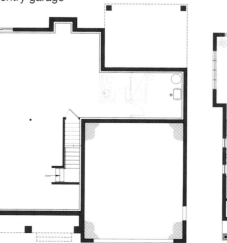

Optional Lower Level
1,126 sq. ft.

© Copyright by designer/architect

First Floor
1,126 sq. ft.

Images provided by designer/architect

houseplansandmore.com

Plan #F11-101D-0089

Dimensions:	70' W x 77'9" D
Heated Sq. Ft.:	2,509
Bonus Sq. Ft.:	1,645
Bedrooms: 4	**Bathrooms:** 2½
Exterior Walls:	2" x 6"
Foundation:	Basement

See index for more information

Special Features

- The wrap-around porch welcomes you into this beautiful airy home designed with a popular Modern Farmhouse flair
- Expansive windows bring so much natural light into every room
- The desirable split bedroom layout of this home is perfect for families
- The dining, kitchen and great room are all open, creating one large open family area
- With a walk-in closet, dual sinks and generously sized bedroom, the master suite makes for a perfect place to retire for the evening
- The optional lower level has an additional 1,645 square feet of living area including a recreation room with a wet bar, two bedrooms and a bath
- 3-car side entry garage

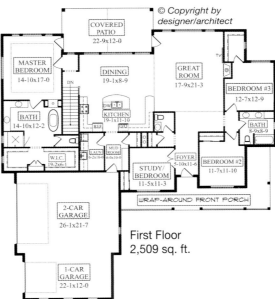

© Copyright by designer/architect

First Floor
2,509 sq. ft.

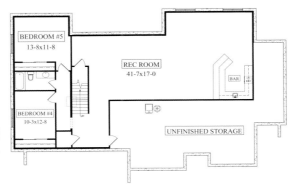

Optional
Lower Level
1,645 sq. ft.

Images provided by designer/architect

Plan #F11-011D-0662

Dimensions: 76' W x 62' D
Heated Sq. Ft.: 2,460
Bedrooms: 3   **Bathrooms:** 2½
Exterior Walls: 2" x 6"
Foundation: Crawl space or slab standard; basement for an additional fee

See index for more information

Special Features

- The covered front porch welcomes you into the interior where you will find a formal dining room right off the foyer
- The vaulted great room enjoys direct access to the amazing vaulted outdoor living area with a fireplace, an outdoor kitchen and a sunny patio
- The bayed breakfast nook right off the kitchen will enjoy views of the outdoors
- The private master suite has a posh bath and a spacious walk-in closet with direct laundry room access
- Two additional bedrooms and a bath complete this home
- 2-car side entry garage

Images provided by designer/architect

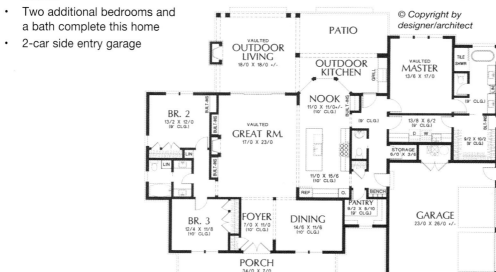

© Copyright by designer/architect

Plan #F11-028D-0112

Dimensions: 56' W x 52' D
Heated Sq. Ft.: 1,611
Bedrooms: 3   **Bathrooms:** 2
Exterior Walls: 2" x 6"
Foundation: Crawl space or slab, please specify when ordering
See index for more information

Special Features

- This Craftsman one-story home has timeless farmhouse appeal
- The cozy great room with fireplace has built-ins on each side of the fireplace for added storage and style
- The kitchen and dining area enjoy a snack bar, great when entertaining in the great room
- The master bedroom enjoys its privacy, and its own bath and walk-in closet
- Two additional bedrooms share the full bath between them
- 2-car side entry garage

Images provided by designer/architect

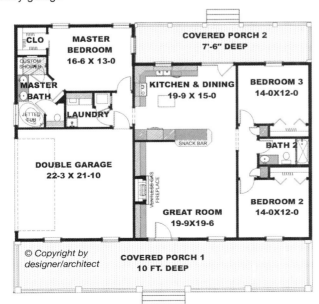

CLO
MASTER BEDROOM 16-6 X 13-0
CUSTOM SHOWER
MASTER BATH
JETTED TUB   LAUNDRY
COVERED PORCH 2 7'-6" DEEP
KITCHEN & DINING 19-9 X 15-0
BEDROOM 3 14-0X12-0
SNACK BAR
BATH 2
DOUBLE GARAGE 22-3 X 21-10
VENT-FREE GAS FIREPLACE
GREAT ROOM 19-9X19-6
BEDROOM 2 14-0X12-0
© Copyright by designer/architect
COVERED PORCH 1 10 FT. DEEP

Second Floor
1,011 sq. ft.

Plan #F11-032D-1143

Dimensions: 37' W x 38' D
Heated Sq. Ft.: 1,891
Bonus Sq. Ft.: 880
Bedrooms: 3 **Bathrooms:** 2½
Exterior Walls: 2" x 6"
Foundation: Basement standard; crawl space, floating slab or monolithic slab for an additional fee

See index for more information

Images provided by designer/architect

Optional
Lower Level
880 sq. ft.

© Copyright by designer/architect

First Floor
880 sq. ft.

Images provided by designer/architect

Plan #F11-148D-0406

Dimensions: 32' W x 35' D
Heated Sq. Ft.: 1,512
Bedrooms: 3 **Bathrooms:** 1½
Exterior Walls: 2" x 6"
Foundation: Basement

See index for more information

Second Floor
827 sq. ft.

© Copyright by designer/architect

First Floor
685 sq. ft.

Optional
Lower Level
1,109 sq. ft.

REC ROOM
18-6x21-9

BEDROOM #6
16-2x12-1

BAR

UNFINISHED
STORAGE/MECH.

UNFINISHED
STORAGE/MECH.

© Copyright by
designer/architect

COVERED
DECK

DINING
14-0x13-1

GREAT
ROOM
18-8x16-3

MASTER
BEDROOM
16-7x16-0

KITCHEN
15-1x12-4

STUDY/
BEDROOM #3
11-4x11-5

LAUNDRY
9-0x12-7

W.I.C
9-0x9-10

ENTRY

3-CAR
GARAGE
24-4x33-1

BEDROOM #2
12-0x13-1

FRONT
PORCH

COVERED
PORCH

First Floor
2,251 sq. ft.

Plan #F11-101D-0115

Dimensions: 60' W x 76' D
Heated Sq. Ft.: 2,251
Bonus Sq. Ft.: 1,109
Bedrooms: 3 **Bathrooms:** 2½
Exterior Walls: 2" x 6"
Foundation: Basement or daylight basement, please specify when ordering

See index for more information

Images provided by designer/architect

Images provided by designer/architect

Plan #F11-170D-0003

Dimensions: 70'9" W x 91' D
Heated Sq. Ft.: 2,672
Bedrooms: 4 **Bathrooms:** 3½
Foundation: Monolithic slab or slab standard; crawl space, basement or daylight basement for an additional fee

See index for more information

STORAGE

STORAGE
11'-5" X 5'-9"

GARAGE
24'-0" X 12'-11"

© Copyright by
designer/architect

GARAGE
24'-0" X 23'-11"

PATIO

PATIO

PATIO

STORAGE

SCREEN PORCH
17'-9" X 15'-0"
10' CEILING

MASTER
BEDROOM
14'-0" X 15'-0"

MASTER
BATH
13'-9" X 11'-1"

PANTRY

LOCKERS

KITCHEN
13'-1" X 16'-5"

ISLAND

EATING
13'-2" X 13'-8"

UTILITY

MASTER
CLOSET
7'-9"
X
15'-9"

FAMILY ROOM
19'-4" X 19'-2"

STUDY/
GUEST ROOM
11'-9"
X
14'-10"

½
BATH

FRONT PORCH
34'-0" X 8'-0"
10' CEILING

First Floor
1,888 sq. ft.

ATTIC
ACCESS

DOWN

BATH
2

BATH
3

BEDROOM
2
11'-9" X 11'-9"

COMMON
AREA
9'-8" X 17'-6"

BEDROOM
3
11'-6" X 11'-9"

SECOND
FLOOR

Second Floor
784 sq. ft.

First Floor
2,230 sq. ft.

Plan #F11-056S-0008

Images provided by designer/architect

Dimensions: 73'4" W x 71'8" D
Heated Sq. Ft.: 3,818
Bonus Sq. Ft.: 386
Bedrooms: 3   **Bathrooms:** 2½
Foundation: Basement standard; crawl space or slab for an additional fee

See index for more information

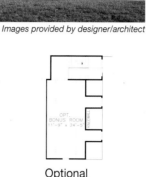

Optional
Second Floor
386 sq. ft.

Lower Level
1,588 sq. ft.

Second Floor
455 sq. ft.

Plan #F11-051D-0926

Dimensions: 41' W x 72' D
Heated Sq. Ft.: 2,025
Bedrooms: 3   **Bathrooms:** 3
Exterior Walls: 2" x 6"
Foundation: Basement standard; slab, crawl space or concrete block for an additional fee

See index for more information

Images provided by designer/architect

First Floor
1,570 sq. ft.

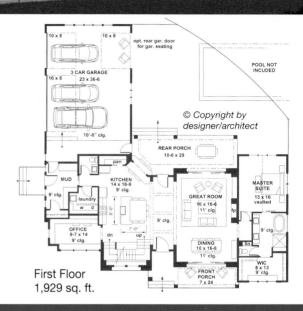

Images provided by designer/architect

Plan #F11-091D-0518

Dimensions: 67' W x 75'2" D
Heated Sq. Ft.: 3,011
Bedrooms: 4   **Bathrooms:** 3½
Exterior Walls: 2" x 6"
Foundation: Crawl space standard; slab, basement or walk-out basement for an additional fee

See index for more information

Second Floor
1,082 sq. ft.

First Floor
1,929 sq. ft.

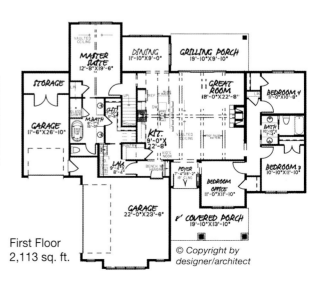

Images provided by designer/architect

Plan #F11-155D-0186

Dimensions: 72'6" W x 64'8" D
Heated Sq. Ft.: 2,113
Bonus Sq. Ft.: 414
Bedrooms: 4   **Bathrooms:** 2
Exterior Walls: 2" x 6"
Foundation: Crawl space or slab standard; basement or daylight basement for an additional fee

See index for more information

Optional
Second Floor
414 sq. ft.

First Floor
2,113 sq. ft.

© Copyright by designer/architect

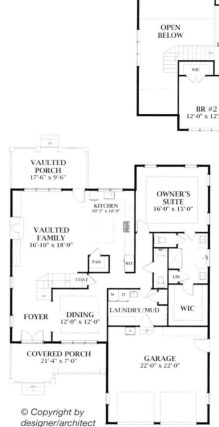

Second Floor
753 sq. ft.

First Floor
1,584 sq. ft.

© Copyright by
designer/architect

Images provided by designer/architect

Plan #F11-139D-0090

Dimensions: 45' W x 64' D
Heated Sq. Ft.: 2,337
Bonus Sq. Ft.: 332
Bedrooms: 3   **Bathrooms:** 2½
Exterior Walls: 2" x 6"
Foundation: Crawl space standard; slab, basement, daylight basement or walk-out basement for an additional fee

See index for more information

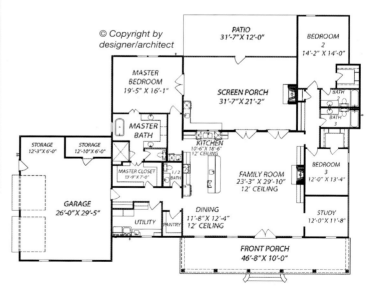

© Copyright by
designer/architect

Images provided by designer/architect

Plan #F11-170D-0016

Dimensions: 95' W x 74' D
Heated Sq. Ft.: 3,013
Bedrooms: 3   **Bathrooms:** 3½
Foundation: Monolithic slab or slab standard; crawl space, basement or daylight basement for an additional fee

See index for more information

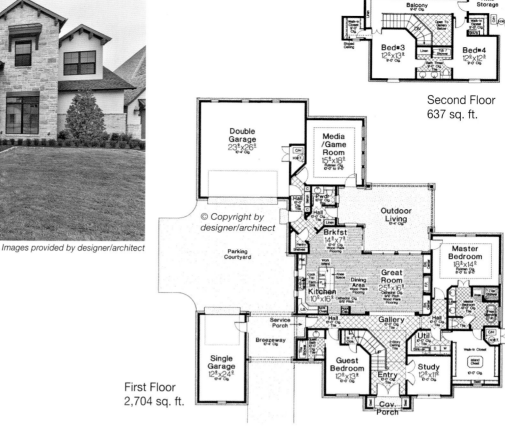

Second Floor
637 sq. ft.

First Floor
2,704 sq. ft.

© Copyright by designer/architect

Images provided by designer/architect

Plan #F11-036D-0242

Dimensions: 80' W x 83'4" D
Heated Sq. Ft.: 3,341
Bedrooms: 4   **Bathrooms:** 3½
Foundation: Slab

See index for more information

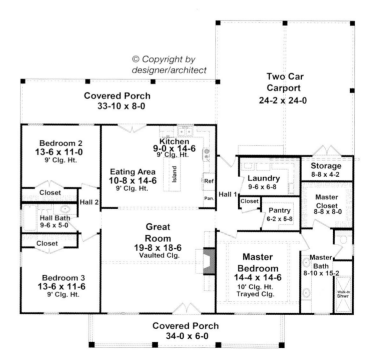

© Copyright by designer/architect

Images provided by designer/architect

Plan #F11-077D-0293

Dimensions: 58' W x 58'6" D
Heated Sq. Ft.: 1,800
Bedrooms: 3   **Bathrooms:** 2
Foundation: Crawl space or slab, please specify when ordering

See index for more information

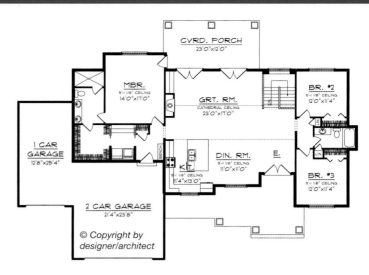

Plan #F11-051D-0979

Dimensions: 81' W x 59' D
Heated Sq. Ft.: 1,921
Bedrooms: 3   **Bathrooms:** 2
Exterior Walls: 2" x 6"
Foundation: Basement standard;
crawl space or slab for an additional
fee

See index for more information

Images provided by designer/architect

Images provided by designer/architect

Plan #F11-169D-0001

Dimensions: 50' W x 30' D
Heated Sq. Ft.: 1,400
Bedrooms: 3   **Bathrooms:** 2
Foundation: Crawl space

See index for more information

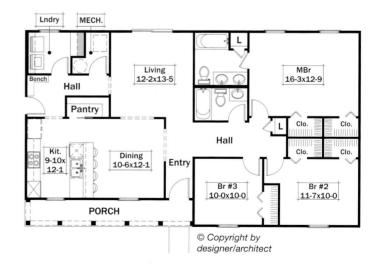

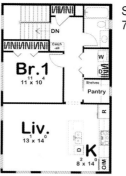

Second Floor
701 sq. ft.

Br. 1
11 x 10

Liv.
13 x 14

K
8 x 14

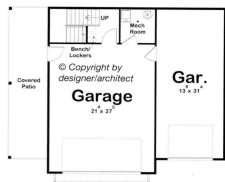

© Copyright by
designer/architect

Covered
Patio

Garage
21⁴ x 27⁰

UP

Mech
Room

Bench/
Lockers

Gar.
13⁸ x 31⁴

First Floor
106 sq. ft.

Images provided by designer/architect

Plan #F11-123D-0255

Dimensions:	44' W x 35' D
Heated Sq. Ft.:	807
Bedrooms: 1	**Bathrooms:** 1
Foundation:	Slab

See index for more information

Optional
Second Floor
412 sq. ft.

Bonus
11 x 22
Cath. Ceiling

First Floor
2,461 sq. ft.

© Copyright by
designer/architect

Mbr.
15 x 15
10'-0" Ceiling

Covered
Patio

Grill

Br. 2
12 x 12

Grt. Rm.
16 x 22
Cath. Ceiling

Bfst
9 x 18
Cath. Ceiling

K.
8 x 18
Cath. Ceiling

Br. 4
11 x 11
10'-0" Ceiling

Entry
10'-0" Ceiling

Din.
11 x 12
10'-0" Ceiling

Mud
Room

Br. 3
12 x 11

Gar.
24 x 22

Covered
Porch

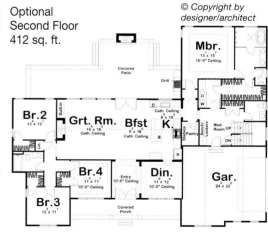

Optional
Lower Level
1,839 sq. ft.

Theater Screen

Theater
22 x 26

High Bar Table

Br. 5
12 x 17

Fam.
17 x 17

Table
15 x 12

Bar
17 x 17

Stor.

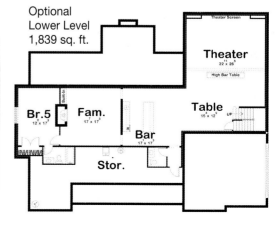

Plan #F11-123D-0151

Dimensions:	74' W x 60' D
Heated Sq. Ft.:	2,461
Bonus Sq. Ft.:	2,251
Bedrooms: 4	**Bathrooms:** 2½

Foundation: Basement standard;
slab, crawl space or walk-out
basement for an additional fee

See index for more information

Images provided by designer/architect

Plan #F11-101D-0132

Dimensions:	89'9" W x 75'6" D
Heated Sq. Ft.:	3,717
Bonus Sq. Ft.:	1,981
Bedrooms: 4	**Bathrooms:** 3½
Exterior Walls:	2" x 6"
Foundation:	Basement

See index for more information

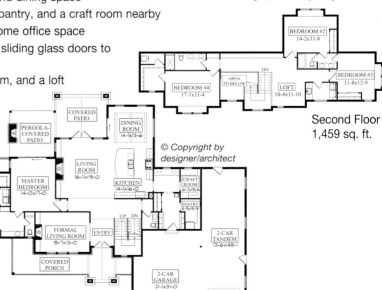

Images provided by designer/architect

Special Features

- The living and dining rooms surround the kitchen in gathering and dining space
- The kitchen has a huge island, great for entertaining, a walk-in pantry, and a craft room nearby
- A formal living room has a fireplace and would make a lovely home office space
- The master bedroom has a posh bath, huge walk-in closet and sliding glass doors to a pergola-covered patio with an outdoor fireplace
- The second floor has three bedrooms, two baths, a laundry room, and a loft
- The optional lower level has an additional 1,981 square feet of living area and features a flex room, a theater, a gym, a rec room, a half bath, storage, and a guest bedroom with a walk-in closet and a full bath
- 2-car front entry garage, and a 2-car front entry tandem garage

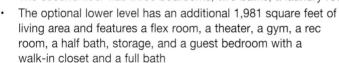

© Copyright by
designer/architect

Second Floor
1,459 sq. ft.

Optional
Lower Level
1,981 sq. ft.

First Floor
2,258 sq. ft.

Plan #F11-032D-1081

Dimensions: 50' W x 38' D
Heated Sq. Ft.: 1,604
Bedrooms: 2   **Bathrooms:** 2
Exterior Walls: 2" x 6"
Foundation: Basement standard;
crawl space, floating slab or
monolithic slab for an additional fee

See index for more information

Special Features

- This one-story Farmhouse home has a great side entrance into a mud room with storage and a built-in bench
- Enter the main front door and walk into a vaulted kitchen, dining and living room combination that is open and spacious with access to an oversized covered porch
- Off the side foyer is the laundry room which also connects directly to the master bath
- The second bedroom has a full bath right outside its door

Images provided by designer/architect

Plan #F11-101D-0146

Dimensions:	58'4" W x 78' D
Heated Sq. Ft.:	2,346
Bedrooms: 2	**Bathrooms:** 2½
Exterior Walls:	2" x 6"
Foundation:	Basement

See index for more information

Special Features

- This rustic Modern Farmhouse has a compact footprint and a charming wrap-around porch
- Upon entering you will be greeted by a home office and bedroom 2 with its own bath on the right
- Straight ahead is a vaulted family room with a fireplace and views of the rear covered patio
- The kitchen features a huge island and has dining to one side that's surrounded in windows
- The master bedroom has covered patio access, a private bath and a large walk-in closet
- 2-car front entry garage

Images provided by designer/architect

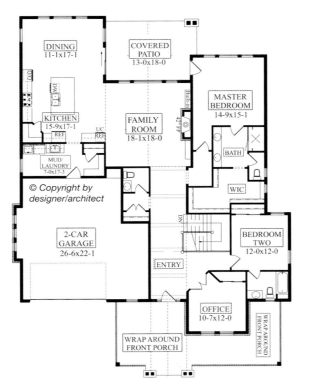

Plan #F11-032D-1137

Dimensions: 46'4" W x 40'4" D
Heated Sq. Ft.: 1,840
Bonus Sq. Ft.: 912
Bedrooms: 3   **Bathrooms:** 2½
Exterior Walls: 2" x 6"
Foundation: Basement standard; crawl space, monolithic slab or floating slab for an additional fee

See index for more information

Second Floor
928 sq. ft.

Special Features

- This stunning Modern Farmhouse has all bedrooms on the second floor for privacy and a first floor just filled with function at every turn
- Off the foyer is an office/den with enough space for two workstations
- The beautiful living room has a center fireplace and plenty of windows
- The second floor master suite is vaulted, has a bath behind a pocket door and a walk-in closet
- The optional lower level has an additional 912 square feet of living area
- 1-car front entry garage

© Copyright by designer/architect

First Floor
912 sq. ft.

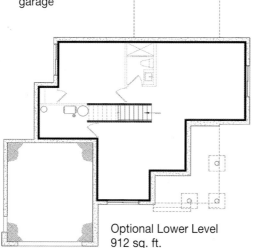

Optional Lower Level
912 sq. ft.

Images provided by designer/architect

Plan #F11-101D-0149

Dimensions:	74'6" W x 65'6" D
Heated Sq. Ft.:	2,105
Bonus Sq. Ft.:	1,872
Bedrooms: 2	**Bathrooms:** 2½
Exterior Walls:	2" x 6"
Foundation:	Basement

See index for more information

Images provided by designer/architect

Special Features

- This stunning home has a simple floor plan that's open and airy the moment you walk in
- One of the main attractions in this home design is the huge mud/laundry room that is filled with tons of storage space
- The great room has sliding glass doors leading to a rear wrap-around covered patio
- The master bedroom has its own patio, a walk-in closet, and a large bath with a unique shower/freestanding tub room
- The optional lower level has an additional 1,872 square feet of living area that includes a rec room, two bedrooms, two full baths, and a gym
- 3-car side entry garage

Optional Lower Level
1,872 sq. ft.

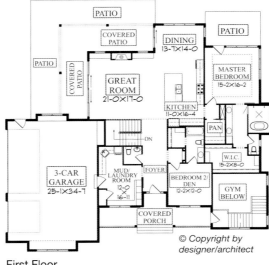

First Floor
2,105 sq. ft.

© Copyright by designer/architect

Plan #F11-091D-0509

Dimensions:	72' W x 69'2" D
Heated Sq. Ft.:	2,886
Bonus Sq. Ft.:	270
Bedrooms: 4	**Bathrooms:** 4½
Exterior Walls:	2" x 6"

Foundation: Crawl space standard; slab, basement or walk-out basement for an additional fee

See index for more information

Special Features

- Simply stunning Modern Farmhouse design includes all the extras on every homeowner's wish list including an office and a mud room
- The remarkable great room has a cozy fireplace visible from the kitchen
- The kitchen features a walk-in pantry with a barn style door, a huge island and dining space
- The luxury private master bedroom has a dressing room sized walk-in closet and a luxurious spa style bath
- The mud room is accessed from a handy side entrance as well as the garage
- The second floor features all of the secondary bedrooms as well as an open loft space, perfect as a teen hang-out spot
- The garage has an overhead door that can be raised on the pool and patio side where outdoor living space can be created in a shady spot that's also convenient to a pool bath
- The future bonus space on the second floor has an additional 270 square feet of living area
- 3-car side entry garage

Images provided by designer/architect

Second Floor
1,086 sq. ft.

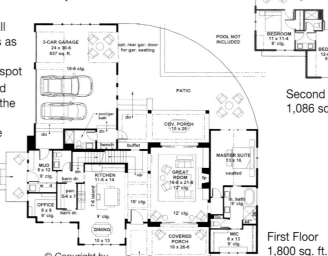

© Copyright by designer/architect

First Floor
1,800 sq. ft.

Plan #F11-028D-0115

Dimensions:	44' W x 36'6" D
Heated Sq. Ft.:	1,035
Bedrooms: 3	**Bathrooms:** 2
Exterior Walls:	2" x 6"
Foundation:	Slab

See index for more information

Images provided by designer/architect

Special Features

- This home has a split bedroom layout for added privacy
- The open kitchen/dining and great room is perfect for entertaining because the open layout creates a larger spacious feel
- The master bedroom is separated from the other bedrooms for privacy and has a walk-in closet
- The master bath has dual sinks, plenty of storage, and a large custom shower
- The laundry room is tucked off the kitchen and hidden with a barn style door
- Bedrooms 2 and 3 share a nice-sized bath
- The rear porch is covered and 6' deep, which is perfect for expanding your living space outdoors

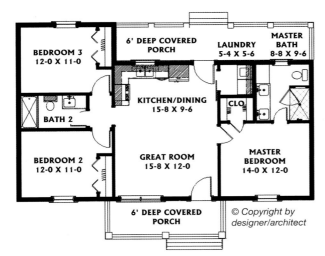

© Copyright by designer/architect

Plan #F11-141D-0290

Dimensions: 72'4" W x 62'4" D
Heated Sq. Ft.: 2,227
Bedrooms: 3   **Bathrooms:** 2½
Foundation: Crawl space or slab standard; basement or walk-out basement for an additional fee

See index for more information

Special Features

- This unforgettable Modern Farmhouse has a symmetrically pleasing covered front porch that's always inviting and draws you in
- The vaulted family room has views of the dining area and kitchen
- The covered back porch mimics the front in size and offers that perfect shady spot to sit with a glass of iced tea on a hot summer day
- The master suite is in a great first floor location and enjoys a private bath with an oversized shower and a walk-in closet behind a pocket door to maximize space
- The second floor features two bedrooms, a full bath, and an office/loft with a walk-in closet

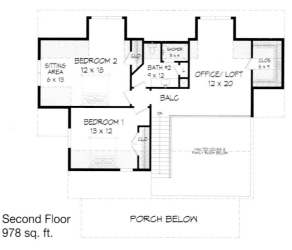

Second Floor
978 sq. ft.

First Floor
1,249 sq. ft.

Images provided by designer/architect

Plan #F11-101D-0126

Dimensions: 102'3" W x 63' D
Heated Sq. Ft.: 3,907
Bonus Sq. Ft.: 2,052
Bedrooms: 4 **Bathrooms:** 3½
Exterior Walls: 2" x 6"
Foundation: Basement, daylight basement or walk-out basement, please specify when ordering

See index for more information

Special Features

- The open kitchen with a huge island enjoys views of the vaulted living room and sunny dining area
- Behind the kitchen is a huge laundry room, a mud room, and a walk-in pantry
- The private master bedroom has a cozy corner fireplace, sliding glass doors to a deck, and a bath with a walk-in closet
- The second floor has three large additional bedrooms, and a loft
- The optional lower level has an additional 2,052 square feet of living area including a rec room, a movie room, a workout room, an office, a bedroom, and a bath
- 3-car side entry garage

First Floor
2,585 sq. ft.

© Copyright by designer/architect

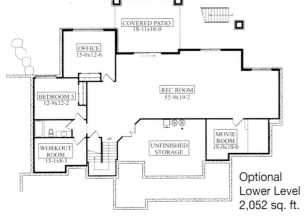

Optional
Lower Level
2,052 sq. ft.

Second Floor
1,322 sq. ft.

Images provided by designer/architect

Plan #F11-155D-0121

Dimensions: 108'2" W x 92'4" D
Heated Sq. Ft.: 6,301
Bedrooms: 6   **Bathrooms:** 5½
Foundation: Walk-out basement or daylight basement standard; crawl space or slab for an additional fee
See index for more information

Special Features

- This luxury home has a balance of Craftsman and farmhouse style
- The great room and kitchen comprise most of the living space on the first floor and are topped with vaulted and beamed ceilings for added ambiance and architectural drama
- The second floor features three secondary bedrooms; one with its own bath and the other two share a full bath
- The lower level includes a kitchen, living area with fireplace, a large mud room, a gym, an office, a sixth bedroom, and a full bath
- 3-car front entry garage

Second Floor
1,245 sq. ft.

© Copyright by designer/architect

First Floor
2,895 sq. ft.

Lower Level
2,161 sq. ft.

Images provided by designer/architect

houseplansandmore.com

Plan #F11-123D-0149

Dimensions:	75' W x 57' D
Heated Sq. Ft.:	2,296
Bonus Sq. Ft.:	2,021
Bedrooms: 3	**Bathrooms:** 2½

Foundation: Basement standard; crawl space, slab or walk-out basement for an additional fee

See index for more information

Special Features

- The appealing double door entry invites guests into this friendly home
- The great room has two sets of French doors leading to the rear covered patio with fireplace
- The master bath has direct access to the laundry room for ease
- The optional lower level has an additional 1,563 square feet of living area and enjoys a large casual family room with a wet bar, space for a game table, a play room, two bedrooms, and a full bath
- The optional second floor has an additional 458 square feet of living area
- 2-car side entry garage

First Floor
2,296 sq. ft.

Optional
Second Floor
458 sq. ft.

Optional
Lower Level
1,563 sq. ft.

Images provided by designer/architect

Plan #F11-123S-0051

Dimensions:	90' W x 78'9" D
Heated Sq. Ft.:	3,958
Bonus Sq. Ft.:	615
Bedrooms: 4	**Bathrooms:** 3½

Foundation: Basement standard; crawl space, slab or walk-out basement for an additional fee

See index for more information

Images provided by designer/architect

Special Features

- This five-star Farmhouse is far from humble and features numerous spaces ideal for stylish entertaining
- The absolutely stunning freestanding two-story stone fireplace is definitely the focal point of the interior since it can be seen from multiple spaces and both floors
- The glorious sun room is a great private retreat rain or shine
- The great room is lined with double doors; three sets on two parallel walls making this space so breathtaking with natural light it will make a lasting impression on all those who enter
- The master bedroom enjoys a first floor location and has a plush bath and outdoor access
- The secondary bedrooms and a loft reside on the second floor
- The bonus room above the garage has an additional 615 square feet of living area
- 3-car side entry garage

Second Floor
1,588 sq. ft.

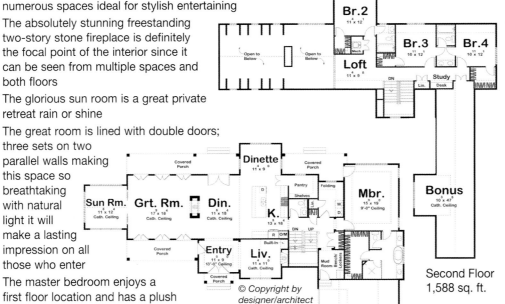

© Copyright by designer/architect

First Floor
2,370 sq. ft.

Plan #F11-101D-0080

Dimensions: 79' W x 97'9" D
Heated Sq. Ft.: 2,682
Bonus Sq. Ft.: 1,940
Bedrooms: 2 **Bathrooms:** 2½
Exterior Walls: 2" x 6"
Foundation: Basement, daylight basement or walk-out basement, please specify when ordering

See index for more information

Images provided by designer/architect

Special Features

- This home typifies the best in design with unique architectural features
- Family can enjoy the outdoors with the expansive rear decks, one complete with a fireplace
- A private den with deck access is a secluded retreat
- The optional lower level has an additional 1,940 square feet of living area including three additional bedrooms, two full baths, a half bath, a laundry room, and a rec room with a kitchenette
- 3-car side entry garage

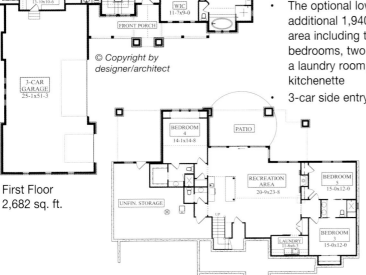

© Copyright by designer/architect

First Floor
2,682 sq. ft.

Optional Lower Level
1,940 sq. ft.

Plan #F11-123D-0146

Dimensions: 66' W x 62' D
Heated Sq. Ft.: 2,309
Bonus Sq. Ft.: 1,706
Bedrooms: 4   **Bathrooms:** 3½
Foundation: Basement standard;
crawl space, slab or walk-out
basement for an additional fee

See index for more information

Special Features

- A huge covered front porch and a covered patio create outdoor living areas that are seamless to the interior
- The mud room by the garage entrance is accompanied by a roomy laundry room, a half bath and a bench with lockers above
- The great room is topped with a cathedral ceiling that opens up the interior tremendously
- The optional lower level has an additional 1,244 square feet of living area and features a family room with bar and a great home theater
- The optional second floor has an additional 462 square feet of living area
- 2-car side entry garage

Bonus Rm.
12'⁰ x 29'⁰

Optional
Second Floor
462 sq. ft.

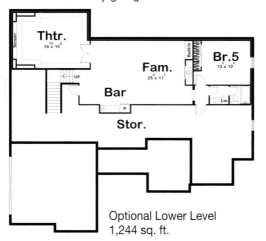

Optional Lower Level
1,244 sq. ft.

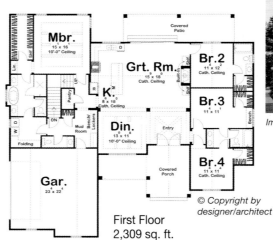

© Copyright by
designer/architect

First Floor
2,309 sq. ft.

Images provided by designer/architect

Plan #F11-172D-0041

Dimensions:	53' W x 47'6" D
Heated Sq. Ft.:	2,313
Bonus Sq. Ft.:	1,615
Bedrooms: 4	**Bathrooms:** 2½
Exterior Walls:	2" x 6"

Foundation: Basement standard; crawl space, monolithic slab, stem wall slab, daylight basement or walk-out basement for an additional fee

See index for more information

Special Features

- This stylish home has tons of curb appeal
- The first floor has an open floor plan with the kitchen island looking into the dining area and beyond to the family room
- The second floor consists of all four bedrooms for convenience with younger children
- The optional lower level has an additional 1,615 square feet of living area and a family room, theater, two bedrooms and a bath
- 3-car front entry garage

Second Floor
1,187 sq. ft.

Images provided by designer/architect

Optional
Lower Level
1,615 sq. ft.

© Copyright by designer/architect

First Floor
1,126 sq. ft.

Plan #F11-123D-0250

Dimensions: 47' W x 64' D
Heated Sq. Ft.: 2,318
Bonus Sq. Ft.: 999
Bedrooms: 4   **Bathrooms:** 3½
Foundation: Basement standard; crawl space, slab or walk-out basement for an additional fee
See index for more information

Special Features

- This stylish two-story home can handle a more narrow lot
- The private master bedroom inhabits the first floor and enjoys a spa style bath with a large shower and a walk-in closet
- The secondary bedrooms all reside on the second floor as well as an open loft space
- The bonus room on the second floor has an additional 204 square feet of living area
- The optional lower level has an additional 795 square feet of living area with a family room, a game table area, a wet bar, a wine room, bedroom and full bath
- 2-car side entry garage

Second Floor
966 sq. ft.

Bonus 9' x 20'
Cath. Ceiling

Narnia Closet

Br.2 12' x 11'

Br.4 11' x 10'

Br.3 13' x 11'

Loft 18' x 9'

Lin.

DN

Images provided by designer/architect

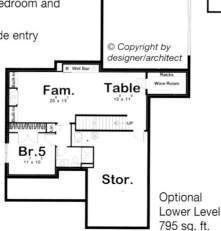

© Copyright by designer/architect

Fam. 20' x 13'

Table 12' x 11'

Wet Bar

Racks

Wine Room

UP

Br.5 11' x 10'

Stor.

Optional Lower Level
795 sq. ft.

Gar. 22' x 22'

Covered Patio

Din. 11' x 13'

Bench/ Lockers

W D

Lin.

Covered Patio

K. 12' x 12'

Liv. 13' x 15'

DN

UP

Entry

Mbr. 15' x 13'
10'-0" Ceiling

Covered Porch

Shoe Rack

First Floor
1,352 sq. ft.

Plan #F11-011D-0627

Dimensions:	52' W x 61' D
Heated Sq. Ft.:	1,878
Bedrooms: 3	**Bathrooms:** 2
Exterior Walls:	2" x 6"

Foundation: Crawl or slab standard; basement for an additional fee

See index for more information

Images provided by designer/architect

Special Features

- Upon entering the foyer that is flanked by benches, there is a soaring 16' ceiling allowing for plenty of natural light to enter the space
- Beautiful family-friendly design with a centrally located great room, dining room and kitchen combination and the sleeping quarters in a private wing
- The master suite is complete with the amenities of a walk-in closet, a double-bowl vanity and separate tub and shower units in the private bath
- Enjoy outdoor living on the covered rear patio that has a built-in barbecue grill and cabinets for ease when cooking outdoors
- 2-car front entry garage

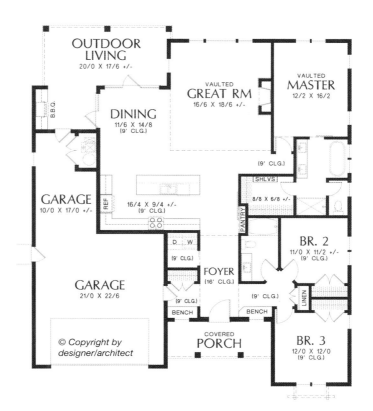

Plan #F11-141D-0202

Dimensions: 81' W x 125'2" D
Heated Sq. Ft.: 5,317
Bedrooms: 5   **Bathrooms:** 4½
Foundation: Slab standard; crawl space, basement or walk-out basement for an additional fee
See index for more information

Special Features

- The double door front foyer is flanked by a formal dining room with built-in hutch space and a parlor for formal entertaining and greeting guests
- The master bedroom retreat has its own hall, storage/safe room, private office, double walk-in closets and a spacious bath with double vanities, a spa tub and a custom shower
- A second master bedroom is a perfect in-law suite with its own bath and walk-in closet
- The family room, kitchen and morning room offer a large open space to gather indoors, while the outdoor space is more than impressive, featuring a screened porch and a covered porch with outdoor kitchen
- 4-car side entry garage

Second Floor
1,759 sq. ft.

© Copyright by
designer/architect

First Floor
3,558 sq. ft.

Images provided by designer/architect

Plan #F11-172S-0003

Dimensions: 73' W x 76' D
Heated Sq. Ft.: 4,658
Bedrooms: 6 **Bathrooms:** 4½
Exterior Walls: 2" x 6"
Foundation: Crawl space standard; stem wall slab, monolithic slab, basement, daylight basement or walk-out basement for an additional fee

See index for more information

Special Features

- So many wonderful features fill this stylish luxury Modern Farmhouse design including a guest room, and a luxurious master suite on the first floor
- The kitchen has a walk-through pantry, a large mud room and an island with dining space
- The second floor has a hobby room with an outdoor balcony that could be a great office
- Three bedrooms enjoy easy access to the washer and dryer closet outside bedroom #1
- There's also a completely separate apartment over the garage with a bedroom, kitchen, family room, bath with laundry space, and an outdoor deck
- 3-car rear entry garage, and a 1-car side entry garage

Images provided by designer/architect

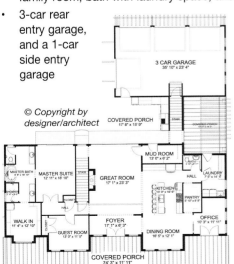

First Floor
2,369 sq. ft.

Second Floor
2,289 sq. ft.

Plan #F11-091D-0534

Dimensions: 76'10" W x 78'2" D
Heated Sq. Ft.: 3,952
Bedrooms: 4 **Bathrooms:** 4
Exterior Walls: 2" x 6"
Foundation: Crawl space standard; slab, basement or walk-out basement for an additional fee

See index for more information

Images provided by designer/architect

Special Features

- Perfect symmetry creates a stunning and stylish Modern Farmhouse facade that is formidable as well as memorable
- The great room is topped with rustic beams creating a warmer interior space and the stone fireplace adds to that cozy feel that's hard to ignore
- The kitchen features a large hidden prep kitchen, a huge island overlooking the great room, and a sizable walk-in pantry
- The master suite enjoys views of the covered rear porch with an outdoor fireplace and also has a large walk-in closet and an elegant spa style bath
- A secluded pocket office is tucked away behind the kitchen
- 3-car side entry garage

© Copyright by designer/architect

Second Floor 1,530 sq. ft.

First Floor 2,422 sq. ft.

Plan #F11-123D-0256

Dimensions: 74' W x 48'8" D
Heated Sq. Ft.: 2,637
Bedrooms: 3   **Bathrooms:** 2½
Foundation: Basement standard; crawl space, slab or walk-out basement for an additional fee
See index for more information

Special Features

- Rustic touches add personality to the exterior of this two-story Modern Farmhouse home
- Step inside and find an unexpectedly light and airy atmosphere in the great room featuring a two-story ceiling with a towering fireplace and multiple floor-to-ceiling windows
- The kitchen is anchored by a long island with dining space, a double sink and dishwasher
- Nearby is a little office with two built-in desks across from one another for great function
- Off the garage is a mud room that gives way to a laundry room
- The master bedroom is private on the first floor away from the other bedrooms; while the second floor houses two additional bedrooms and a central loft space with views of the great room below
- 2-car side entry garage

Br. 2
12'4 x 11'1

Loft
12'8 x 11'10

Open To Below
Cath. Ceiling

Br. 3
12'4 x 11'1

DN
Desk

Second Floor
787 sq. ft.

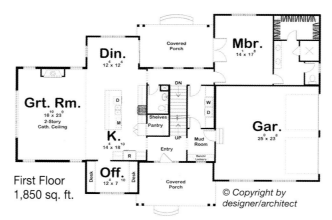

Din.
12' x 12'

Grt. Rm.
16'10 x 23'0
2-Story
Cath. Ceiling

K.
14'4 x 18'10

Off.
12'4 x 7'10

Covered Porch

Mbr.
14'4 x 17'8

Gar.
25'0 x 23'8

Shelves
Pantry
Mud Room
Bench/Lockers
Entry

Covered Porch

First Floor
1,850 sq. ft.

© Copyright by designer/architect

Images provided by designer/architect

Plan #F11-032D-1170

Dimensions:	54' W x 46' D
Heated Sq. Ft.:	1,487
Bonus Sq. Ft.:	1,487
Bedrooms: 2	**Bathrooms:** 1
Exterior Walls:	2" x 6"

Foundation: Basement standard; crawl space, floating slab or monolithic slab for an additional fee

See index for more information

Images provided by designer/architect

Special Features

- This modern one-level home has a memorable exterior and just as remarkable interior
- The living room has a vaulted ceiling, a stylish fireplace surrounded in built-in bookcases, and an entire wall of sliding glass doors
- The master bedroom enjoys a private place within the home and includes a pampering spa style bath with a freestanding tub
- A quiet office is tucked near the front hall
- The optional lower level has an additional 1,487 square feet of living area
- 1-car front entry garage

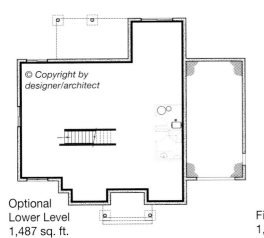

© Copyright by designer/architect

Optional
Lower Level
1,487 sq. ft.

First Floor
1,487 sq. ft.

Call toll-free 1-800-373-2646

Second Floor
1,514 sq. ft.

Br.3
13³ x 10⁶

Br.2
13³ x 11⁰

Loft
14⁷ x 8⁰

Mbr.
19 x 14⁷
Cath. Ceiling

© Copyright by
designer/architect

Gar.
19 x 23

Catch All

Mech.

Bench/
Lockers

Mud Room
5 x 13

Pantry

Shelves

UP

Desk

Hrth.
7 x 16

Din.
11⁵ x 16⁰

K.
11 x 16⁰

Grt. Rm.
19 x 15⁰

Covered
Porch

First Floor
1,113 sq. ft.

Plan #F11-123D-0244

Dimensions: 30' W x 71' D
Heated Sq. Ft.:   2,627
Bedrooms: 3   **Bathrooms:** 2½
Foundation: Crawl space standard;
slab, basement or walk-out
basement for an additional fee

See index for more information

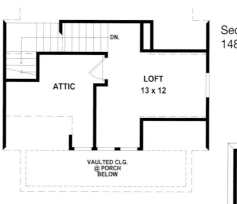

Images provided by designer/architect

Plan #F11-087D-1682

Dimensions: 25' W x 32' D
Heated Sq. Ft.:   740
Bedrooms: 1   **Bathrooms:** 1
Foundation: Slab

See index for more information

Images provided by designer/architect

Second Floor
148 sq. ft.

DN.

ATTIC

LOFT
13 x 12

VAULTED CLG.
@ PORCH
BELOW

CLO.
4 x 3

BEDROOM
10 x 10

BATH
5 x 10

LAUNDRY

HALL

KITCHEN
8 x 15

CTS.

UP

LIVING AREA
16 x 11

PAN.

"VAULTED"
PORCH
21 x 5

First Floor
592 sq. ft.

© Copyright by
designer/architect

Images provided by designer/architect

Plan #F11-026D-2149

Dimensions: 54' W x 51'4" D
Heated Sq. Ft.: 1,603
Bedrooms: 3 **Bathrooms:** 2
Foundation: Basement standard; slab, crawl space or walk-out basement for an additional fee

See index for more information

Images provided by designer/architect

Plan #F11-170D-0012

Dimensions: 74'8" W x 87'7" D
Heated Sq. Ft.: 2,605
Bedrooms: 4 **Bathrooms:** 3
Foundation: Slab or monolithic slab standard; crawl space, basement or daylight basement for an additional fee

See index for more information

First Floor
916 sq. ft.

Second Floor
939 sq. ft.

Plan #F11-011D-0692

Dimensions: 29' W x 54'6" D
Heated Sq. Ft.: 1,855
Bedrooms: 4   **Bathrooms:** 3
Exterior Walls: 2" x 6"
Foundation: Crawl space or slab standard; basement for an additional fee

See index for more information

Second Floor
773 sq. ft.

PORCH BELOW

Plan #F11-141D-0345

Images provided by designer/architect

Dimensions: 85' W x 46'6" D
Heated Sq. Ft.: 1,972
Bedrooms: 3   **Bathrooms:** 3½
Foundation: Crawl space, slab or daylight basement, please specify when ordering

See index for more information

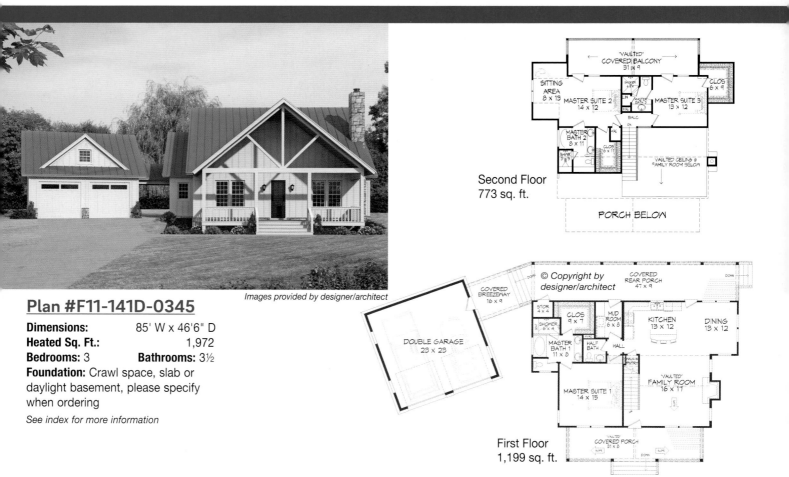

First Floor
1,199 sq. ft.

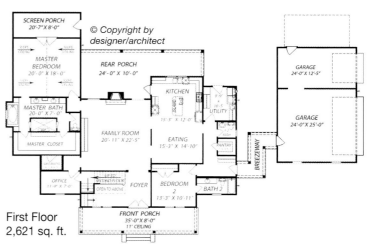

Second Floor
1,005 sq. ft.

BEDROOM 3
12'-3" X 13'-0"

BATH 3

BEDROOM 4
11'-11" X 13'-0"

ATTIC ACCESS

ATTIC ACCESS

STAIRS DOWN

LOFT AREA
13'-4 X 11'-0"
OPEN TO BELOW

Images provided by designer/architect

© Copyright by designer/architect

SCREEN PORCH
20'-7" X 8'-0"

MASTER BEDROOM
20'-0" X 18'-0"

REAR PORCH
24'-0" X 10'-0"

KITCHEN
15'-3" X 12'-0"

UTILITY

GARAGE
24'-0" X 12'-5"

MASTER BATH
20'-7" X 0"

FAMILY ROOM
20'-11" X 22'-5"

EATING
15'-3" X 14'-10"

PANTRY

GARAGE
24'-0" X 25'-0"

MASTER CLOSET

BREEZEWAY

OFFICE
11'-0" X 7'-0"

FOYER

BEDROOM 2
13'-3" X 10'-11"

BATH 2

First Floor
2,621 sq. ft.

FRONT PORCH
35'-0" X 8'-0"
11' CEILING

Plan #F11-170D-0020

Dimensions: 105'4" W x 69'3" D
Heated Sq. Ft.:   3,626
Bedrooms: 4   **Bathrooms:** 3½
Foundation: Slab or monolithic slab standard; crawl space, basement or daylight basement for an additional fee

See index for more information

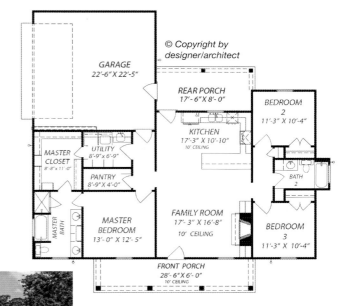

© Copyright by designer/architect

GARAGE
22'-6" X 22'-5"

REAR PORCH
17'-6" X 8'-0"

KITCHEN
17'-3" X 10'-10"
10' CEILING

BEDROOM 2
11'-3" X 10'-4"

MASTER CLOSET
8'-8" X 11'-0"

UTILITY
8'-9" x 6'-9"

PANTRY
8'-9" X 4'-0"

BATH 2

MASTER BATH

MASTER BEDROOM
13'-0" X 12'-5"

FAMILY ROOM
17'-3" X 16'-8"
10' CEILING

BEDROOM 3
11'-3" X 10'-4"

FRONT PORCH
28'-6" X 6'-0"
10' CEILING

Plan #F11-170D-0005

Dimensions: 54' W x 53' D
Heated Sq. Ft.:   1,422
Bedrooms: 3   **Bathrooms:** 2
Foundation: Slab or monolithic slab standard; crawl space, basement or daylight basement for an additional fee

See index for more information

Images provided by designer/architect

Plan #F11-101D-0140

Dimensions: 101'9" W x 78'1" D
Heated Sq. Ft.: 4,626
Bedrooms: 4
Bathrooms: 3 full, 2 half
Exterior Walls: 2" x 6"
Foundation: Basement

See index for more information

Special Features

- This marvelous Modern Farmhouse design promises to surprise with stylish and trendy details at every turn
- The completely open first floor has a huge kitchen with double islands, a massive walk-through pantry and access to the covered patio with an outdoor fireplace
- An unexpected craft room would also make a great spot for home schooling and homework time
- The second floor features a large media room with covered deck access, a piano room, and an exercise room
- The master bath is five-star and features a huge walk-through shower
- 2-car front entry garage, and a 1-car drive-through garage

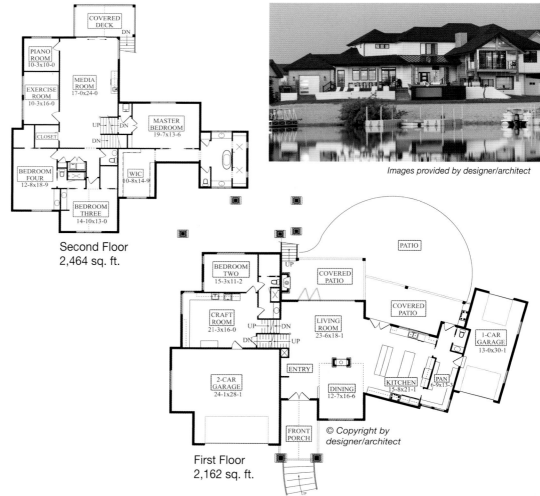

Images provided by designer/architect

Second Floor
2,464 sq. ft.

First Floor
2,162 sq. ft.

© Copyright by designer/architect

Plan #F11-123D-0144

Dimensions: 66' W x 54' D
Heated Sq. Ft.: 2,025
Bedrooms: 3   **Bathrooms:** 2
Foundation: Basement standard; crawl space, slab or walk-out basement for an additional fee

See index for more information

Special Features

- You will fall in love the minute you lay your eyes of this unique farmhouse style home
- The great room has a coffered ceiling and cozy fireplace viewable from the kitchen
- The private master bedroom enjoys a large bath and walk-in closet
- There's a large pantry off the kitchen that really expands the square footage and storage needs required for most home chefs
- The laundry room can be access from the master walk-in closet through a pocket door
- 2-car side entry garage

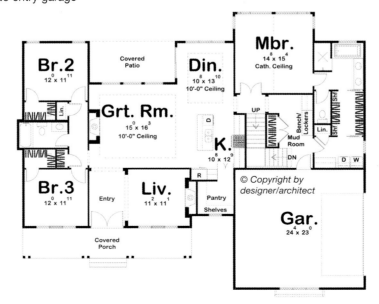

Images provided by designer/architect

houseplansandmore.com

Images provided by designer/architect

Plan #F11-032D-1145

Dimensions: 41' W x 46' D
Heated Sq. Ft.: 2,814
Bedrooms: 3   **Bathrooms:** 2½
Exterior Walls: 2" x 6"
Foundation: Basement standard; crawl space, floating slab or monolithic slab for an additional fee
See index for more information

Special Features

- This stunning Modern Farmhouse style home has a terrific layout with tons of great amenities
- The living room is completely open to the dining room with the kitchen island just behind the dining table
- The first floor master suite enjoys a walk-in closet and private bath with both a free-standing tub and a walk-in shower
- A private home office is near the master suite
- A large walk-in pantry keeps the kitchen organized
- The lower level features an open family room, a large laundry room, two bedrooms, and a bath
- 1-car front entry garage

First Floor
1,407 sq. ft.

Lower Level
1,407 sq. ft.

© Copyright by designer/architect

Plan #F11-161D-0016

Dimensions:	76' W x 120' D
Heated Sq. Ft.:	3,275
Bedrooms: 4	**Bathrooms:** 3½
Exterior Walls:	2" x 6"
Foundation:	Crawl space

See index for more information

Special Features

- The kitchen, dining area and great room are open to one another creating an overwhelming sense of spaciousness
- Stair-stepped rooms and walls of windows at the rear of this home create amazing views from every angle
- A centrally located great room takes center stage and does not disappoint with its built-in niches and cabinets providing space to display art and family treasures
- The laundry room features not only a large bench with hooks above, but cubbies and an L-shaped counter for folding and sorting clothes
- The master suite has floor-to-ceiling windows and a luxury bath with a shower, tub, walk-in closet and double bowl vanity
- The second floor has a den/studio, a guest room/TV room and a full bath
- 3-car side entry garage

Images provided by designer/architect

© Copyright by designer/architect

Second Floor
546 sq. ft.

First Floor
2,729 sq. ft.

Call toll-free 1-800-373-2646

houseplansandmore.com

Plan #F11-055S-0115

Dimensions: 126'2" W x 110'11" D
Heated Sq. Ft.: 4,501
Bonus Sq. Ft.: 501
Bedrooms: 5 **Bathrooms:** 5½
Exterior Walls: 2" x 6"
Foundation: Crawl space or slab standard; basement or daylight basement for an additional fee

See index for more information

Special Features

- The two-story great room boasts double-doors that open to the rear covered porch, a fireplace, and built-in flanking shelves
- A walk-in pantry and a breakfast bar with seating for seven are some awesome features of the well-equipped kitchen
- The bonus room on the second floor has an additional 501 square feet of living area and is perfect for a home theater or game room
- 3-car front entry garage

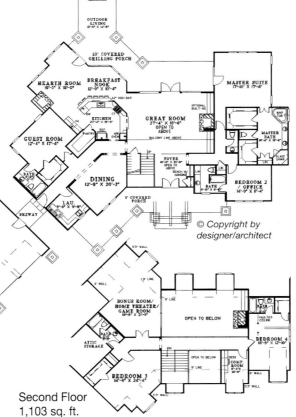

First Floor
3,398 sq. ft.

Second Floor
1,103 sq. ft.

© Copyright by designer/architect

Images provided by designer/architect

First Floor
2,073 sq. ft.

Plan #F11-155D-0147

Dimensions: 70'6" W x 58'2" D
Heated Sq. Ft.: 2,073
Bonus Sq. Ft.: 316
Bedrooms: 3 **Bathrooms:** 2½
Foundation: Crawl space or slab standard; basement or daylight basement for an additional fee

See index for more information

Images provided by designer/architect

Optional
Second Floor
316 sq. ft.

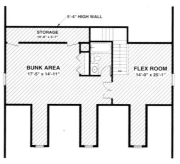

Second Floor
911 sq. ft.

First Floor
1,059 sq. ft.

Plan #F11-013D-0253

Dimensions: 40'3" W x 42'4" D
Heated Sq. Ft.: 2,943
Bedrooms: 3 **Bathrooms:** 3
Foundation: Basement standard; crawl space or slab for an additional fee for an additional fee

See index for more information

Lower Level
973 sq. ft.

Images provided by designer/architect

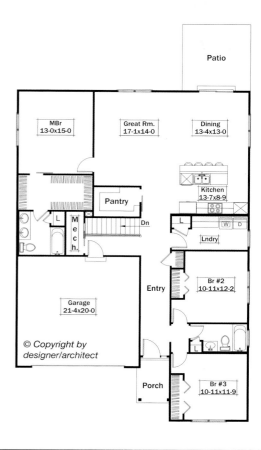

Plan #F11-169D-0003

Dimensions: 41' W x 60'4" D
Heated Sq. Ft.: 1,762
Bedrooms: 3   **Bathrooms:** 2
Foundation: Basement standard; crawl space or slab for an additional fee

See index for more information

Images provided by designer/architect

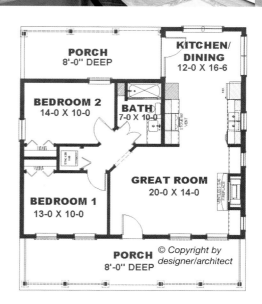

Images provided by designer/architect

Plan #F11-028D-0108

Dimensions: 33' W x 40' D
Heated Sq. Ft.: 890
Bedrooms: 2   **Bathrooms:** 1
Exterior Walls: 2" x 6"
Foundation: Slab or crawl space, please specify when ordering

See index for more information

Plan #F11-111D-0095

Dimensions: 46' W x 50'8" D
Heated Sq. Ft.: 2,458
Bedrooms: 3   **Bathrooms:** 3
Foundation: Slab standard; crawl space for an additional fee

See index for more information

Images provided by designer/architect

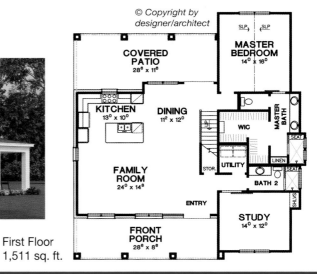

Second Floor
947 sq. ft.

© Copyright by designer/architect

First Floor
1,511 sq. ft.

Plan #F11-141D-0326

Dimensions: 97'6" W x 65'2" D
Heated Sq. Ft.: 2,835
Bedrooms: 3   **Bathrooms:** 3
Foundation: Crawl space standard; slab, basement or walk-out basement for an additional fee

See index for more information

Images provided by designer/architect

© Copyright by designer/architect

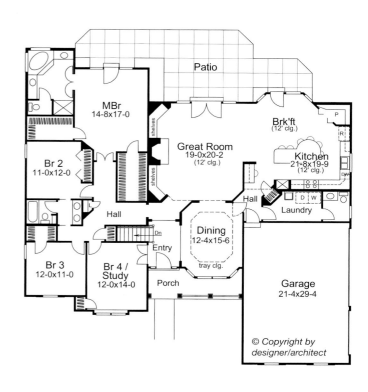

Plan #F11-007D-0113

Dimensions: 66' W x 66' D
Heated Sq. Ft.: 2,547
Bedrooms: 4   **Bathrooms:** 2½
Foundation: Basement standard; crawl space or slab for an additional fee

See index for more information

Images provided by designer/architect

Plan #F11-026D-2079

Dimensions: 42' W x 42' D
Heated Sq. Ft.: 1,600
Bonus Sq. Ft.: 336
Bedrooms: 3   **Bathrooms:** 2½
Foundation: Basement standard; crawl space, slab or walk-out basement for an additional fee

See index for more information

Images provided by designer/architect

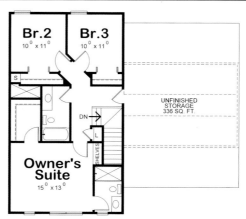

Second Floor
752 sq. ft.

First Floor
848 sq. ft.

Plan #F11-026D-2091

Dimensions: 42' W x 51'4" D
Heated Sq. Ft.: 1,603
Bedrooms: 3   **Bathrooms:** 2
Foundation: Basement standard;
crawl space, slab or walk-out
basement for an additional fee

See index for more information

Images provided by designer/architect

OPTIONAL COVERED PATIO

Dining Area
13⁰ x 11⁰

Family Room
15⁰ x 18⁴
10'-0" CEILING

Owner's Suite
13⁰ x 14⁰
10'-0" CEILING

Kit.
13⁰ x 11⁰

R
P

DN

DROP ZONE

W D

Br.3
10⁰ x 11⁰

POCKET OFFICE

Br.2
10⁰ x 12⁰

Garage
20⁸ x 22⁰

© Copyright by designer/architect

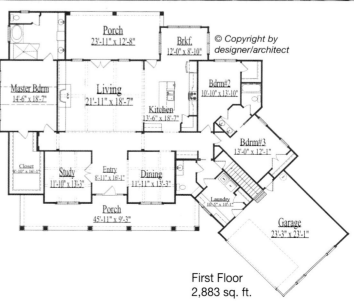

Plan #F11-157D-0006

Dimensions: 89'11" W x 75' D
Heated Sq. Ft.: 2,883
Bonus Sq. Ft.: 397
Bedrooms: 3   **Bathrooms:** 2½
Exterior Walls: 2" x 6"
Foundation: Crawl space standard;
slab for an additional fee

See index for more information

Images provided by designer/architect

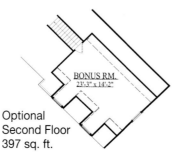

BONUS RM.
23'-3" x 14'-2"

Optional
Second Floor
397 sq. ft.

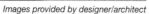

© Copyright by designer/architect

Porch
23'-11" x 12'-8"

Brkf.
12'-0" x 8'-10"

Master Bdrm
14'-6" x 18'-7"

Living
21'-11" x 18'-7"

Bdrm#2
10'-10" x 13'-10"

Kitchen
13'-6" x 18'-7"

Closet
8'-10" x 16'-1"

Study
11'-10" x 13'-3"

Entry
8'-11" x 16'-1"

Dining
11'-11" x 13'-3"

Bdrm#3
13'-0" x 12'-1"

Laundry
10'-5" x 10'-1"

Porch
45'-11" x 9'-3"

Garage
23'-3" x 23'-1"

First Floor
2,883 sq. ft.

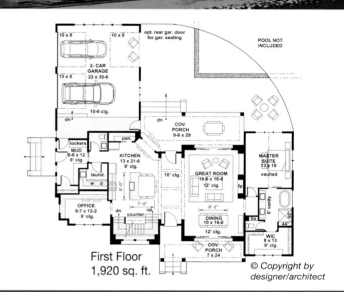

Plan #F11-091D-0515

Dimensions:	67' W x 69'2" D
Heated Sq. Ft.:	2,837
Bedrooms: 4	**Bathrooms:** 2½
Exterior Walls:	2" x 6"

Foundation: Crawl space standard; slab or basement for an additional fee

See index for more information

Second Floor
917 sq. ft.

First Floor
1,920 sq. ft.

© Copyright by designer/architect

Second Floor
1,263 sq. ft.

Plan #F11-052D-0170

Dimensions:	88' W x 49' D
Heated Sq. Ft.:	3,290
Bonus Sq. Ft.:	2,315
Bedrooms: 4	**Bathrooms:** 3½
Foundation:	Walk-out basement

See index for more information

Optional Lower Level
2,315 sq. ft.

© Copyright by designer/architect

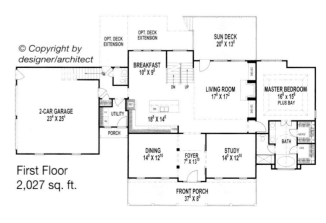

First Floor
2,027 sq. ft.

Plan #F11-011D-0674

Dimensions: 40' W x 60'6" D
Heated Sq. Ft.:   1,552
Bedrooms: 3   **Bathrooms:** 2
Exterior Walls: 2" x 6"
Foundation: Crawl space or slab standard; basement for an additional fee

See index for more information

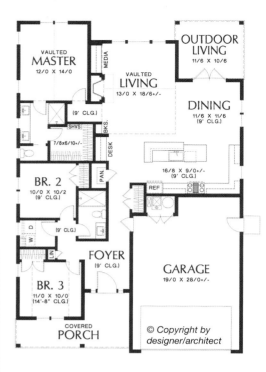

Images provided by designer/architect

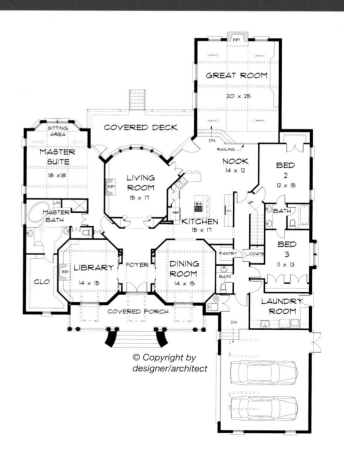

Images provided by designer/architect

Plan #F11-164D-0044

Dimensions: 69' W x 98' D
Heated Sq. Ft.:   3,287
Bedrooms: 3   **Bathrooms:** 2½
Foundation: Slab

See index for more information

Second Floor
560 sq. ft.

Images provided by designer/architect

Plan #F11-141D-0405

Dimensions: 90' W x 54'10" D
Heated Sq. Ft.: 2,365
Bonus Sq. Ft.: 1,805
Bedrooms: 3 **Bathrooms: 2½**
Exterior Walls: 2" x 6"
Foundation: Basement standard; crawl space, slab or walk-out basement for an additional fee

See index for more information

Optional Lower Level
1,805 sq. ft.

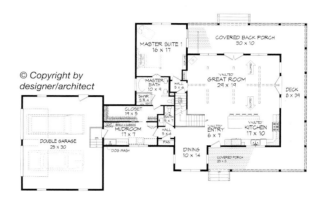

© Copyright by designer/architect

First Floor
1,805 sq. ft.

Images provided by designer/architect

Plan #F11-159D-0014

Dimensions: 87'8" W x 56'8" D
Heated Sq. Ft.: 2,340
Bonus Sq. Ft.: 1,480
Bedrooms: 3 **Bathrooms: 2½**
Exterior Walls: 2" x 6"
Foundation: Basement or walk-out basement, please specify when ordering

See index for more information

© Copyright by designer/architect

First Floor
2,340 sq. ft.

Optional Lower Level
1,480 sq. ft.

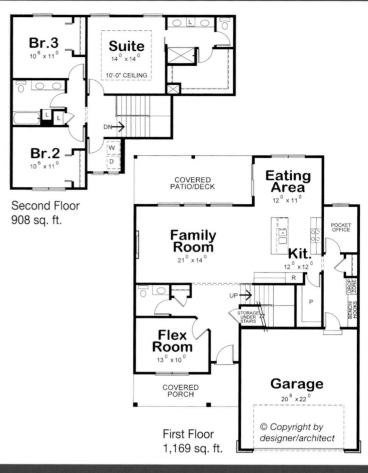

Br.3
10⁶ x 11⁰

Suite
14⁰ x 14⁰
10'-0" CEILING

Br.2
10⁶ x 11⁰

DN →

W
D

Second Floor
908 sq. ft.

COVERED PATIO/DECK

Eating Area
12⁰ x 11⁰

POCKET OFFICE

Family Room
21⁰ x 14⁰

Kit.
12⁰ x 12⁰

UP →

R

P

BENCH HOOKS

DROP ZONE

STORAGE UNDER STAIRS

Flex Room
13⁰ x 10⁰

COVERED PORCH

Garage
20⁸ x 22⁰

First Floor
1,169 sq. ft.

© Copyright by designer/architect

Plan #F11-026D-2158

Images provided by designer/architect

Dimensions: 40' W x 54' D
Heated Sq. Ft.: 2,077
Bedrooms: 3 **Bathrooms:** 2½
Exterior Walls: 2" x 6"
Foundation: Basement standard; crawl space, slab or walk-out basement for an additional fee

See index for more information

Covered Patio

Din.
12⁰ x 12⁴

Mbr.
15 x 12
Cath. Ceiling

Br.3
12 x 12

B.

Grt. Rm.
17 x 17
Cath. Ceiling

D

K.
8 x 13

B.

DN

R

Pantry

Br.2
12 x 12⁰

Covered Porch

Catch-all

Bench/ Lockers

D W

Gar.
22⁰ x 23⁰

© Copyright by designer/architect

Plan #F11-123D-0112

Dimensions: 49' W x 64' D
Heated Sq. Ft.: 1,797
Bedrooms: 3 **Bathrooms:** 2
Foundation: Basement standard; crawl space, slab or walk-out basement for an additional fee

See index for more information

Images provided by designer/architect

Plan #F11-139D-0087

Dimensions:	76'10" W x 68'9" D
Heated Sq. Ft.:	3,409
Bonus Sq. Ft.:	332
Bedrooms: 4	**Bathrooms:** 3½
Exterior Walls:	2" x 6"

Foundation: Crawl space standard; slab, basement, daylight basement or walk-out basement for an additional fee

See index for more information

Images provided by designer/architect

© Copyright by designer/architect

Second Floor
471 sq. ft.

First Floor
2,938 sq. ft.

Plan #F11-155D-0159

Dimensions:	70'6" W x 60'2" D
Heated Sq. Ft.:	2,073
Bonus Sq. Ft.:	283
Bedrooms: 3	**Bathrooms:** 2½

Foundation: Crawl space or slab standard; basement or daylight basement for an additional fee

See index for more information

Images provided by designer/architect

Optional Second Floor
283 sq. ft.

© Copyright by designer/architect

First Floor
2,073 sq. ft.

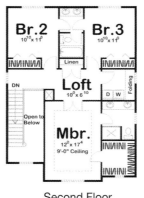

Second Floor
919 sq. ft.

First Floor
858 sq. ft.

Plan #F11-123D-0139

Dimensions:	34'4" W x 46' D
Heated Sq. Ft.:	1,777
Bonus Sq. Ft.:	584
Bedrooms: 3	**Bathrooms:** 2½

Foundation: Basement standard; crawl space, slab or walk-out basement for an additional fee

See index for more information

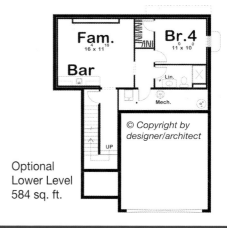

© Copyright by designer/architect

Optional
Lower Level
584 sq. ft.

Images provided by designer/architect

Second Floor
533 sq. ft.

© Copyright by
designer/architect

Plan #F11-155D-0114

Dimensions:	55' W x 139'9" D
Heated Sq. Ft.:	3,414
Bedrooms: 3	**Bathrooms:** 3½

Foundation: Crawl space or slab standard; basement or daylight basement for an additional fee

See index for more information

First Floor
2,881 sq. ft.

Images provided by designer/architect

Plan #F11-026D-2072

Dimensions: 45' W x 62' D
Heated Sq. Ft.: 1,619
Bedrooms: 3   **Bathrooms:** 2
Exterior Walls: 2" x 6"
Foundation: Slab standard; crawl space, basement or walk-out basement for an additional fee

See index for more information

Images provided by designer/architect

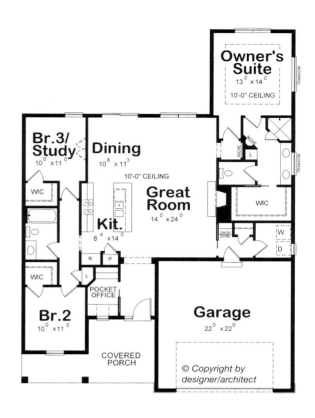

© Copyright by designer/architect

Plan #F11-167D-0006

Dimensions: 68'11" W x 69'10" D
Heated Sq. Ft.: 2,939
Bedrooms: 4   **Bathrooms:** 3½
Exterior Walls: 2" x 6"
Foundation: Slab standard; crawl space for an additional fee

See index for more information

© Copyright by designer/architect

Images provided by designer/architect

Plan #F11-011D-0687

Images provided by designer/architect

Dimensions:	74' W x 55' D
Heated Sq. Ft.:	1,975
Bedrooms: 4	**Bathrooms:** 2
Exterior Walls:	2" x 6"

Foundation: Crawl space or slab standard; basement for an additional fee

See index for more information

Plan #F11-144D-0017

Images provided by designer/architect

Dimensions:	42' W x 34'6" D
Heated Sq. Ft.:	1,043
Bedrooms: 2	**Bathrooms:** 1
Exterior Walls:	2" x 6"

Foundation: Crawl space or slab, please specify when ordering

See index for more information

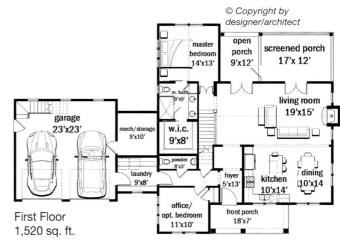

First Floor
1,520 sq. ft.

Floor plan labels: garage 23'x23', master bedroom 14'x13', open porch 9'x12', screened porch 17'x 12', m. bath 9'x9', living room 19'x15', mech/storage 9'x10', w.i.c. 9'x8', laundry 9'x8', powder 8'x3', foyer 5'x5', kitchen 10'x14', dining 10'x14, office/opt. bedroom 11'x10', front porch 18'x7'

Plan #F11-167D-0002

Dimensions:	74' W x 49'5" D
Heated Sq. Ft.:	2,063
Bedrooms: 3	**Bathrooms:** 2½
Exterior Walls:	2" x 6"

Foundation: Slab standard; crawl space for an additional fee

See index for more information

Images provided by designer/architect

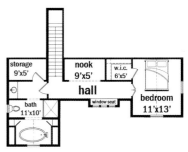

Second Floor
543 sq. ft.

Floor plan labels: storage 9'x5', nook 9'x5', w.i.c. 6'x5', hall, bath 11'x10', window seat, bedroom 11'x13'

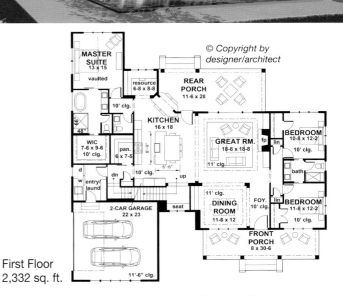

Images provided by designer/architect

Plan #F11-091D-0521

Dimensions:	67' W x 67'8" D
Heated Sq. Ft.:	2,332
Bonus Sq. Ft.:	286
Bedrooms: 3	**Bathrooms:** 2½
Exterior Walls:	2" x 6"

Foundation: Crawl space standard; slab, basement or walk-out basement for an additional fee

See index for more information

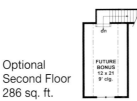
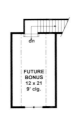

**Optional
Second Floor**
286 sq. ft.

FUTURE BONUS 12 x 21 9' clg.

First Floor
2,332 sq. ft.

Floor plan labels: MASTER SUITE 13 x 15 vaulted, resource 6-8 x 8-8, REAR PORCH 11-6 x 28, KITCHEN 16 x 18, GREAT RM. 18-8 x 18-8, BEDROOM 10-8 x 12-2, WIC 7-6 x 9-6, pan. 6 x 7-5, entry/laund, DINING ROOM 11-6 x 12, FOY., BEDROOM 11-8 x 12-2, 2-CAR GARAGE 22 x 23, FRONT PORCH 8 x 30-6

Plan #F11-123D-0241

Dimensions: 87' W x 52' D
Heated Sq. Ft.: 2,835
Bedrooms: 4   **Bathrooms:** 3½
Foundation: Basement standard; crawl space, slab or walk-out basement for an additional fee

See index for more information

Images provided by designer/architect

Special Features

- This unique home blends today's Modern Farmhouse architecture with classic barn style design elements on the exterior for a truly "down home" feel
- Traditionally designed on the interior to include formal spaces flanking the foyer, and the more casual spaces are in the back of the home
- The open kitchen overlooks the breakfast area and the great room with built-in fireplace
- All bedrooms reside on the second floor ensuring privacy from day-to-day household activities
- A handy mud room connects the large garage to the rest of the home
- 3-car front entry garage

First Floor
1,513 sq. ft.

Second Floor
1,322 sq. ft.

Plan #F11-141D-0314

Dimensions: 81'1" W x 124'4" D
Heated Sq. Ft.: 5,400
Bedrooms: 6   **Bathrooms:** 4½
Foundation: Crawl space or slab standard; basement or walk-out basement for an additional fee

See index for more information

Second Floor
1,823 sq. ft.

© Copyright by designer/architect

First Floor
3,577 sq. ft.

Special Features

- This luxury Modern Farmhouse incorporates so many great amenities including an outdoor kitchen, office, parlor, screened porch, friend's entry, and a media room
- The huge beamed family room is cozy and inviting thanks to the fireplace
- The vaulted screened porch is a showstopper with a cozy fireplace
- The home office is tucked away near the master bedroom for peace and quiet
- There's a large utility room in additional to a mud area by the friend's entry
- The second floor media area is bound to be a favorite spot to hang-out
- 4-car side entry garage

Plan #F11-101D-0117

Dimensions: 98' W x 81'2" D
Heated Sq. Ft.: 2,925
Bonus Sq. Ft.: 1,602
Bedrooms: 3   **Bathrooms:** 2½
Exterior Walls: 2" x 6"
Foundation: Basement, daylight basement or walk-out basement, please specify when ordering

See index for more information

Special Features

- This stunning Prairie inspired rustic Modern Farmhouse has a welcoming front porch and leads into an open foyer with beautiful views of the great room
- The luxury master bedroom has covered deck access, a massive bath with a freestanding tub, and a huge walk-in closet with direct laundry and mud room access
- The kitchen maintains a feeling of openness and enjoys the added function of the large island
- Two bedrooms can be found behind the kitchen and they share a large Jack and Jill style bath
- The optional lower level has an additional 1,602 square feet of living area including a rec room with a fireplace and wet bar, and two private bedrooms with their own walk-in closets and baths
- 3-car side entry garage

© Copyright by designer/architect

First Floor
2,925 sq. ft.

Optional Lower Level
1,602 sq. ft.

Images provided by designer/architect

Plan #F11-028D-0099

Dimensions:	30' W x 49' D
Heated Sq. Ft.:	1,320
Bedrooms: 3	**Bathrooms:** 2
Exterior Walls:	2" x 6"

Foundation: Crawl space or monolithic slab, please specify when ordering

See index for more information

Special Features

- In a sensible size, this cottage can easily incorporate popular modern farmhouse style trends into its floor plan with a barn style door from the master bedroom into the bath and rustic floating shelves for storage in the kitchen

- The great room and kitchen/dining area blend together making the interior feel larger than its true size

- All three of the bedrooms are located near each other for convenience

- A laundry room is centrally located adding ease with this frequent chore

Images provided by designer/architect

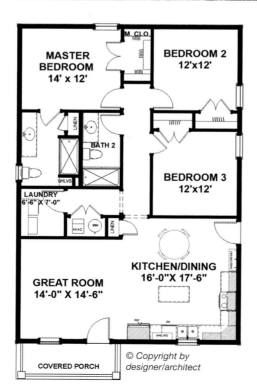

MASTER BEDROOM 14' x 12'

BEDROOM 2 12'x12'

M. CLO.

LINEN

BATH 2

SHLVS

LAUNDRY 6'-6" X 7'-0"

HVAC WH LINEN

BEDROOM 3 12'x12'

GREAT ROOM 14'-0" X 14'-6"

KITCHEN/DINING 16'-0"X 17'-6"

REF DW

SHELVES

COVERED PORCH

© Copyright by designer/architect

Plan #F11-123D-0257

Dimensions:	108' W x 52' D
Heated Sq. Ft.:	2,155
Bedrooms: 3	**Bathrooms:** 2½
Exterior Walls:	2" x 6"

Foundation: Slab standard; crawl space, basement or walk-out basement for an additional fee

See index for more information

Special Features

- This rustic, barn-like dwelling is sure to stand out and provide you with a casual living environment that merges nicely with the outdoors thanks to four large garage style overhead doors in the sun room that can be lifted and opened to the outdoors
- The great room has one large overhead door that can open the home even further when both the sun room and the great room are opened up at the same time
- The kitchen is in the center of the action and has dining space near the great room
- The master bedroom is in a private first floor location
- The second floor includes two bedrooms and a full bath
- 3-car front entry garage

© Copyright by designer/architect

Second Floor
603 sq. ft.

First Floor
1,552 sq. ft.

Images provided by designer/architect

Call toll-free 1-800-373-2646

Plan #F11-032D-0887

Dimensions:	42' W x 40' D
Heated Sq. Ft.:	1,212
Bonus Sq. Ft.:	1,212
Bedrooms: 2	**Bathrooms:** 1
Exterior Walls:	2" x 6"

Foundation: Basement standard; crawl space, floating slab or monolithic slab for an additional fee

See index for more information

Images provided by designer/architect

Special Features

- This highly efficient home offers an open floor plan with beamed ceilings above adding a tremendous amount of architectural interest to the interior
- A fireplace acts like a partition between the bedroom hall and the main gathering spaces
- The large covered porch is a wonderful extension of the interior living spaces to the outdoors
- The island in the kitchen includes casual dining space and a double basin sink and dishwasher
- The optional lower level has an additional 1,212 square feet of living area

First Floor
1,212 sq. ft.

© Copyright by designer/architect

Optional
Lower Level
1,212 sq. ft.

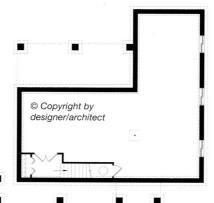

Plan #F11-101D-0097

Dimensions:	70' W x 86' D
Heated Sq. Ft.:	2,526
Bonus Sq. Ft.:	1,938
Bedrooms: 2	**Bathrooms:** 2½
Exterior Walls:	2" x 6"
Foundation:	Basement

See index for more information

Special Features

- This Craftsman inspired ranch home has a sleek, rustic exterior and a refreshingly open and modern interior

- The kitchen has an oversized island with space for prepping meals and dining

- An office is found right off the foyer and it connects to a Jack and Jill bath making it also ideal as a bedroom

- The master bedroom enjoys a private sitting area with covered patio views, a posh bath with a free-standing tub and separate walk-in shower, and a large walk-in closet

- The optional lower level has an additional 1,938 square feet of living area and includes a recreation room, a wet bar, a wine room, two additional bedrooms with walk-in closets, a full bath and a half bath

- 3-car front entry garage

© Copyright by designer/architect

First Floor
2,526 sq. ft.

Optional Lower Level
1,938 sq. ft.

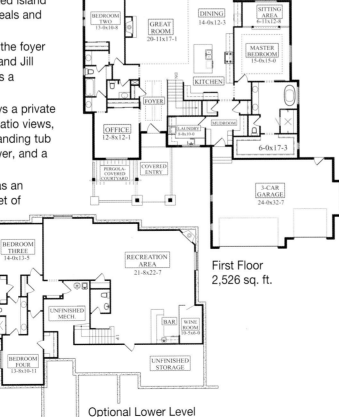

Images provided by designer/architect

MASTER
BEDROOM
10⁴ x 12¹⁰

BEDROOM
3
9⁸ x 10⁸

Second Floor
605 sq. ft.

MSTR.
BATH

BEDROOM
2
10⁰ x 11⁰

BATH
2

© Copyright by
designer/architect

Plan #F11-111D-0042

Dimensions: 29' W x 30' D
Heated Sq. Ft.: 1,074
Bedrooms: 3   **Bathrooms:** 2½
Foundation: Slab standard; crawl
space for an additional fee

See index for more information

Images provided by designer/architect

PATIO

KITCHEN
9⁰ x 10⁰

PWDR

DINING &
LIVING
14⁰ x 19⁰

GARAGE
10⁰ x 19⁸

PORCH

First Floor
469 sq. ft.

Images provided by designer/architect

Plan #F11-148D-0404

Dimensions: 48' W x 42' D
Heated Sq. Ft.: 1,282
Bedrooms: 3   **Bathrooms:** 2
Exterior Walls: 2" x 6"
Foundation: Basement

See index for more information

© Copyright by
designer/architect

BALCONY
20'-0" X 8'-0"

MASTER BEDROOM
13'-2" X 12'-2"

BEDROOM #2
10'-6" X 10'-4"

KITCHEN
8'-6" X 12'-0"

DINNING ROOM
11'-2" X 14'-0"

BATHROOM #2
9'-0" X 5'-0"

BEDROOM #3
12'-4" X 9'-0"

LIVING ROOM
13'-2" X 14'-6"

SHOWER
36"X78"

BATHROOM #1
8'-2" X 6'-6"

GARAGE
13'-4" X 21'-0"

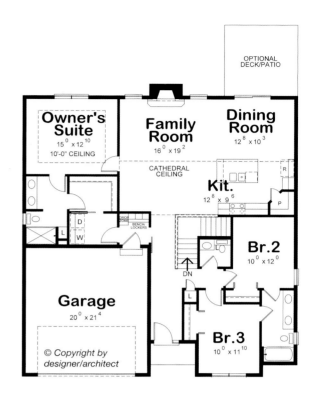

Images provided by designer/architect

Plan #F11-026D-2143

Dimensions: 45' W x 47'8" D
Heated Sq. Ft.: 1,642
Bedrooms: 3   **Bathrooms:** 2½
Exterior Walls: 2" x 6"
Foundation: Basement standard; crawl space, slab or walk-out basement for an additional fee

See index for more information

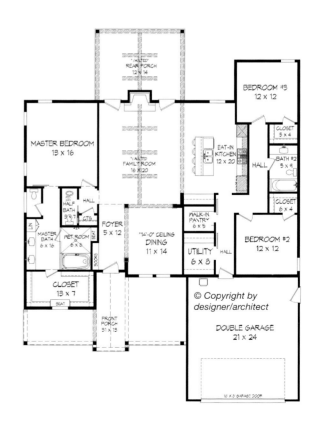

Images provided by designer/architect

Plan #F11-141D-0223

Dimensions: 52'10" W x 67'2" D
Heated Sq. Ft.: 2,095
Bedrooms: 3   **Bathrooms:** 2½
Exterior Walls: 2" x 6"
Foundation: Crawl space or slab standard; basement or walk-out basement for an additional fee

See index for more information

OPEN TO BELOW

LOFT
Vaulted Ceiling
18'8"x17'8"

LIN.

BR. #2
Vaulted Ceiling
15'0"x14'0"

GRT. RM.
Vaulted Ceiling
21'6"x15'0"

KIT.
Vaulted Ceiling
13'6"x15'0"

PAN.

LOCKERS

BR. #1
10'-1 1/8" Ceiling
13'0"x11'4"

BENCH

3 CAR GARAGE
35'4"x23'8"

© Copyright by
designer/architect

First Floor
1,080 sq. ft.

Plan #F11-051D-0978

Dimensions:	47' W x 54' D
Heated Sq. Ft.:	1,871
Bedrooms: 2	**Bathrooms:** 2
Exterior Walls:	2" x 6"
Foundation:	Slab

See index for more information

Images provided by designer/architect

Images provided by designer/architect

Plan #F11-056D-0104

Dimensions:	63'1" W x 41'10" D
Heated Sq. Ft.:	1,925
Bedrooms: 3	**Bathrooms:** 2½
Foundation:	Slab

See index for more information

BREAKFAST
11'-5"x12'-7"
10' CLG

COVERED PORCH
12'-3" x 11'-8"
VAULTED

© Copyright by
designer/architect

MASTER BEDROOM
15'-5" x 14'-3"
PLUS OFFSET
10' CLG

LODGE ROOM
VAULTED
17'-7" x 24'-3"
PLUS OFFSET

BEDROOM#2
11'-8" x 12'-4"
10' CLG

KITCHEN
11'-5"x15'-5"
10' CLG

BATH

MSTR. BATH

PAN.

SITTING
VAULTED

P.R

W.I.C

L.R

COVR'D PORCH
20'-0" x 5'-5"

BEDROOM#3
11'-8" x 12'-4"
10' CLG

Images provided by designer/architect

Plan #F11-139D-0091

Dimensions: 64'5" W x 83'9" D
Heated Sq. Ft.: 3,163
Heated Sq. Ft.: 447
Bedrooms: 4   **Bathrooms:** 3½
Exterior Walls: 2" x 6"
Foundation: Crawl space standard; slab, basement, daylight basement or walk-out basement for an additional fee

See index for more information

© Copyright by designer/architect

First Floor
2,362 sq. ft.

Second Floor
801 sq. ft.

Images provided by designer/architect

Plan #F11-163D-0019

Dimensions: 73' W x 51' D
Heated Sq. Ft.: 2,689
Bedrooms: 4   **Bathrooms:** 3½
Exterior Walls: 2" x 6"
Foundation: Crawl space

See index for more information

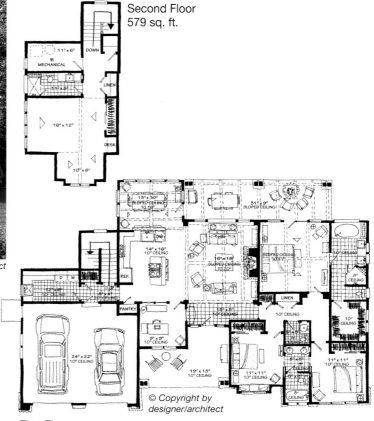

Second Floor
579 sq. ft.

© Copyright by designer/architect

First Floor
2,110 sq. ft.

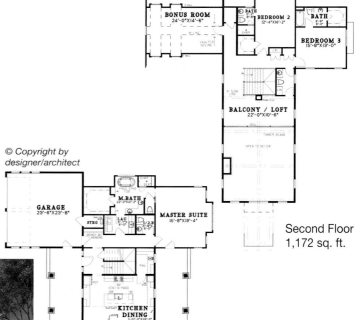

Second Floor
1,172 sq. ft.

Plan #F11-155D-0232

Images provided by designer/architect

Dimensions: 65' W x 82' D
Heated Sq. Ft.: 3,014
Bonus Sq. Ft.: 381
Bedrooms: 3
Bathrooms: 3 full, 2 half
Exterior Walls: 2" x 6"
Foundation: Crawl space or slab standard; basement or daylight basement for an additional fee

See index for more information

© Copyright by designer/architect

First Floor
1,842 sq. ft.

Images provided by designer/architect

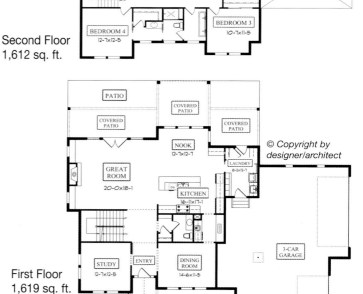

Second Floor
1,612 sq. ft.

© Copyright by designer/architect

First Floor
1,619 sq. ft.

Plan #F11-101D-0068

Dimensions: 71'6" W x 64' D
Heated Sq. Ft.: 3,231
Bonus Sq. Ft.: 368
Bedrooms: 4   **Bathrooms:** 2½
Exterior Walls: 2" x 6"
Foundation: Basement

See index for more information

Plan #F11-091D-0523

Dimensions: 69' W x 57'6" D
Heated Sq. Ft.: 2,514
Bonus Sq. Ft.: 390
Bedrooms: 4   **Bathrooms:** 3½
Exterior Walls: 2" x 6"
Foundation: Crawl space standard; slab, basement, daylight basement or walk-out basement for an additional fee

See index for more information

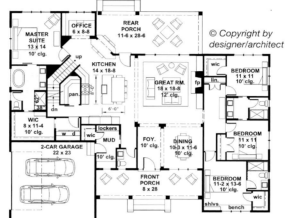

© Copyright by designer/architect

First Floor
2,514 sq. ft.

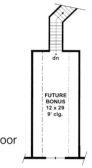

Optional Second Floor
390 sq. ft.

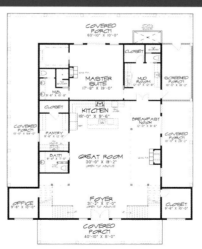

© Copyright by designer/architect

First Floor
2,670 sq. ft.

Second Floor
1,402 sq. ft.

Plan #F11-155D-0052

Dimensions: 60'10" W x 78' D
Heated Sq. Ft.: 4,072
Bedrooms: 3   **Bathrooms:** 3½
Foundation: Crawl space or slab, please specify when ordering

See index for more information

Plan #F11-011D-0579

Dimensions: 60' W x 64' D
Heated Sq. Ft.: 2,292
Bedrooms: 3   **Bathrooms:** 2½
Exterior Walls: 2" x 6"
Foundation: Crawl space or slab standard; basement for an additional fee

See index for more information

Images provided by designer/architect

Special Features

- An attractive front porch and large dormer window adds curb appeal, undeniable charm and a Modern Farmhouse feel
- As you enter this home there is a convenient office and half bath
- The vaulted living and dining areas join forces and surround the kitchen with gathering space
- Below the large window in the dining room is a built-in seat adding character to the space
- The large L-shaped kitchen has a long center island and features a walk-in pantry
- The master bedroom and bath are tucked away in the rear of this home, offering plenty of peace and quiet
- Two bedrooms on the second floor share a bath and large loft
- Charming extras can be found throughout this design including a bench and locker style storage in the mud room
- 2-car front entry garage

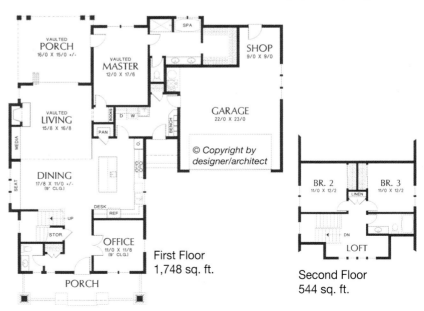

First Floor
1,748 sq. ft.

Second Floor
544 sq. ft.

Plan #F11-123D-0200

Dimensions: 62' W x 86' D
Heated Sq. Ft.: 3,205
Bonus Sq. Ft.: 970
Bedrooms: 4   **Bathrooms:** 3½
Exterior Walls: 2" x 6"
Foundation: Slab standard; crawl space, basement or walk-out basement for an additional fee

See index for more information

Special Features

- This barn home offers that rural feel and large open spaces with cathedral ceilings
- Double doors flank each side of the fireplace in the towering two-story great room
- The kitchen features a huge island that has enough space for dining and fantastic views of the great room
- The second floor features a loft overlooking the great room below
- The bonus room on the second floor has an additional 970 square feet of living area
- 3-car side entry garage, and a 1-car side entry garage

First Floor
1,943 sq. ft.

Second Floor
1,262 sq. ft.

Images provided by designer/architect

Plan #F11-056S-0010

Dimensions: 74'10" W x 83'5" D
Heated Sq. Ft.: 2,795
Bonus Sq. Ft.: 3,297
Bedrooms: 3   **Bathrooms:** 3½
Foundation: Basement standard;
crawl space or slab for an additional
fee

See index for more information

Images provided by designer/architect

Special Features

- This fairytale farmhouse design has so much character it feels as though it was built a century ago thanks to its stone accents, arched paned windows, and gingerbread style gable woodwork
- The lodge room is the main gathering spot with a cozy fireplace, views of the covered porch and only steps from the kitchen island
- The master bedroom enjoys a plush bath with a stunning tub, two vanities and double walk-in closets
- The optional lower level has an additional 2,795 square feet of living area; while the optional second floor has an additional 502 square feet of living area
- 2-car side entry garage

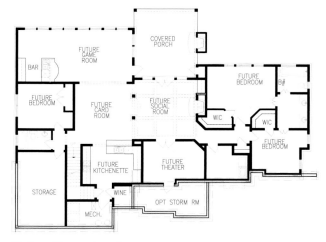

Optional Lower Level
2,795 sq. ft.

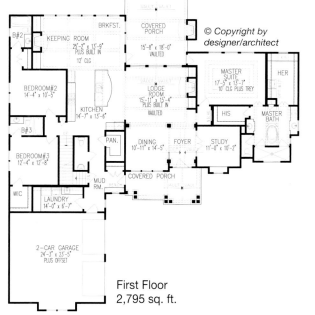

First Floor
2,795 sq. ft.

**Optional
Second Floor**
502 sq. ft.

Plan #F11-101D-0050

Dimensions:	110'6" W x 84' D
Heated Sq. Ft.:	4,784
Bonus Sq. Ft.:	1,926
Bedrooms: 5	**Bathrooms:** 4½
Exterior Walls:	2" x 6"
Foundation:	Basement

See index for more information

Special Features

- Rustic beams above the entry give this home a lodge feel
- The first floor enjoys an open floor plan that has the kitchen in the center of activity surrounded by the great room and casual dining area with a fireplace
- The private master bedroom and bath enjoy covered deck access and his and hers walk-in closets
- A quiet home office is hidden behind the kitchen
- The second floor loft is a nice place to hang-out, and the laundry room is located near the second floor bedrooms for ease with this ongoing chore
- The optional lower level has an additional 1,926 square feet of living area and enjoys a wet bar and family room for entertaining, and for hobbies there's a climbing room and craft room
- 2-car side entry garage, and a 1-car front entry garage

Images provided by designer/architect

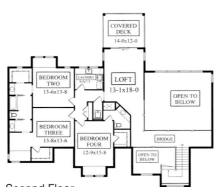

Second Floor
1,753 sq. ft.

© Copyright by
designer/architect

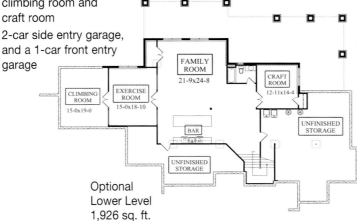

Optional
Lower Level
1,926 sq. ft.

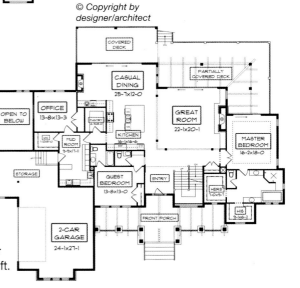

First Floor
3,031 sq. ft.

Plan #F11-032D-1165

Dimensions:	48' W x 31' D
Heated Sq. Ft.:	1,810
Bonus Sq. Ft.:	908
Bedrooms: 3	**Bathrooms:** 1½
Exterior Walls:	2" x 6"

Foundation: Basement standard; crawl space, floating slab or monolithic slab for an additional fee

See index for more information

Special Features

- Utilitarian simplicity creates a Modern Farmhouse that's functional, stylish and no-fuss
- Step into the front hall and find a cozy office to the right, and the living room to the left
- The kitchen has a walk-in pantry and a huge island that spans its entire length with seating for five people to relax and enjoy casual dining
- The second floor is comprised of all of the bedrooms, and a handy second floor laundry room is centrally located
- The optional lower level has an additional 908 square feet of living area
- 1-car front entry garage

Second Floor
902 sq. ft.

© Copyright by designer/architect

First Floor
908 sq. ft.

Optional Lower Level
908 sq. ft.

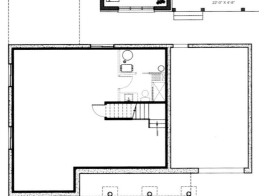

Images provided by designer/architect

Images provided by designer/architect

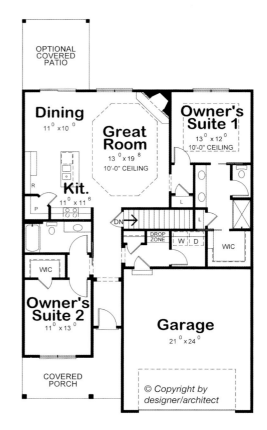

Plan #F11-026D-2134

Dimensions: 38' W x 55' D
Heated Sq. Ft.: 1,387
Bedrooms: 2   **Bathrooms:** 2
Foundation: Basement standard; crawl space, slab or walk-out basement for an additional fee

See index for more information

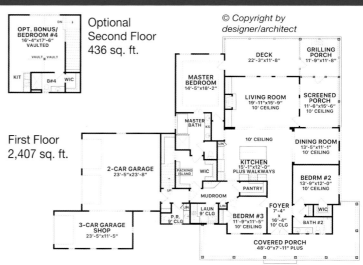

Images provided by designer/architect

Plan #F11-056D-0107

Dimensions: 94' W x 70'4" D
Heated Sq. Ft.: 2,407
Bonus Sq. Ft.: 436
Bedrooms: 3   **Bathrooms:** 2½
Foundation: Slab standard; crawl space or basement for an additional fee

See index for more information

Images provided by designer/architect

Plan #F11-163D-0018

Dimensions: 93' W x 64' D
Heated Sq. Ft.: 2,760
Bedrooms: 3   **Bathrooms:** 3½
Exterior Walls: 2" x 6"
Foundation: Crawl space

See index for more information

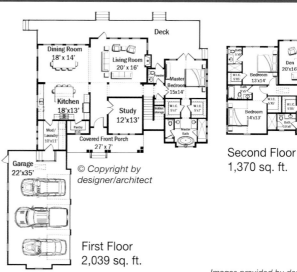

First Floor
2,039 sq. ft.

Second Floor
1,370 sq. ft.

Images provided by designer/architect

Plan #F11-167D-0010

Dimensions: 70'11" W x 84'10" D
Heated Sq. Ft.: 3,409
Bedrooms: 4   **Bathrooms:** 4½
Exterior Walls: 2" x 6"
Foundation: Crawl space standard; slab for an additional fee

See index for more information

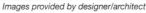

First Floor
1,108 sq. ft.

© Copyright by designer/architect

Images provided by designer/architect

Plan #F11-032D-1164

Dimensions: 54'4" W x 33' D
Heated Sq. Ft.: 2,041
Bonus Sq. Ft.: 1,180
Bedrooms: 3 **Bathrooms:** 1½
Exterior Walls: 2" x 6"
Foundation: Basement standard; crawl space, floating slab or monolithic slab for an additional fee

See index for more information

Second Floor
933 sq. ft.

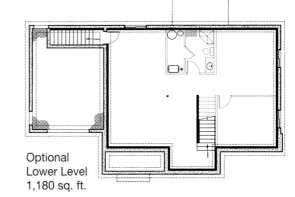

Optional
Lower Level
1,180 sq. ft.

Plan #F11-155D-0170

Dimensions: 60'6" W x 64'8" D
Heated Sq. Ft.: 1,897
Bedrooms: 4 **Bathrooms:** 2
Foundation: Crawl space or slab standard; basement or daylight basement for an additional fee

See index for more information

© Copyright by designer/architect

Images provided by designer/architect

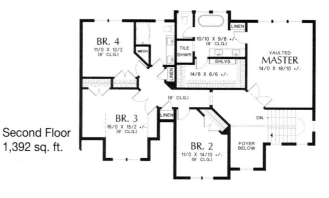

Second Floor
1,392 sq. ft.

BR. 4
11/0 X 12/2
(9' CLG.)

10/10 X 9/8 +/-
(9' CLG.)

VAULTED
MASTER
14/0 X 18/10 +/-

14/8 X 6/6 +/-

(9' CLG.)

BR. 3
16/0 X 15/2 +/-
(9' CLG.)

BR. 2
11/0 X 14/10 +/-
(9' CLG.)

DN.

FOYER
BELOW

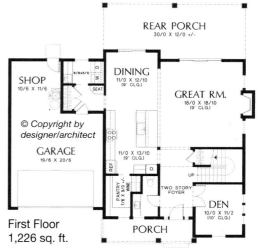

REAR PORCH
30/0 X 12/0 +/-

SHOP
10/6 X 11/6

DINING
11/0 X 12/10
(9' CLG.)

GREAT RM.
18/0 X 18/10
(9' CLG.)

© Copyright by
designer/architect

GARAGE
19/6 X 20/6

11/0 X 13/10
(9' CLG.)

UP

TWO STORY
FOYER

DEN
10/0 X 11/2
(10' CLG.)

PANTRY
7/6 X 9/0 +/-

First Floor
1,226 sq. ft.

PORCH

Plan #F11-011D-0658

Images provided by designer/architect

Dimensions:	50' W x 52' D
Heated Sq. Ft.:	2,618
Bedrooms: 4	**Bathrooms:** 2½
Exterior Walls:	2" x 6"

Foundation: Crawl space or slab standard; basement for an additional fee

See index for more information

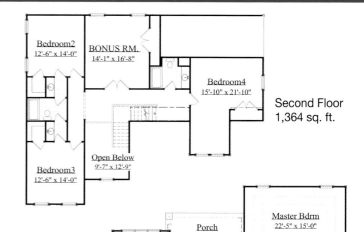

Bedroom2
12'-6" x 14'-0"

BONUS RM.
14'-1" x 16'-8"

Bedroom4
15'-10" x 21'-10"

Second Floor
1,364 sq. ft.

Open Below
9'-7" x 12'-9"

Bedroom3
12'-6" x 14'-0"

Master Bdrm
22'-5" x 15'-0"

Porch
16'-3" x 8'-10"

Nook
12'-6" x 10'-2"

Family
16'-7" x 20'-6"

Kitchen
13'-8" x 12'-2"

© Copyright by
designer/architect

Garage
22'-5" x 22'-8"

Dining
12'-6" x 13'-0"

Study
12'-6" x 12'-0"

Porch
16'-9" x 8'-6"

First Floor
1,923 sq. ft.

Plan #F11-157D-0010

Images provided by designer/architect

Dimensions:	52'7" W x 61'10" D
Heated Sq. Ft.:	3,287
Bedrooms: 4	**Bathrooms:** 3½

Foundation: Crawl space standard; slab for an additional fee

See index for more information

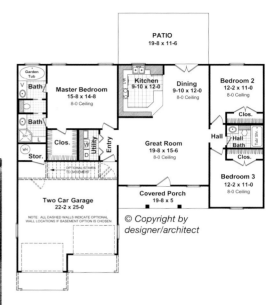

Plan #F11-077D-0019

Dimensions: 54' W x 47' D
Heated Sq. Ft.:   1,400
Bedrooms: 3   **Bathrooms:** 2
Foundation: Slab, crawl space or basement, please specify when ordering

See index for more information

Images provided by designer/architect

© Copyright by designer/architect

First Floor 2,278 sq. ft.

Optional Second Floor 430 sq. ft.

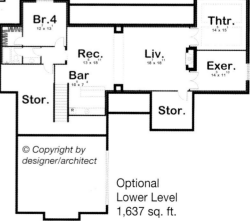

Optional Lower Level 1,637 sq. ft.

© Copyright by designer/architect

Plan #F11-123D-0141

Dimensions: 73' W x 68'4" D
Heated Sq. Ft.:   2,278
Bonus Sq. Ft.:   2,067
Bedrooms: 3   **Bathrooms:** 2½
Foundation: Basement standard; crawl space, slab or walk-out basement for an additional fee

See index for more information

Images provided by designer/architect

Optional
Second Floor
1,535 sq. ft.

Images provided by designer/architect

Plan #F11-013D-0255

Dimensions: 71'2" W x 64'6" D
Heated Sq. Ft.: 2,156
Bonus Sq. Ft.: 3,887
Bedrooms: 3 **Bathrooms:** 3
Foundation: Basement standard; daylight basement for an additional fee

See index for more information

Optional Lower Level
2,352 sq. ft.

First Floor
2,156 sq. ft.

© Copyright by designer/architect

Images provided by designer/architect

Plan #F11-155D-0118

Dimensions: 121'6" W x 65'7" D
Heated Sq. Ft.: 3,310
Bedrooms: 4 **Bathrooms:** 3½
Foundation: Crawl space or slab standard; basement or daylight basement for an additional fee

See index for more information

First Floor
2,301 sq. ft.

Second Floor
1,009 sq. ft.

© Copyright by designer/architect

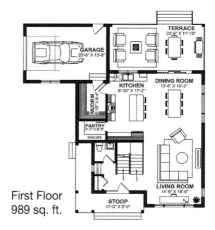

Second Floor
925 sq. ft.

First Floor
989 sq. ft.

Plan #F11-032D-1167

Dimensions: 45' W x 46'10" D
Heated Sq. Ft.: 1,914
Bonus Sq. Ft.: 989
Bedrooms: 3 **Bathrooms:** 2½
Exterior Walls: 2" x 6"
Foundation: Basement standard; crawl space, floating slab or monolithic slab for an additional fee

See index for more information

Images provided by designer/architect

Optional
Lower Level
989 sq. ft.

DECK

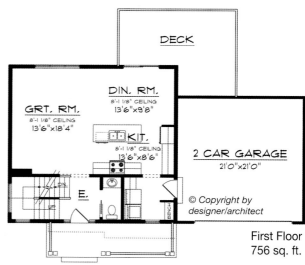

First Floor
756 sq. ft.

Plan #F11-051D-0947

Dimensions: 49'4" W x 33' D
Heated Sq. Ft.: 1,495
Bedrooms: 3 **Bathrooms:** 2½
Exterior Walls: 2" x 6"
Foundation: Basement standard; crawl space or slab for an additional fee

See index for more information

Images provided by designer/architect

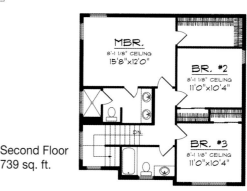

Second Floor
739 sq. ft.

Plan #F11-155D-0210

Dimensions:	81'4" W x 67'8" D
Heated Sq. Ft.:	2,191
Bonus Sq. Ft.:	193
Bedrooms:	3
Bathrooms:	2 full, 2 half
Exterior Walls:	2" x 6"

Foundation: Crawl space or slab, please specify when ordering

See index for more information

Images provided by designer/architect

© Copyright by designer/architect

Images provided by designer/architect

Plan #F11-111D-0081

Dimensions:	54'6" W x 54'9" D
Heated Sq. Ft.:	2,137
Bonus Sq. Ft.:	247
Bedrooms: 3	**Bathrooms:** 2

Foundation: Slab standard; crawl space for an additional fee

See index for more information

Optional Second Floor 247 sq. ft.

Detached Garage

First Floor 2,137 sq. ft.

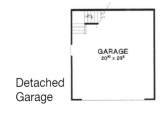

© Copyright by designer/architect

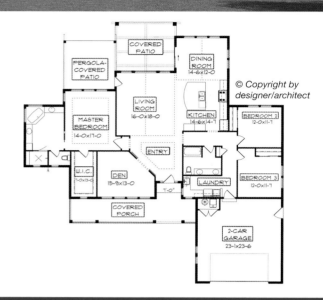

Plan #F11-101D-0150

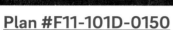

Images provided by designer/architect

© Copyright by designer/architect

Dimensions:	71'6" W x 74'6" D
Heated Sq. Ft.:	2,290
Bedrooms: 3	**Bathrooms:** 2
Exterior Walls:	2" x 6"
Foundation:	Slab

See index for more information

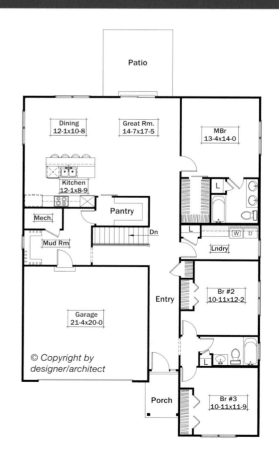

Plan #F11-169D-0002

Images provided by designer/architect

© Copyright by designer/architect

Dimensions:	41' W x 60'4" D
Heated Sq. Ft.:	1,762
Bedrooms: 3	**Bathrooms:** 2
Foundation:	Basement standard; crawl space or slab for an additional fee

See index for more information

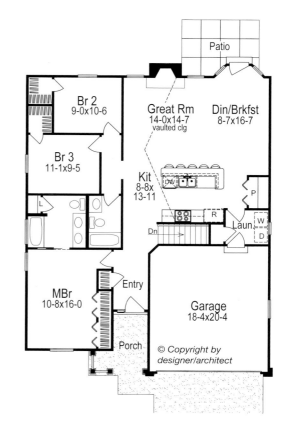

Images provided by designer/architect

Plan #F11-007D-5060

Dimensions: 38' W x 48'4" D
Heated Sq. Ft.: 1,344
Bedrooms: 3 **Bathrooms:** 2
Foundation: Basement standard;
crawl space or slab for an additional
fee

See index for more information

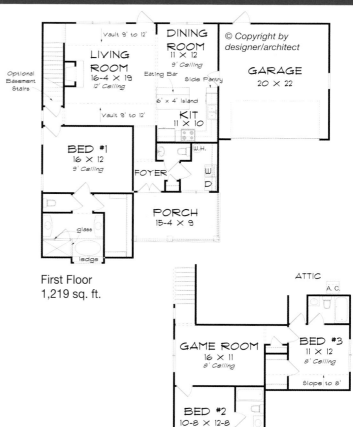

Images provided by designer/architect

First Floor
1,219 sq. ft.

Second Floor
659 sq. ft.

Plan #F11-130D-0387

Dimensions: 52' W x 44' D
Heated Sq. Ft.: 1,878
Bedrooms: 3 **Bathrooms:** 3½
Foundation: Slab standard;
basement or crawl space for an
additional fee

See index for more information

Plan #F11-101D-0145

Dimensions:	40' W x 58' D
Heated Sq. Ft.:	2,413
Bonus Sq. Ft.:	1,052
Bedrooms: 4	**Bathrooms:** 3
Exterior Walls:	2" x 6"
Foundation:	Basement

See index for more information

Images provided by designer/architect

Special Features

- This modern masterpiece has its bedrooms separated from each other for the utmost privacy
- The sleek and open kitchen overlooks the living room with fireplace
- The large second floor laundry room is ideal for the family on-the-go
- The master bedroom is vaulted and enjoys a large sitting area
- The optional lower level has an additional 1,052 square feet of living area including a family room with wet bar, a bedroom, and a full bath
- 3-car front entry tandem garage

Optional Lower Level
1,052 sq. ft.

First Floor
1,195 sq. ft.

Second Floor
1,218 sq. ft.

Plan #F11-123D-0147

Dimensions: 73' W x 89' D
Heated Sq. Ft.: 2,388
Bonus Sq. Ft.: 1,827
Bedrooms: 3   **Bathrooms:** 2
Foundation: Basement standard;
crawl space, slab or walk-out
basement for an additional fee

See index for more information

Special Features

- The kitchen has great room views, a walk-in pantry and is surrounded in dining options from casual to formal
- A cheerful and quiet sun room is found off the great room
- The master bedroom is in a private location and has the laundry room nearby for ease
- The optional lower level has an additional 1,447 square feet of living area; while the optional second floor has an additional 380 square feet of living area
- 2-car side entry garage

Images provided by designer/architect

First Floor
2,388 sq. ft.

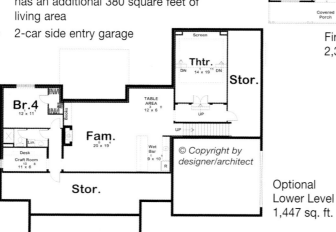

© Copyright by
designer/architect

Optional
Lower Level
1,447 sq. ft.

Optional
Second Floor
380 sq. ft.

Plan #F11-032D-1135

Dimensions:	65' W x 50' D
Heated Sq. Ft.:	1,788
Bonus Sq. Ft.:	1,788
Bedrooms: 2	**Bathrooms:** 2
Exterior Walls:	2" x 6"

Foundation: Basement standard; crawl space, floating slab or monolithic slab for an additional fee

See index for more information

Special Features

- Stylish modern living with an open feel that's easy to come home to
- Directly off the foyer is the office/den with easy access when business associates arrive
- The master suite enjoys double walk-in closets leading to a private bath
- The kitchen has an open feel to the nearby dining room and beyond to the living room featuring a fireplace
- A handy mud room connects the garage to the rest of the home
- The optional lower level has an additional 1,788 square feet of living area
- 2-car front entry garage

First Floor
1,788 sq. ft.

Optional
Lower Level
1,788 sq. ft.

© Copyright by
designer/architect

Images provided by designer/architect

designing & decorating a
modern farmhouse
inside & out

You've built your dream Modern Farmhouse and now it's time to decorate! How do you create that interior that "wows" just as much as the exterior does? How do you make the rooms feel seamless with the exterior and offer a full Modern Farmhouse experience from the front sidewalk all the way through to the back covered porch?

on the outside

not so subtle Modern Farmhouse style may seem low-key at first glance, but all those low key elements combine and form quite a bold statement. Bold, rustic beams, copper gutters, contrasting paint colors such as black and white, copper and metal light fixtures in angular shapes and oversized sizes all seem subtle on their own, but together create a personality all their own.

all the feels Although Modern Farmhouses are simple in overall design, texture really plays a prominent role in creating the relaxed vibe of the Modern Farmhouse's style. Whether its vertical and horizontal siding, rustic shingle siding, Industrial metal roofing, or black metal paned windows, textures of all types come together to form a truly one-of-a-kind Modern Farmhouse experience each time.

Unless noted, all images copyrighted by designer/architect. Page 114, top to bottom: Plan #F11-139D-0090, page 28; Plan #F11-091D-0509, page 38, Royal Oaks Design, Inc.; Plan #F11-101D-0149, page 37; Page 115: left, top to bottom: Plan #F11-101D-0126, page 41; Plan #F11-101D-0121, page 157; Plan #F11-101D-0132, page 32; right, top to bottom: Plan F11-101D-0131, page 191, Damon Searles, photographer; Plan #F11-101D-0050, page 98; See additional photos and purchase plans at houseplansandmore.com.

let there be light and dark

White is still the most popular choice for Modern Farmhouse exteriors, but black and various shades of gray are really gaining popularity, too. Color usually takes a supporting role to all of the texture provided by the various siding styles being used, but now look for black, charcoal, olive green, blue and dark plum to start trending in exterior colors.

one-of-a-kind design

Quirky comes to mind with today's Modern Farmhouse style. A classic farmhouse planter could sit outside the front door right alongside a hanging crochet swinging seat or full length colorful bench seat. This style truly merges eclectic styles and mixes neutrals in various textures to create a welcoming, inviting feel. Thick pile rugs, cozy loosely knit blankets, and fluffy pillows may decorate a front entry or seating creating an inviting feel to a front entry that may have a sharp, angular metal staircase.

love the outdoors

Often referred to as "outdoor living spaces," large front and back covered porches are common and an important feature because they offer additional living space for dining, entertaining, or relaxing. Add a porch swing, or an updated rocking chair in black or a bold or pastel color, and these porches are less "Grandma's house," and more today's modern family.

stay transparent

As discussed, windows are an important design element that allow for the interior to feel light and airy. Typically, double-hung and seen with black framing that stands out against the stark white exterior and interior finishes, windows play an important role in keeping the home bright, friendly and open. Traditional double-hung style keep the design grounded to its original farmhouse roots.

on the inside

less and more Most Modern Farmhouse designs have a laid-back personality that's friendly, inviting and promote a simple lifestyle. Homeowners now more than ever want their homes to be a refuge and sanctuary. A Modern Farmhouse is meant to be a peaceful, inviting retreat like an oasis that shelters you from the outside world. But, since the pandemic, some Modern Farmhouse style has started incorporating cozier elements such as color and prints, and textures such as fur and velvet. The decor has even become a bit more playful, and a bit less stark.

decor, neutral no more? When Modern Farmhouses first hit the scene they were almost entirely neutral - think all white or cream with little or no color at all. But, Modern Farmhouses are becoming a little more playful and starting to incorporate color into their decor. Fun, unexpected places like the kitchen, mud room, home office and laundry room are adding calming and inviting hues of blue and green for a refreshing change of pace to Modern Farmhouse living.

cool color comeback Still a neutral color palette reigns supreme in a Modern Farmhouse, but if color creeps into the home, you can bet it's a calm , soothing blue or green. Shades of blue and green, many that you would see in nature seem to be most popular. For those of you less daring, a contrasting gray or black island in the kitchen island also creates a dramatic look when paired with an all-white kitchen. Bold blues, rich greens and other more neutral variations of these hues are being splashed all over kitchen islands, laundry room cabinets, counter-tops and bookcases. Whatever color Modern Farmhouse kitchen you prefer, it will still include large windows, Shaker-style cabinets, quartz counter-tops, a tile back-splash, Industrial-style or statement light fixtures, a large island, and open shelving. Think uncomplicated and less cluttered.

still holding onto the past

If there's the chance to use reclaimed wood, stone, wrought iron, and other materials from buildings of the past, then continue to use these pieces as statement items and highlight them in your design. Whether it's rustic timber beams or rafters, "Ship Lap," original wood flooring, an antique fireplace, or salvaged antiqued doors, go ahead and use these special items for architectural interest. Even steel and polished concrete have a place in these homes because of their industrial look and durability.

go big or go home

The accessories including lighting in a Modern Farmhouse are not overly matching, but are more complementary with tons of character. Modern Farmhouse décor uses carefully placed, thoughtful elements that add personality to a space. The decor mixes sleek, modern accessories often mixed haphazardly with timeless ones. Artwork may be the one thing that adds a pop of color. The majority of the texture comes from throw rugs, and the fabric used on the sofas and chairs. Bold, often oversized light fixtures are a must, and if you're looking for a sleeker vibe, then add steel, wrought iron or sputnik style lighting to create an Industrial or retro feel.

you don't live in a barn, or do you?

Besides being a space-saving option, barn doors can be a decorative addition to any space, too. Use natural wood for a rustic feel, or paint it white, black, or even a bold color and add black hardware for a more sleek, decorative look. Either way, "barn doors" are a staple in Modern Farmhouse style and offer plenty of character while taking up less space and maximizing your home's square footage.

The Modern Farmhouse has taken the world by storm with its simplistic style and aesthetic. It is a sustainable choice that feels custom and tranquil and offers a relaxed way of life creating the perfect escape from today's chaotic world. Pairing down design and decorating, the Modern Farmhouse provides a kind of living that is appealing to so many homeowners today whether they're just starting out, or looking to transform and simplify their life.

Images provided by designer/architect

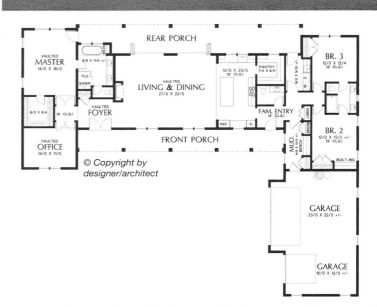

© Copyright by designer/architect

Plan #F11-011D-0630

Dimensions: 90' W x 75' D
Heated Sq. Ft.: 2,495
Bedrooms: 3   **Bathrooms:** 2½
Exterior Walls: 2" x 6"
Foundation: Craw space or slab standard; basement for an additional fee

See index for more information

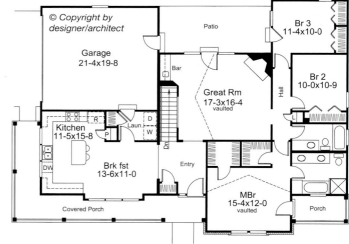

Plan #F11-007D-0140

Dimensions: 62' W x 45' D
Heated Sq. Ft.: 1,591
Bedrooms: 3   **Bathrooms:** 2
Foundation: Basement standard; crawl space or slab for an additional fee

See index for more information

Images provided by designer/architect

Images provided by designer/architect

Plan #F11-167D-0001

Dimensions: 59'6" W x 60' D
Heated Sq. Ft.: 2,017
Bedrooms: 3   **Bathrooms:** 3
Exterior Walls: 2" x 6"
Foundation: Crawl space standard; slab for an additional fee

See index for more information

Second Floor
1,144 sq. ft.

Plan #F11-139D-0088

Dimensions: 63'7" W x 61'6" D
Heated Sq. Ft.: 3,121
Bonus Sq. Ft.: 461
Bedrooms: 3   **Bathrooms:** 2½
Exterior Walls: 2" x 6"
Foundation: Crawl space standard; slab, basement, daylight basement or walk-out basement for an additional fee

See index for more information

Images provided by designer/architect

First Floor
1,977 sq. ft.

Second Floor
637 sq. ft.

© Copyright by designer/architect

First Floor
980 sq. ft.

Images provided by designer/architect

Plan #F11-032D-1083

Dimensions: 30' W x 36' D
Heated Sq. Ft.: 1,617
Bedrooms: 4   **Bathrooms:** 2
Exterior Walls: 2" x 6"
Foundation: Basement standard; crawl space, floating slab or monolithic slab for an additional fee

See index for more information

Optional Second Floor
436 sq. ft.

© Copyright by designer/architect

First Floor
2,407 sq. ft.

Images provided by designer/architect

Plan #F11-056D-0106

Dimensions: 94' W x 70'4" D
Heated Sq. Ft.: 2,407
Bonus Sq. Ft.: 436
Bedrooms: 3   **Bathrooms:** 2½
Foundation: Slab standard; crawl space or basement for an additional fee

See index for more information

Images provided by designer/architect

Plan #F11-058D-0266

Dimensions:	60'8" W x 59'8" D
Heated Sq. Ft.:	2,176
Bedrooms: 3	**Bathrooms:** 2½
Exterior Walls:	2" x 6"
Foundation:	Basement

See index for more information

Images provided by designer/architect

Plan #F11-077D-0288

Dimensions:	57' W x 74' D
Heated Sq. Ft.:	2,107
Bonus Sq. Ft.:	461
Bedrooms: 3	**Bathrooms:** 2½

Foundation: Crawl space or slab, please specify when ordering

See index for more information

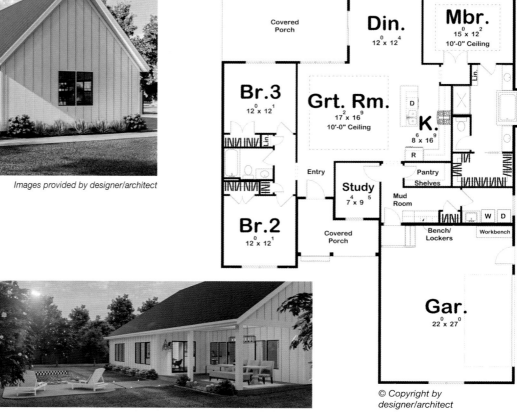

Plan #F11-123D-0176

Dimensions: 50' W x 68' D
Heated Sq. Ft.: 1,797
Bedrooms: 3   **Bathrooms:** 2
Foundation: Slab standard; crawl space, basement or walk-out basement for an additional fee

See index for more information

Images provided by designer/architect

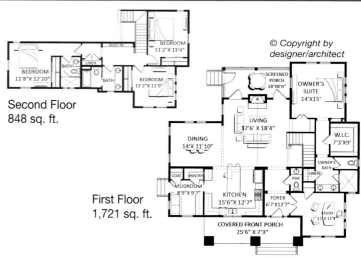

Second Floor
848 sq. ft.

First Floor
1,721 sq. ft.

Images provided by designer/architect

Plan #F11-167D-0003

Dimensions: 50'6" W x 50'5" D
Heated Sq. Ft.: 2,569
Bedrooms: 4   **Bathrooms:** 3½
Exterior Walls: 2" x 6"
Foundation: Crawl space standard; slab or basement for an additional fee

See index for more information

REF

T.W.H

8/0 X 9/0
(9' CLG.)

PAN

SHLVS

LIV/DIN
11/6 X 20/0
(9' CLG.)

STOR

UP

BR. 2
11/6 X 10/0
(8' CLG.)

W/D

LIN

DN.

BR. 1
11/6 X 10/0
(8' CLG.)

SEAT

Second Floor
455 sq. ft.

First Floor
489 sq. ft.

PORCH

Images provided by designer/architect

Plan #F11-011D-0683

Dimensions: 17' W x 41' D
Heated Sq. Ft.: 944
Bedrooms: 2   **Bathrooms:** 1½
Exterior Walls: 2" x 6"
Foundation: Crawl space or slab standard; basement for an additional fee

See index for more information

Images provided by designer/architect

Plan #F11-111D-0084

Dimensions: 77'11" W x 54'11" D
Heated Sq. Ft.: 2,169
Bedrooms: 3   **Bathrooms:** 2
Foundation: Slab standard; crawl space for an additional fee

See index for more information

MASTER BEDROOM
15⁰ x 16⁰

COVERED PATIO
11⁰ x 21⁶

FIREPLACE

DINING
12⁸ x 11⁹

MASTER BATH

WIC

TUB

SHLVS

BATH #2

SHLVS

GREAT ROOM
20⁰ x 21⁰

KITCHEN
12⁸ x 17⁰

DBL OVENS

PANTRY

GARAGE
22⁴ x 31⁴

BEDROOM #3
12⁰ x 12⁶

BEDROOM #2
11⁸ x 12⁰

GALLERY
DORMER WINDOWS ABOVE

PORCH

MUD ROOM

BENCH

UTILITY

Call toll-free 1-800-373-2646

Plan #F11-155D-0070

Dimensions:	60' W x 80'8" D
Heated Sq. Ft.:	2,464
Bonus Sq. Ft.:	758
Bedrooms: 4	**Bathrooms:** 3½

Foundation: Crawl space or slab standard; basement or daylight basement for an additional fee

See index for more information

Special Features

- The best in Farmhouse living, this home has a welcoming covered front porch offering extra charm and curb appeal
- The cheerful breakfast room has a functional computer desk and views of the rear grilling porch
- The combining of the great room, kitchen and breakfast room create a space that no doubt will be the central hub of this home
- The master suite offers all the amenities a homeowner needs
- The private bedroom 4 has its own bath, a built-in desk and a nearby TV/media room
- The optional bonus space on the second floor has an additional 758 square feet of living area
- 2-car side entry garage

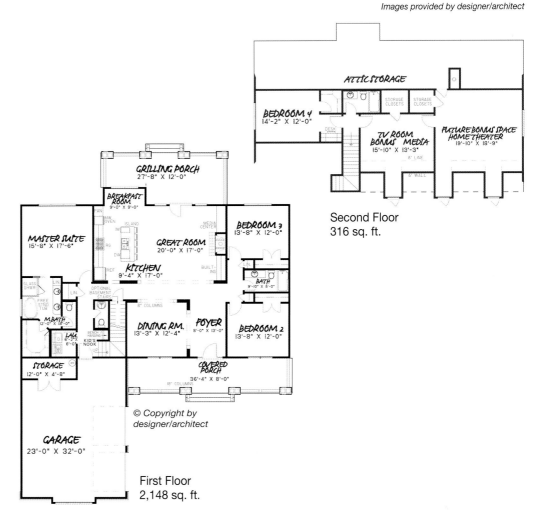

Second Floor
316 sq. ft.

First Floor
2,148 sq. ft.

© Copyright by designer/architect

Plan #F11-155D-0116

Dimensions: 107'8" W x 57'10" D
Heated Sq. Ft.: 3,277
Bonus Sq. Ft.: 603
Bedrooms: 5   **Bathrooms:** 3½
Foundation: Crawl space or slab, please specify when ordering

See index for more information

Special Features

- This totally unique barn-style home has a central gathering space and bedrooms on each side
- The great room and kitchen blend together to form the core of this home
- A huge laundry/mud room includes a shower, a sink, and a walk-in pantry
- The master suite is comprised of a private bath and two large walk-in closets
- The optional second floor has an additional 503 square feet of living area
- 2-car front entry garage

Images provided by designer/architect

Optional
Second Floor
603 sq. ft.

First Floor
3,277 sq. ft.

Plan #F11-011D-0660

Dimensions: 52' W x 53' D
Heated Sq. Ft.: 1,704
Bedrooms: 3 **Bathrooms:** 2½
Exterior Walls: 2" x 6"
Foundation: Crawl space or slab standard; basement for an additional fee

See index for more information

Special Features

- Stylish Modern Farmhouse living has never been easier than with this perfectly-sized one-story
- The vaulted great room has a corner fireplace and windows on two walls for an airy atmosphere
- A large island in the kitchen faces towards the great room and provides casual dining space
- The secluded master bedroom enjoys a large walk-in closet, and a private bath
- 2-car side entry garage

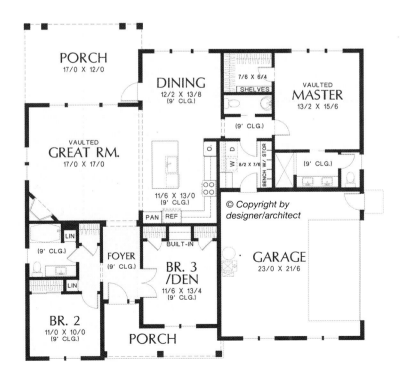

PORCH
17/0 X 12/0

DINING
12/2 X 13/8
(9' CLG.)

7/6 X 6/4
SHELVES

VAULTED
MASTER
13/2 X 15/6

(9' CLG.)

(9' CLG.)

VAULTED
GREAT RM.
17/0 X 17/0

11/6 X 13/0
(9' CLG.)

BENCH W/ STOR

8/2 X 7/6

(9' CLG.)

PAN REF

© Copyright by designer/architect

LIN
(9' CLG.)

BUILT-IN

FOYER
(9' CLG.)

BR. 3
/DEN
11/6 X 13/4
(9' CLG.)

GARAGE
23/0 X 21/6

LIN

BR. 2
11/0 X 10/0
(9' CLG.)

PORCH

Images provided by designer/architect

Plan #F11-032D-1151

Dimensions:	45' W x 38' D
Heated Sq. Ft.:	2,113
Bonus Sq. Ft.:	1,056
Bedrooms: 3	**Bathrooms:** 2½
Exterior Walls:	2" x 6"

Foundation: Basement standard; crawl space, floating slab or monolithic slab for an additional fee

See index for more information

Special Features

- The open living room features a beautiful modern fireplace creating dramatic ambiance
- The kitchen has an island and large walk-in pantry
- Sliding glass doors make the dining room cheerful and bright
- The optional lower level has an additional 1,056 square feet of living area
- 1-car side entry garage

Second Floor
1,057 sq. ft.

Images provided by designer/architect

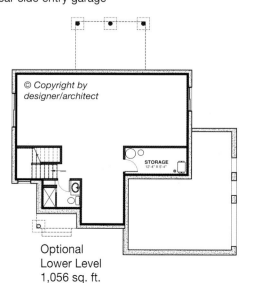

Optional
Lower Level
1,056 sq. ft.

First Floor
1,056 sq. ft.

Plan #F11-101D-0125

Dimensions:	118'3" W x 70' D
Heated Sq. Ft.:	2,970
Bonus Sq. Ft.:	2,014
Bedrooms: 2	**Bathrooms:** 2½
Exterior Walls:	2" x 6"
Foundation:	Walk-out basement

See index for more information

Special Features

- This rustic Modern masterpiece has an open floor plan with the utmost style and distinction
- The stylish kitchen has a huge island, rustic beams above, and plenty of storage for maintaining a sleek appearance free of clutter
- The master bedroom has a beamed ceiling, covered deck access, a luxury bath and a huge walk-in closet
- A guest room has its own private bath
- The optional lower level has an additional 2,014 square feet of living area including a rec room with a huge wet bar, a game nook, two bedrooms, and a Jack and Jill style bath
- 2-car front entry garage, and a 1-car side entry garage

Optional Lower Level
2,014 sq. ft.

First Floor
2,970 sq. ft.

Images provided by designer/architect

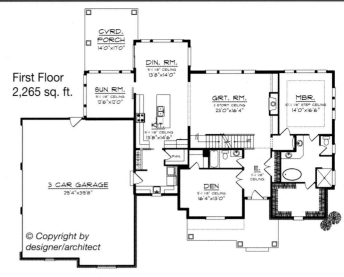

First Floor
2,265 sq. ft.

© Copyright by
designer/architect

Plan #F11-051D-0962

Second Floor
940 sq. ft.

Dimensions: 82'4" W x 70' D
Heated Sq. Ft.: 3,205
Bedrooms: 4   **Bathrooms:** 4
Exterior Walls: 2" x 6"
Foundation: Basement standard; crawl space or slab for an additional fee

See index for more information

Images provided by designer/architect

Images provided by designer/architect

Plan #F11-028D-0117

Dimensions: 50' W x 42'6" D
Heated Sq. Ft.: 1,425
Bedrooms: 3   **Bathrooms:** 2
Exterior Walls: 2" x 6"
Foundation: Crawl space or slab, please specify when ordering

See index for more information

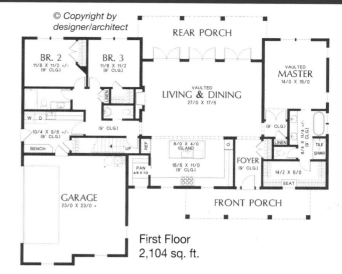

© Copyright by designer/architect

First Floor
2,104 sq. ft.

Plan #F11-011D-0617

Dimensions: 69' W x 58' D
Heated Sq. Ft.: 2,104
Bonus Sq. Ft.: 268
Bedrooms: 3   **Bathrooms:** 2½
Exterior Walls: 2" x 6"
Foundation: Crawl space or slab standard; basement for an additional fee

See index for more information

Images provided by designer/architect

Optional
Second Floor
268 sq. ft.

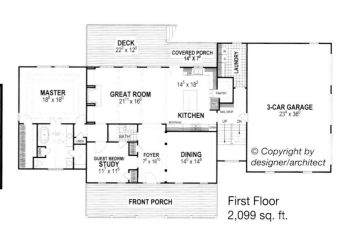

Second Floor
1,463 sq. ft.

Plan #F11-052D-0171

Images provided by designer/architect

Dimensions: 88' W x 54' D
Heated Sq. Ft.: 3,562
Bonus Sq. Ft.: 1,899
Bedrooms: 5   **Bathrooms:** 4
Foundation: Walk-out basement

See index for more information

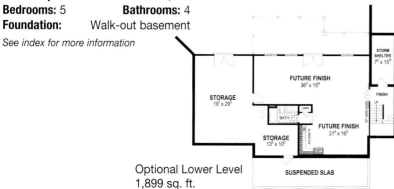

© Copyright by designer/architect

Optional Lower Level
1,899 sq. ft.

First Floor
2,099 sq. ft.

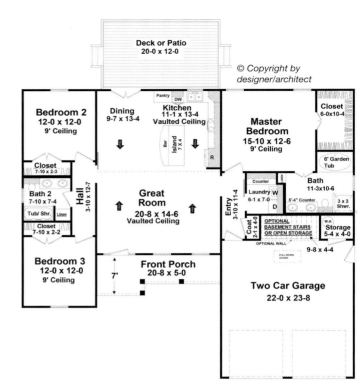

© Copyright by designer/architect

Deck or Patio 20-0 x 12-0

Bedroom 2 12-0 x 12-0 9' Ceiling

Dining 9-7 x 13-4

Pantry

DW

Kitchen 11-1 x 13-4 Vaulted Ceiling

Bar Island 7 X 4

Master Bedroom 15-10 x 12-6 9' Ceiling

Closet 6-0x10-4

6' Garden Tub

Closet 7-10 x 2-3

Bath 2 7-10 x 7-4

Tub/ Shr.

Linen

Hall 3-10 x 12-7

Great Room 20-8 x 14-6 Vaulted Ceiling

Counter

Laundry W 6-1 x 7-0

Entry 3-10 x 11-4

Bath 11-3x10-6

5'-4" Counter

D

3 x 3 Shwr.

Coat 2-1 x 4-0

OPTIONAL BASEMENT STAIRS OR OPEN STORAGE

OPTIONAL WALL

W.H.

Storage 5-4 x 4-0

9-8 x 4-4

Closet 7-10 x 2-2

Bedroom 3 12-0 x 12-0 9' Ceiling

7'

Front Porch 20-8 x 5-0

PULL-DOWN STAIRS

Two Car Garage 22-0 x 23-8

Images provided by designer/architect

Plan #F11-077D-0294

Dimensions: 56' W x 62'4" D
Heated Sq. Ft.: 1,600
Bedrooms: 3   **Bathrooms:** 2
Foundation: Crawl space, slab or basement, please specify when ordering

See index for more information

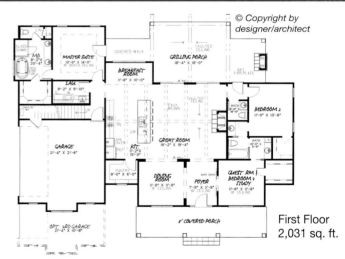

© Copyright by designer/architect

First Floor 2,031 sq. ft.

Plan #F11-155D-0145

Dimensions: 70'6" W x 56'2" D
Heated Sq. Ft.: 2,031
Bonus Sq. Ft.: 406
Bedrooms: 3   **Bathrooms:** 2½
Foundation: Crawl space or slab standard; basement or daylight basement for an additional fee

See index for more information

Images provided by designer/architect

Optional Second Floor 406 sq. ft.

Second Floor
521 sq. ft.

Plan #F11-032D-1060

Dimensions:	66' W x 80' D
Heated Sq. Ft.:	3,249
Bedrooms: 3	**Bathrooms:** 2½
Exterior Walls:	2" x 6"

Foundation: Crawl space standard; basement, floating slab or monolithic slab for an additional fee

See index for more information

Images provided by designer/architect

© Copyright by designer/architect

First Floor
2,728 sq. ft.

Optional
Second Floor
572 sq. ft.

© Copyright by designer/architect

Images provided by designer/architect

Plan #F11-056D-0092

Dimensions:	86'6" W x 90'6" D
Heated Sq. Ft.:	3,152
Bonus Sq. Ft.:	572
Bedrooms:	3
Bathrooms:	3 full, 2 half
Exterior Walls:	2" x 6"

Foundation: Slab standard; crawl space for an additional fee

See index for more information

First Floor
3,152 sq. ft.

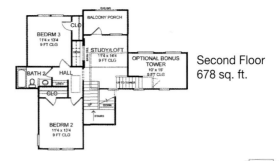

Second Floor
678 sq. ft.

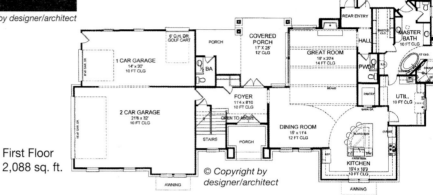

Plan #F11-019D-0049

Dimensions: 96' W x 62' D
Heated Sq. Ft.: 2,766
Bonus Sq. Ft.: 155
Bedrooms: 3
Bathrooms: 2 full, 2 half
Foundation: Slab standard; crawl space or basement for an additional fee

See index for more information

First Floor
2,088 sq. ft.

© Copyright by designer/architect

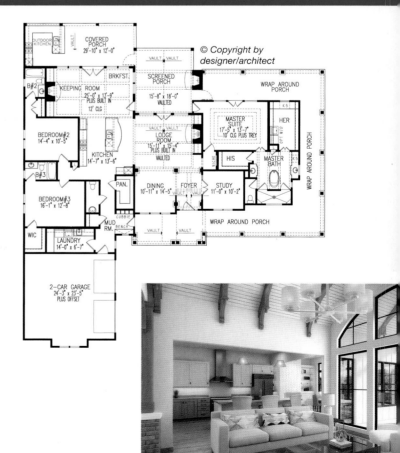

Plan #F11-056D-0138

Dimensions: 81'6" W x 93'5" D
Heated Sq. Ft.: 2,795
Bedrooms: 3   **Bathrooms:** 3½
Foundation: Slab

See index for more information

houseplansandmore.com

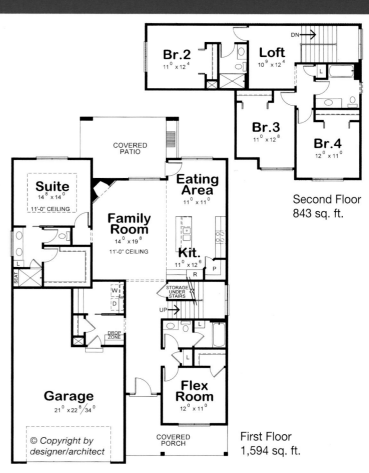

Second Floor
843 sq. ft.

First Floor
1,594 sq. ft.

© Copyright by designer/architect

Plan #F11-026D-2161

Dimensions: 41' W x 68' D
Heated Sq. Ft.: 2,437
Bedrooms: 4   **Bathrooms:** 4
Foundation: Slab standard; crawl space, basement or walk-out basement for an additional fee

See index for more information

Images provided by designer/architect

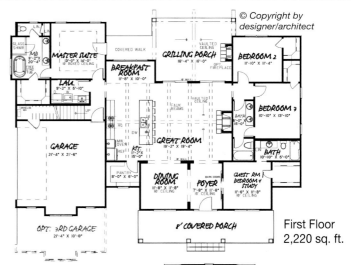

© Copyright by designer/architect

First Floor
2,220 sq. ft.

Plan #F11-155D-0129

Dimensions: 70'4" W x 56'2" D
Heated Sq. Ft.: 2,220
Bonus Sq. Ft.: 432
Bedrooms: 4   **Bathrooms:** 3
Foundation: Crawl space or slab standard; basement or daylight basement for an additional fee

See index for more information

Images provided by designer/architect

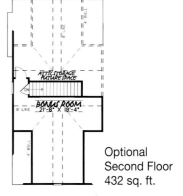

Optional
Second Floor
432 sq. ft.

stylish & functional
laundry & mud rooms

When it comes to starting the day right, most homeowners would agree that seeking lost keys and stumbling over wayward toys are not on the list of things to do.

Homeowners everywhere dream of a home where the day's necessary items are easily accessed without frustration or extreme exertion. Imagine the surprise when this dream becomes a reality – all it takes is some creative organization and attention to routine.

For many homeowners the front entryway is no longer the primary center of traffic for entering or exiting the home. Garage entries allow families to pile immediately into vehicles upon take-off and subsequently spill back into the house when landing back at home. Mud rooms and laundry areas have become the "catch alls," teaming with belongings that have no home, or are forgotten upon drop-off. Day after day, this constantly growing clutter makes it more difficult to get in and out of the house efficiently. In order to combat the expanding mess (and increasing stress), it is time to take control of your mud room or laundry room space in just a few simple steps.

evaluate your needs

Before you even glance at the mud room, sit down and construct a list of every item that leaves your house daily. Break it down by person to evaluate each family member's individual needs. Then turn it around and create a second list with each item that regularly enters the house (again, by person). It may sound tedious, but this approach will help ensure that regularly needed belongings will have a place in your newly organized space.

With lists in hand, it is time to turn toward the space itself. What does the area need to make the lives of your family easier? Is there adequate floor space to install seating for removing muddy shoes? Is closet space accessible, or will you need to install a storage system? Keep in mind that each item needs a designated space to reside without stuffing or overflowing, so take your time researching what hardware can best serve your needs.

these storage solutions can include:

hooks are great for storing objects that require easy access on the move, such as keys, purses, umbrellas, or even dog leashes.

shelving units such as cubbies and locker systems come in a variety of sizes making them useful for any mud room. Whether supplementary storage or a primary source of storing gear, these units can be custom for every member of your family.

baskets & bins come in numerous shapes, sizes, and materials, allowing your family to divide items efficiently. Clear, over-the-door hangers, are ideal for sorting small items like hats and mittens, making use of vertical space and keeping everything in sight.

cull the clutter

After you have devised what you need, it is time to remove what you do not. Begin cleaning out the current space, banishing those objects that do not belong in the entryway. Be careful to not let them pile up elsewhere! Make a rule that every item removed from the space is given a proper home; putting forth a small effort now will save time in the future.

Also use this time to categorize certain belongings and seek out a better storage spot. For example, if closet space is limited, is it really necessary to store infrequently used dress coats in the entryway? It makes much more sense to limit that closet to everyday wear while relocating the dress coats to another storage space.

move forward - slowly

Now that you know what storage is needed, "installation" can begin. Take your time and be deliberate with your placements. Slowly adjusting to your new space allows your family to form a routine, ensuring your rear foyer is used to its fullest capacity.

re-evaluate

While establishing a routine allows your family to get the most from a storage system, it is important to re-evaluate your organizational needs regularly. Upon examination, is each space still being utilized as intended? Have you noticed any frustrations with the system? For example, are there hooks for backpacks, but no place to store this season's sports bag? If one storage solution is not as convenient as before, this is your opportunity to try something else. As life changes so will your storage needs, so be on the look out for reoccurring issues and easy resolutions.

Unless noted, all images copyrighted by designer/architect. Page 136: top to bottom: Erin Crain Interiors, erincrain.com, Bernard Andre, photographer; Plan F11-101D-0090, page 167; Page 137, top, left: Plan #F11-091D-0534, page 52, photo courtesy of Royal Oaks Design, Inc.; top, right: Better Homes & Gardens®; Plan F11-055D-0342, page 173; ClosetMaid® System, closetmaid.com; Plan #F11-091D-0509, page 38, photo courtesy of Royal Oaks Design, Inc.; Page 138, top to bottom, left: ClosetMaid® Drop Zone Center, closetmaid.com; Electronic charging station, ikea.com; Plan F11-051D-0960, page 262; Plan F11-055D-0990, page 244; top to bottom, right: thehappyhousie.com; lookwhatidid.blogspot.ca; Plan F11-101D-0150, page 108, Warren Diggles Photography; Page 139, top to bottom: washer and dryer, designamerica.com; ClosteMaid® Built-In Hamper, closetmaid.com; meritagehomes.com; Built-In Dog Food Bowls, Terracotta Design Build, terracottadesignbuild.com; Built-In Cage and Dog Bed, maisonderevebuilders.com; All plans available for purchase at houseplansandmore.com.

just drop it

Beyond the need for organization of shoes, coats, bags, and other daily gear, some homeowners find themselves in need of a separate "drop zone," or a message center. Drop zones are typically a three to four foot wide surface where small items are put upon entering the home. Valets keep charger cords under control and accessible, and small dishes or hooks organize different sets of keys. The drop zone is an excellent place to toss junk mail into a recycle bin while keeping important letters handy in a mail tray. If drawers are available, drop zones can be used to store emergency items, spare keys, and extra office supplies.

commanding performance

Message centers may or may not be a part of the drop zone depending on the space available. For some families, a simple white board is perfect for passing information and tracking one another's daily activities. Other families may expand the message center to utilize cork, magnet boards, or chalkboards while keeping track of schedules, notes, homework, grocery and chore lists. Whatever the use, the message center can play a vital role in keeping your home running smoothly.

Making the most of your mud room is not a difficult task, but it does require an initial time investment. Putting in time now will certainly save you future headaches and wasted efforts. Research the available storage options and seek suggestions from friends and even organizational professionals. As you begin this process, remember that there is not one "perfect" method for organizing your rear foyer. However, a little patience and flexibility will certainly help you find the best solution for your lifestyle.

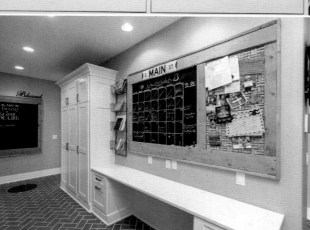

the down & dirty on great
laundry rooms

Many homeowners recall when laundry rooms were located in unfinished basements, spare closets, or limited space found in the garage or kitchen. These laundry areas were often cramped, impractical, and continuously frustrating for families. Though it's often a task that is approached with little enthusiasm, today's home designs are embracing laundry and mud rooms and making them the most functional spaces under a home's roof. In order to arrange the most efficient laundry area in your home, below are a few aspects to keep in mind.

function
Heavy traffic areas can include the laundry facilities as long as there is adequate space. Even the most organized laundry room has a tendency to harbor piles of clothing, which are inconvenient with people moving through the space so often. So, if you have a combined mud room/laundry room consider placing the laundry portion of the space as far from the entry as possible for better function and ease of movement. Install bins or hampers for dirty clothes and towels to avoid clothing piling up on the floor. Many homes have multiple hampers, with each family member being responsible for gathering their dirty items. If space allows, place a sorter in the laundry room with each slot dedicated to various laundry loads that family members can sort in an organized fashion.

Once the appropriate space is set aside, utilize vertical space just as efficiently as floor space. Some washers and dryers are stackable, allowing smaller spaces to include folding tables or utility sinks. Install overhead cabinetry for storing laundry accessories from detergents to drying racks. At least 48 inches should be left in front of laundry units for easy movement and to provide extra space for future appliances to easily fit in the same location.

amenities
Today's laundry rooms are multi-taskers and can include home offices, crafting spaces, plant potting or gift wrapping stations. They are larger and have plenty of built-in storage. Gone are the days of leaving the laundry room the minute the machine is started, now homeowners can work on their latest craft project while waiting for the towels to dry.

Another popular trend for mud rooms and laundry spaces is creating an accommodating spot for your furry family member. Homeowners are getting super creative when it comes to providing a comfortable environment for their pet. In fact, spending on our furry friends is steadily on the rise and that includes spending for their accommodations within the home, too. Have fun creating a built-in "crate," food and water dishes, or even a dog wash station. The possibilities are endless and not only add great function, but look much more attractive than throwing a dog bed on the floor that everyone trips over.

Though laundry is not necessarily a fun task, the space itself does not need to be a drag. Today's appliances are more sleek than ever, and come in numerous shapes, sizes, and colors that allow you to customize your laundry room to better match your home's decor. Reserve wall space for artwork and install attractive, yet functional flooring.

Though the average family does eight to ten loads of laundry per week, there is no reason it has to be overwhelming. Create a space equipped to tackle your family's needs, while including hobby and organization space, and suddenly the dreaded chore will feel less of a hassle and more of an escape to your happy place.

Plan #F11-032D-1169

Dimensions:	40' W x 46' D
Heated Sq. Ft.:	1,487
Bonus Sq. Ft.:	1,487
Bedrooms: 2	**Bathrooms:** 1
Exterior Walls:	2" x 6"

Foundation: Basement standard; crawl space, floating slab or monolithic slab for an additional fee

See index for more information

Special Features

- This sleek one-story home has all of the extras even though it only has two bedrooms
- Enter the hallway and discover an office with a barn style door
- The mudroom has the laundry room off of it and makes storage and organizing a breeze
- The kitchen, dining area and living room all come together creating the hub of this home
- The master bedroom enjoys a roomy walk-through closet that leads to the bath
- The optional lower level has an additional 1,476 square feet of living area

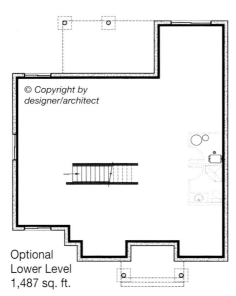

© Copyright by designer/architect

Optional Lower Level
1,487 sq. ft.

First Floor
1,487 sq. ft.

Images provided by designer/architect

Call toll-free 1-800-373-2646   houseplansandmore.com

Plan #F11-051D-0977

Dimensions: 58' W x 64'4" D
Heated Sq. Ft.: 1,837
Bedrooms: 3   **Bathrooms:** 2
Exterior Walls: 2" x 6"
Foundation: Basement standard; crawl space or slab for an additional fee

See index for more information

Special Features

- Clean lines and attention to detail create an exterior that's timeless and Modern all at the same time
- The covered entrance opens into the great room with its impressive 11' ceiling, a fireplace and large windows for a great view of the covered porch and deck
- An appealing split bedroom floor plan offers privacy from the central living space
- The kitchen features a large hidden pantry, nearby lockers and a laundry space, as well as a unique curved breakfast bar and dining space
- 3-car front entry garage

© Copyright by designer/architect

Images provided by designer/architect

Plan #F11-019D-0048

Dimensions: 89'3" W x 48'8" D
Heated Sq. Ft.: 2,248
Bedrooms: 3   **Bathrooms:** 2
Foundation: Slab standard; crawl space or basement for an additional fee

See index for more information

Special Features

- This sprawling one-story Modern Farmhouse inspired design has a great split bedroom floor plan with large entertaining spaces between the bedrooms
- The spacious and open great room has a sloped ceiling with beams and stunning clerestory windows above the entry for a dramatic effect
- The vaulted master suite has a posh bath with double walk-in closets, an oversized shower and two vanities
- There's a large utility room behind the kitchen with a drop zone outside its doors
- Two secondary bedroom share a full bath behind the garage
- 2-car side entry garage

© Copyright by designer/architect

Images provided by designer/architect

Plan #F11-011D-0682

Dimensions:	69' W x 68' D
Heated Sq. Ft.:	2,451
Bedrooms: 3	**Bathrooms:** 3½
Exterior Walls:	2" x 6"

Foundation: Crawl space or slab standard; basement for an additional fee

See index for more information

Special Features

- A truly unique Modern Farmhouse with the dining and living spaces completely separated from the sleeping spaces
- Enter the foyer and choose between either going to the right where all of the bedrooms will be found, or go left and discover the kitchen and vaulted living/dining area where entertaining and daily living will take place
- The kitchen features an oversized island, a walk-in pantry and great views of the dining and living spaces
- The vaulted master bedroom enjoys access to a center outdoor courtyard and has a large bath with a freestanding tub
- 2-car side entry garage

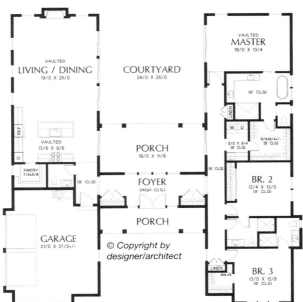

Images provided by designer/architect

Plan #F11-011D-0684

Dimensions: 40' W x 59' D
Heated Sq. Ft.: 1,373
Bedrooms: 3   **Bathrooms:** 2
Exterior Walls: 2" x 6"
Foundation: Crawl space or slab standard; basement for an additional fee

See index for more information

Special Features

- A compact, yet stylish Modern Farmhouse is just the right size for the empty nester, or the first-time home buyer
- The split bedroom floor plan ensures privacy for the home-owners and guests
- The vaulted great room has wonderful covered porch views through a trio of large windows
- The kitchen enjoys an island with sink, and a pantry with washer and dryer space behind a pocket door
- Two secondary bedrooms share a full bath near the front of the home to complete the design
- 2-car front entry garage

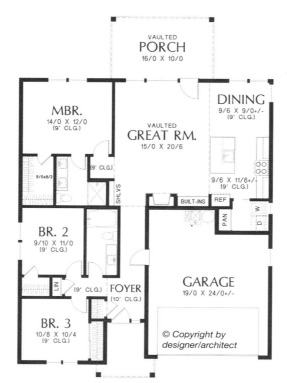

Images provided by designer/architect

© Copyright by designer/architect

Plan #F11-028D-0116

Dimensions: 28' W x 48' D
Heated Sq. Ft.: 1,120
Bedrooms: 2   **Bathrooms:** 2
Exterior Walls: 2" x 6"
Foundation: Slab

See index for more information

Special Features

- This small and stylish Modern Farmhouse is ideal for those wanting to simplify their lifestyle, while wanting to maintain great design and function
- The bedrooms are at the back of the home and both have direct access to a full bath
- The open great room feels even larger thanks to merging with the kitchen
- The kitchen has an island with casual dining space for four people to dine comfortably
- The deep covered front porch offers a great spot to retreat to the outdoors for some fresh air

BEDROOM 1
11-8 x 12-0

BEDROOM 2
11-8 x 12-0

BATH 1   HALL   BATH 2

LAUNDRY
11-8 x 6-8

GREAT ROOM/
DINING AREA
16-4 x 22-0

STOVE WITH
VENT HOOD
COMBO ABOVE

KITCHEN
11-8 X 15-6

8 FT. DEEP PORCH

© Copyright by designer/architect

Images provided by designer/architect

Plan #F11-123S-0039

Dimensions:	48' W x 52' D
Heated Sq. Ft.:	3,319
Bonus Sq. Ft.:	885
Bedrooms: 4	**Bathrooms:** 3½

Foundation: Basement standard; crawl space, slab or walk-out basement for an additional fee

See index for more information

Special Features

- This two-story has curb appeal on the exterior and will definitely stand out in any neighborhood
- The kitchen has an island with dining space, and around the corner is a huge walk-in pantry and a half bath
- The covered patio has a built-in grill for those summer nights when the weather is perfect for outdoor dining
- The second floor features all of the bedrooms plus a large loft space that includes a more private office with a wrap-around desk
- The optional lower level has an additional 885 square feet of living area including a family room, a wet bar, a play room, a bedroom, and a full bath
- 2-car side entry garage

© Copyright by designer/architect

Images provided by designer/architect

Optional Lower Level
885 sq. ft.

First Floor
1,422 sq. ft.

Second Floor
1,897 sq. ft.

Plan #F11-032D-1140

Dimensions: 76' W x 53' D
Heated Sq. Ft.: 2,965
Bonus Sq. Ft.: 1,642
Bedrooms: 3 **Bathrooms:** 2½
Exterior Walls: 2" x 6"
Foundation: Basement standard; crawl space or floating slab for an additional fee

See index for more information

Special Features

- The large front entrance creates an inviting way to be greeted by the interior spaces
- The first floor has both a laundry room as well as a large mud room space and both are right around the corner from the kitchen pantry
- The optional lower level has an additional 1,642 square feet of living area
- 2-car front entry garage

Second Floor
1,252 sq. ft.

Images provided by designer/architect

© Copyright by
designer/architect

Optional Lower Level
1,642 sq. ft.

First Floor
1,713 sq. ft.

Images provided by designer/architect

Plan #F11-091D-0525

Dimensions: 50' W x 56'2" D
Heated Sq. Ft.: 2,453
Bedrooms: 3   **Bathrooms:** 3½
Exterior Walls: 2" x 6"
Foundation: Crawl space standard; basement or slab for an additional fee

See index for more information

Second Floor
931 sq. ft.

First Floor
1,522 sq. ft.

Second Floor
879 sq. ft.

Plan #F11-011D-0678

Dimensions: 40' W x 56' D
Heated Sq. Ft.: 2,055
Bonus Sq. Ft.: 321
Bedrooms: 4   **Bathrooms:** 3
Exterior Walls: 2" x 6"
Foundation: Crawl space or slab standard; basement for an additional fee

See index for more information

Images provided by designer/architect

First Floor
1,176 sq. ft.

Second Floor
1,336 sq. ft.

Owner's Suite
16⁴ x 14⁰
10'-0" CEILING

Br.3
11⁰ x 11⁸

Br.4
11⁸ x 12⁴

Br.2
12⁴ x 12⁴

Family Room
16⁴ x 18⁶

Dining Area
10⁰ x 11⁸

Kit.
12⁴ x 12⁹

PATIO

Garage
21⁸ x 23¹⁰/33⁸

STORAGE

Flex Room
12² x 10⁴

COVERED PORCH

First Floor
1,112 sq. ft.

© Copyright by designer/architect

Images provided by designer/architect

Plan #F11-026D-2092

Dimensions: 45' W x 59'8" D
Heated Sq. Ft.: 2,448
Bedrooms: 4   **Bathrooms:** 3½
Foundation: Basement standard; crawl space or slab for an additional fee

See index for more information

Images provided by designer/architect

BEDROOM 2
11-4 X 11-2

BEDROOM 3
11-4 X 11-2

BATH ROOM

MASTER BATH

WALK-IN

MASTER SUITE
11-4 X 14-8

Second Floor
886 sq. ft.

© Copyright by designer/architect

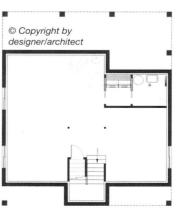

COVERED PORCH

PWD. ROOM

DINING ROOM
10-8 X 11-6

KITCHEN
11-0 X 17-10

LIVING ROOM
11-0 X 26-8

FOYER
10-2 X 4-10

FRONT PORCH

Optional Lower Level
938 sq. ft.

First Floor
938 sq. ft.

Plan #F11-032D-1032

Dimensions: 34' W x 32' D
Heated Sq. Ft.: 1,824
Bonus Sq. Ft.: 938
Bedrooms: 3   **Bathrooms:** 2½
Exterior Walls: 2" x 6"
Foundation: Basement standard; crawl space, floating slab or monolithic slab for an additional fee

See index for more information

Second Floor
715 sq. ft.

© Copyright by
designer/architect

First Floor
1,777 sq. ft.

Plan #F11-011D-0651

Dimensions: 46' W x 79' D
Heated Sq. Ft.: 2,492
Bonus Sq. Ft.: 481
Bedrooms: 3 **Bathrooms:** 2½
Exterior Walls: 2" x 6"
Foundation: Crawl space or slab standard; basement for an additional fee

See index for more information

Images provided by designer/architect

© Copyright by
designer/architect

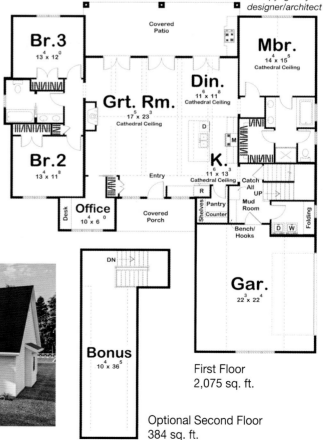

First Floor
2,075 sq. ft.

Plan #F11-123D-0166

Dimensions: 60' W x 69' D
Heated Sq. Ft.: 2,075
Bonus Sq. Ft.: 384
Bedrooms: 3 **Bathrooms:** 2
Foundation: Slab standard; crawl space, basement or walk-out basement for an additional fee

See index for more information

Optional Second Floor
384 sq. ft.

Images provided by designer/architect

© Copyright by designer/architect

Images provided by designer/architect

Plan #F11-056D-0095

Dimensions:	91'6" W x 70' D
Heated Sq. Ft.:	2,510
Bonus Sq. Ft.:	2,172
Bedrooms: 3	**Bathrooms:** 2½

Foundation: Basement standard; crawl space or slab for an additional fee

See index for more information

Optional Lower Level
2,172 sq. ft.

First Floor
2,510 sq. ft.

Second Floor
661 sq. ft.

Plan #F11-139D-0093

Dimensions:	73'3" W x 88'9" D
Heated Sq. Ft.:	3,556
Bonus Sq. Ft.:	721
Bedrooms: 4	**Bathrooms:** 4½
Exterior Walls:	2" x 6"

Foundation: Crawl space standard; slab, basement, daylight basement or walk-out basement for an additional fee

See index for more information

Images provided by designer/architect

© Copyright by designer/architect

First Floor
2,895 sq. ft.

First Floor
2,230 sq. ft.

Plan #F11-056S-0009

Dimensions:	73'4" W x 71'8" D
Heated Sq. Ft.:	3,818
Bonus Sq. Ft.:	386
Bedrooms: 4	**Bathrooms: 4½**

Foundation: Basement standard; crawl space or slab for an additional fee

See index for more information

Optional
Second Floor
386 sq. ft.

Lower Level
1,588 sq. ft.

First Floor
1,856 sq. ft.

Plan #F11-123D-0202

Dimensions:	64' W x 89' D
Heated Sq. Ft.:	1,856
Bonus Sq. Ft.:	1,032
Bedrooms: 2	**Bathrooms: 2**

Foundation: Walk-out basement standard; crawl space, slab or basement for an additional fee

See index for more information

Optional
Lower Level
1,032 sq. ft.

Images provided by designer/architect

© Copyright by designer/architect

First Floor
2,798 sq. ft.

Second Floor
2,168 sq. ft.

Plan #F11-101D-0122

Dimensions:	82' W x 101'9" D
Heated Sq. Ft.:	4,966
Bonus Sq. Ft.:	1,200
Bedrooms:	6
Bathrooms:	4 full, 2 half
Exterior Walls:	2" x 6"
Foundation:	Crawl space

See index for more information

Images provided by designer/architect

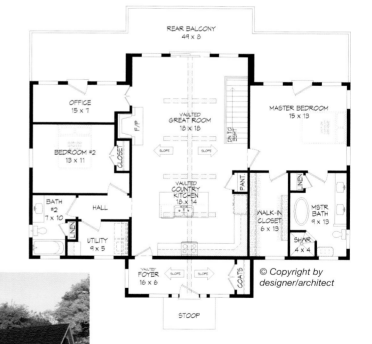

© Copyright by designer/architect

Plan #F11-141D-0340

Dimensions:	49'3" W x 46' D
Heated Sq. Ft.:	1,586
Bedrooms: 2	**Bathrooms:** 2
Exterior Walls:	2" x 6"

Foundation: Slab standard; crawl space or walk-out basement for an additional fee

See index for more information

Images provided by designer/architect

Plan #F11-139D-0086

Images provided by designer/architect

Dimensions: 92' W x 64'7" D
Heated Sq. Ft.: 4,357
Bonus Sq. Ft.: 579
Bedrooms: 5
Bathrooms: 4 full, 2 half
Exterior Walls: 2" x 6"
Foundation: Crawl space standard; slab, basement, daylight basement or walk-out basement for an additional fee

See index for more information

Special Features

- This classic farmhouse home has a grand appearance thanks to its covered front porch spanning across the entire front facade
- The first floor features a study off the foyer ideal when working from home
- Off the garage are many special features including a workshop, a pet kennel and wash, and a mud room with a laundry room attached
- The kitchen has a massive party-sized island for entertaining and a walk-in pantry nearby
- The second floor includes a media area that can overlook the living room below
- The optional loft above the garage has an additional 579 square feet of living area
- 3-car side entry garage

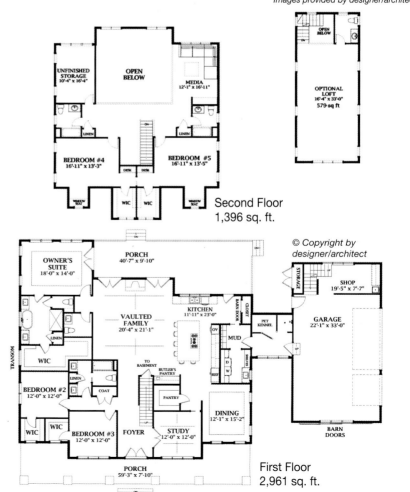

Second Floor
1,396 sq. ft.

© Copyright by designer/architect

First Floor
2,961 sq. ft.

Plan #F11-032D-0963

Dimensions:	34' W x 38' D
Heated Sq. Ft.:	1,178
Bonus Sq. Ft.:	1,178
Bedrooms: 1	**Bathrooms:** 1
Exterior Walls:	2" x 6"

Foundation: Basement standard; crawl space, floating slab or monolithic slab for an additional fee

See index for more information

Images provided by designer/architect

Special Features

- This small Modern Farmhouse design takes simplicity and style to a whole new level
- Step into the entry from the covered front porch and discover an oversized walk-in closet for keeping the entry clutter-free
- The open-concept floor plan has the kitchen and dining area blended perfectly
- The kitchen has a large walk-in pantry with a barn style door for a farmhouse feel
- The bedroom enjoys close proximity to the pampering bath that features a shower as well as a free-standing tub in one corner
- The optional lower level has an additional 1,178 square feet of living area

First Floor
1,178 sq. ft.

© Copyright by designer/architect

Optional
Lower Level
1,178 sq. ft.

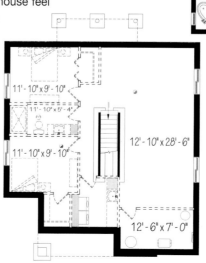

Plan #F11-101D-0121

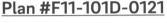

Dimensions:	116'6" W x 62' D
Heated Sq. Ft.:	3,380
Bonus Sq. Ft.:	2,027
Bedrooms: 2	**Bathrooms:** 2½
Exterior Walls:	2" x 6"

Foundation: Basement, daylight basement or walk-out basement, please specify when ordering

See index for more information

Images provided by designer/architect

Special Features

- This stunning Modern home has a touch of Modern Farmhouse flair
- This unique floor plan has a separate apartment style suite that features its own living room, a separate entrance, a covered patio, and a kitchen with an island
- The main home offers an open kitchen with a massive island, a cozy great room with fireplace, a casual dining space, a laundry room and a master bedroom and bath in a private location
- There's also a first floor study, ideal as a home office
- 3-car side entry garage

© Copyright by designer/architect

First Floor
3,380 sq. ft.

Optional Lower Level
2,027 sq. ft.

Plan #F11-172D-0008

Dimensions:	78' W x 47' D
Heated Sq. Ft.:	3,016
Bonus Sq. Ft.:	1,515
Bedrooms: 4	**Bathrooms:** 2½
Exterior Walls:	2" x 6"

Foundation: Basement standard; crawl space, stem wall slab, monolithic slab, daylight basement or walk-out basement for an additional fee

See index for more information

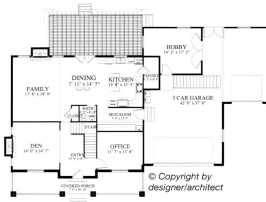

First Floor
1,532 sq. ft.

© Copyright by designer/architect

Second Floor
1,484 sq. ft.

Optional Lower Level
1,515 sq. ft.

Special Features

- The first floor features extras like a home office, a den with fireplace, a family room with a fireplace and an extraordinary hobby room
- The kitchen is super-efficient thanks to a walk-in pantry and the mud room nearby
- The master bedroom located on the second floor has a cozy fireplace
- The second floor laundry room is a handy feature for chore day
- The optional lower level has an additional 1,515 square feet of living area and a large family room with fireplace, two additional bedrooms and a full bath
- 3-car front entry garage

Images provided by designer/architect

Plan #F11-123D-0212

Dimensions:	85' W x 52'8" D
Heated Sq. Ft.:	3,124
Bonus Sq. Ft.:	296
Bedrooms: 5	**Bathrooms:** 3½

Foundation: Basement standard; crawl space, slab or walk-out basement for an additional fee

See index for more information

Special Features

- This noteworthy design has a central great room as the main focal point as you enter the home
- The kitchen enjoys an open atmosphere, a huge island, great room views and dining nearby
- A private in-law suite is tucked near the garage and includes a walk-in closet and a full bath with a walk-in shower
- A cozy living room with fireplace could also be converted to a home office
- The second floor has three additional bedrooms, a full bath, and a study great for getting the kids to do their homework
- The optional bonus room on the second has an additional 296 square feet of living area
- 2-car side entry garage

Bonus
11' x 14'

Second Floor
838 sq. ft.

Br.2
14' x 14'

Study
7' x 12'

Br.3
12' x 12'

Open to Below
Cath. Ceiling

Br.4
12' x 11'
Cath. Ceiling

Gar.
23' x 20'

Din.
12' x 12'

Covered
Patio

Mbr.
14' x 15'
9'-0" Ceiling

Storage
6' x 12'

Mud
Room
Bench/
Lockers

Shelves
Pantry

Grt. Rm.
17' x 20'
2 Story Cathedral Ceiling

K.
12' x 21'
10'-0" Ceiling

Entry

**In-Law
Suite**
11' x 15'
10'-0" Ceiling

Covered
Porch

Liv.
14' x 11'

© *Copyright by
designer/architect*

First Floor
2,286 sq. ft.

Images provided by designer/architect

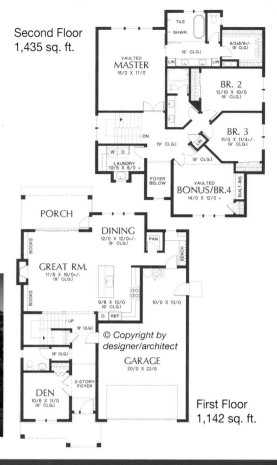

Second Floor
1,435 sq. ft.

VAULTED MASTER 15/2 X 17/0

BR. 2 13/10 X 10/0 (9' CLG.)

BR. 3 11/0 X 11/4+/- (9' CLG.)

LAUNDRY 10/6 X 6/0

VAULTED BONUS/BR.4 14/0 X 12/0 +

PORCH

DINING 12/0 X 12/0+/- (9' CLG.)

GREAT RM. 17/6 X 19/0+/- (9' CLG.)

GARAGE 20/0 X 22/6

DEN 10/6 X 11/0 (9' CLG.)

2-STORY FOYER

© Copyright by designer/architect

First Floor
1,142 sq. ft.

Plan #F11-011D-0681

Dimensions: 38' W x 55' D
Heated Sq. Ft.: 2,577
Bedrooms: 4 **Bathrooms:** 2½
Exterior Walls: 2" x 6"
Foundation: Crawl space or slab standard; basement for an additional fee

See index for more information

Images provided by designer/architect

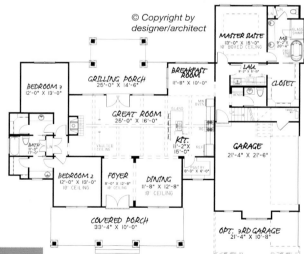

© Copyright by designer/architect

MASTER SUITE 13'-0" X 15'-0" 10' BOXED CEILING

GRILLING PORCH 25'-0" X 14'-6"

BREAKFAST ROOM 11'-8" X 10'-0"

BEDROOM 3 12'-0" X 13'-0"

GREAT ROOM 25'-0" X 16'-0"

LAU. CLOSET

GARAGE 21'-4" X 21'-6"

KIT. 11'-2" X 15'-0"

PANTRY 8'-0" X 6'-0"

BEDROOM 2 12'-0" X 13'-0" 10' CEILING

FOYER 8'-0" X 12'-8" 10' CEILING

DINING 11'-8" X 12'-8" 10' CEILING

COVERED PORCH 33'-4" X 10'-0"

OPT. 3RD GARAGE 21'-4" X 10'-8"

First Floor
2,269 sq. ft.

Plan #F11-155D-0143

Dimensions: 75'6" W x 63'10" D
Heated Sq. Ft.: 2,269
Bonus Sq. Ft.: 456
Bedrooms: 3 **Bathrooms:** 2½
Foundation: Crawl space or slab standard; basement or daylight basement for an additional fee

See index for more information

Images provided by designer/architect

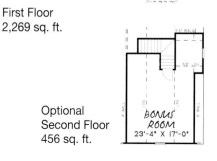

Optional Second Floor
456 sq. ft.

BONUS ROOM 23'-4" X 17'-0"

Second Floor
1,381 sq. ft.

Plan #F11-141D-0403

Dimensions: 85'5" W x 48' D
Heated Sq. Ft.: 3,403
Bedrooms: 5 **Bathrooms:** 3½
Exterior Walls: 2" x 6"
Foundation: Slab standard; crawl space, basement or walk-out basement for an additional fee

See index for more information

Images provided by designer/architect

First Floor
2,022 sq. ft.

Images provided by designer/architect

Plan #F11-056D-0137

Dimensions: 62'10" W x 68'5" D
Heated Sq. Ft.: 2,342
Bonus Sq. Ft.: 1,054
Bedrooms: 3 **Bathrooms:** 2
Foundation: Basement standard; crawl space or slab for an additional fee

See index for more information

First Floor
2,342 sq. ft.

Optional Lower Level
1,054 sq. ft.

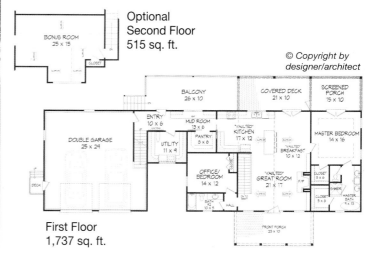

Optional Second Floor 515 sq. ft.

BONUS ROOM 25 x 15

CLOSET

© Copyright by designer/architect

First Floor 1,737 sq. ft.

Plan #F11-141D-0349

Dimensions:	90'9" W x 50' D
Heated Sq. Ft.:	2,806
Bonus Sq. Ft.:	515
Bedrooms: 4	**Bathrooms:** 3

Foundation: Daylight basement standard; crawl space, slab or basement for an additional fee

See index for more information

Images provided by designer/architect

Lower Level 1,069 sq. ft.

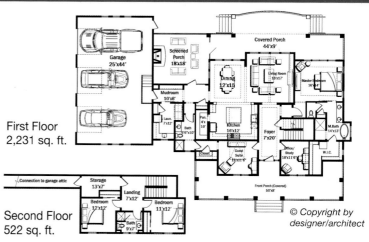

First Floor 2,231 sq. ft.

Second Floor 522 sq. ft.

© Copyright by designer/architect

Images provided by designer/architect

Plan #F11-167D-0005

Dimensions:	94'1" W x 70'8" D
Heated Sq. Ft.:	2,753
Bedrooms: 4	**Bathrooms:** 3
Exterior Walls:	2" x 6"

Foundation: Crawl space standard; basement for an additional fee

See index for more information

houseplansandmore.com

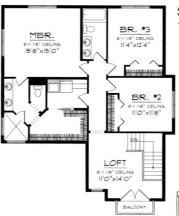

Second Floor
1,172 sq. ft.

First Floor
1,006 sq. ft.

© Copyright by designer/architect

Plan #F11-051D-0956

Dimensions: 36' W x 52' D
Heated Sq. Ft.: 2,178
Bedrooms: 3   **Bathrooms:** 2½
Exterior Walls: 2" x 6"
Foundation: Basement standard; crawl space or slab for an additional fee

See index for more information

Images provided by designer/architect

Plan #F11-163D-0020

Dimensions: 97'6" W x 74'1" D
Heated Sq. Ft.: 3,306
Bedrooms: 5   **Bathrooms:** 2½
Exterior Walls: 2" x 6"
Foundation: Crawl space

See index for more information

Images provided by designer/architect

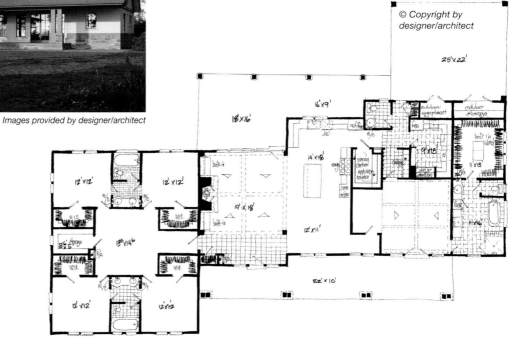

© Copyright by designer/architect

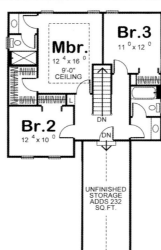

Second Floor
780 sq. ft.

Mbr.
12⁴ x 16⁰
9'-0"
CEILING

Br.3
11⁰ x 12⁰

Br.2
12⁴ x 10⁰

DN

DN

UNFINISHED
STORAGE
ADDS 232
SQ. FT.

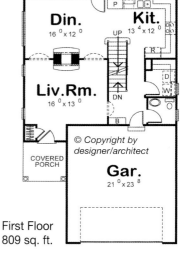

Din.
16⁰ x 12⁰

Kit.
13⁴ x 12⁰

UP

DN

Liv.Rm.
16⁰ x 13⁰

© Copyright by
designer/architect

COVERED
PORCH

Gar.
21⁰ x 23⁸

First Floor
809 sq. ft.

Plan #F11-123D-0234

Dimensions: 30' W x 50' D
Heated Sq. Ft.:   1,589
Bonus Sq. Ft.:   232
Bedrooms: 3   **Bathrooms:** 2½
Foundation: Basement standard;
crawl space, slab or walk-out
basement for an additional fee

See index for more information

Images provided by designer/architect

Second Floor
1,192 sq. ft.

OPEN
BELOW

CLOSET

LOFT/
OFFICE
8'-2" x 13'-4"

BR #3
11'-4" x 11'-0"

WIC

LINEN

BR #2
11'-6" x 12'-0"

FINISHED
BONUS
10'-0" x 20'-4"

© Copyright by
designer/architect

KITCHEN
10'-3" x 18'-9"

LAUNDRY
7'-4" x 10'-11"

VAULTED
FAMILY
15'-4" x 18'-9"

LOCKERS

COAT

CLOSET

WIC
9'-0" x 7'-5"

LIN

FOYER

DINING
11'-9" x 12'-0"

STORAGE

MBATH
9'-1" x 15'-6"

8' PORCH

MASTER BDRM
15'-0" x 15'-0"

First Floor
1,524 sq. ft.

Plan #F11-139D-0104

Dimensions: 35'11" W x 51' D
Heated Sq. Ft.:   2,716
Bonus Sq. Ft.:   203
Bedrooms: 3   **Bathrooms:** 2½
Exterior Walls: 2" x 6"
Foundation: Crawl space standard;
slab, basement, daylight basement
or walk-out basement for an
additional fee

See index for more information

Images provided by designer/architect

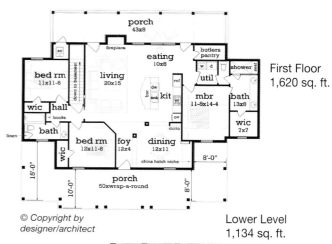

First Floor
1,620 sq. ft.

Lower Level
1,134 sq. ft.

Plan #F11-020D-0386

Dimensions:	58' W x 50' D
Heated Sq. Ft.:	2,754
Bedrooms: 4	**Bathrooms:** 3
Exterior Walls:	2" x 6"
Foundation:	Walk-out basement

See index for more information

Images provided by designer/architect

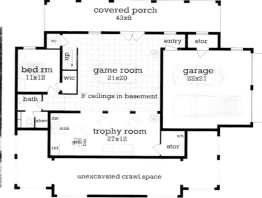

Plan #F11-052D-0157

Dimensions:	40'4" W x 42' D
Heated Sq. Ft.:	2,067
Bonus Sq. Ft.:	356
Bedrooms: 4	**Bathrooms:** 2½
Foundation:	Walk-out basement

See index for more information

Images provided by designer/architect

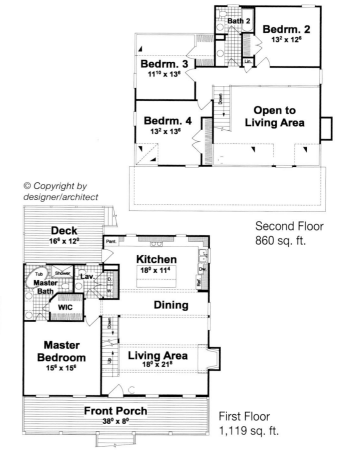

Second Floor
860 sq. ft.

Lower Level
88 sq. ft.

First Floor
1,119 sq. ft.

First Floor
1,008 sq. ft.

Second Floor
504 sq. ft.

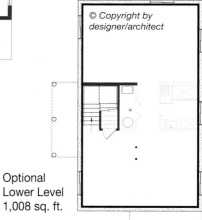

Optional
Lower Level
1,008 sq. ft.

Plan #F11-032D-1127

Dimensions: 24' W x 42' D
Heated Sq. Ft.: 1,512
Bonus Sq. Ft.: 1,008
Bedrooms: 3   **Bathrooms:** 2½
Exterior Walls: 2" x 6"
Foundation: Basement standard; crawl space floating slab or monolithic slab for an additional fee

See index for more information

Images provided by designer/architect

Images provided by designer/architect

Plan #F11-123S-0027

Dimensions: 66' W x 69' D
Heated Sq. Ft.: 4,332
Bedrooms: 5   **Bathrooms:** 4½
Foundation: Basement standard; crawl space, slab or walk-out basement for an additional fee

See index for more information

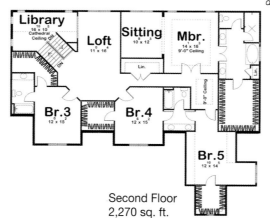

Second Floor
2,270 sq. ft.

First Floor
2,062 sq. ft.

Plan #F11-101D-0090

Dimensions:	78' W x 79' D
Heated Sq. Ft.:	2,875
Bonus Sq. Ft.:	1,611
Bedrooms: 3	**Bathrooms:** 3½
Exterior Walls:	2" x 6"

Foundation: Basement or daylight basement, please specify when ordering

See index for more information

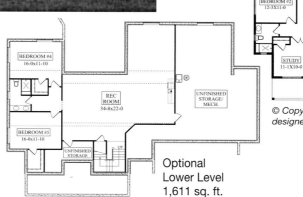

Optional
Lower Level
1,611 sq. ft.

First Floor
2,875 sq. ft.

© Copyright by
designer/architect

© Copyright by
designer/architect

First Floor
2,572 sq. ft.

Plan #F11-123D-0251

Dimensions:	71' W x 74' D
Heated Sq. Ft.:	2,572
Bonus Sq. Ft.:	260
Bedrooms: 4	**Bathrooms:** 2½

Foundation: Crawl space standard; slab, basement or walk-out basement for an additional fee

See index for more information

Images provided by designer/architect

Optional
Second Floor
260 sq. ft.

Plan #F11-026D-2013

Dimensions: 57'8" W x 58' D
Heated Sq. Ft.: 1,925
Bedrooms: 3   **Bathrooms:** 2
Exterior Walls: 2" x 6"
Foundation: Basement standard;
crawl space, slab or walk-out
basement for an additional fee

See index for more information

Images provided by designer/architect

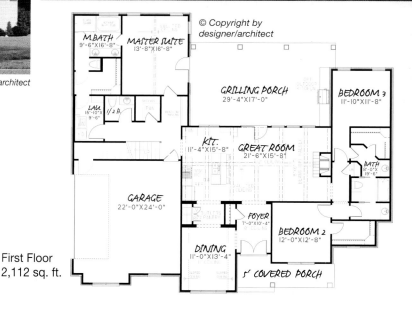

Plan #F11-155D-0157

Dimensions: 65'10" W x 58'10" D
Heated Sq. Ft.: 2,112
Bonus Sq. Ft.: 347
Bedrooms: 3   **Bathrooms:** 2½
Foundation: Crawl space or slab
standard; basement or daylight
basement for an additional fee

See index for more information

Images provided by designer/architect

Optional
Second Floor
347 sq. ft.

First Floor
2,112 sq. ft.

Plan #F11-011D-0653

Dimensions: 60' W x 53'6" D
Heated Sq. Ft.: 3,032
Bedrooms: 4   **Bathrooms:** 3½
Exterior Walls: 2" x 6"
Foundation: Crawl space or slab standard; basement for an additional fee

See index for more information

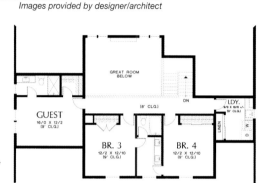

Second Floor
1,073 sq. ft.

First Floor
1,959 sq. ft.

© Copyright by designer/architect

Plan #F11-121D-0025

Dimensions: 50' W x 34'6" D
Heated Sq. Ft.: 1,368
Bedrooms: 3   **Bathrooms:** 2
Foundation: Basement standard; crawl space or slab for an additional fee

See index for more information

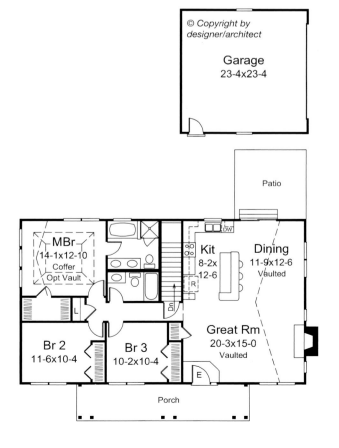

© Copyright by designer/architect

Garage
23-4x23-4

Plan #F11-141D-0323

Dimensions: 86'9" W x 52' D
Heated Sq. Ft.: 1,787
Bonus Sq. Ft.: 1,787
Bedrooms: 2 **Bathrooms:** 2
Foundation: Slab standard; crawl space, basement or walk-out basement for an additional fee

See index for more information

Special Features

- Perfect symmetry embodies this truly special Modern Farmhouse design
- From the large covered front covered porch, step right into the vaulted great room featuring a stunning window above the front door
- The vaulted breakfast room is steps from the kitchen island and enjoys covered deck views
- The private master bedroom has direct screened porch access, and a private bath with a roomy walk-in closet
- Off the garage is both a large utility room and a large mud room area filled with storage space
- The optional lower level has an additional 1,787 square feet of living area
- 2-car front entry garage

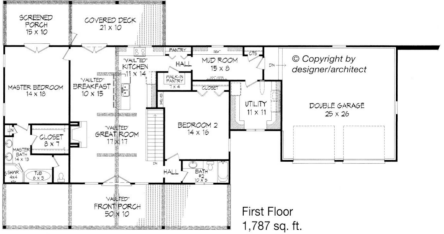

First Floor
1,787 sq. ft.

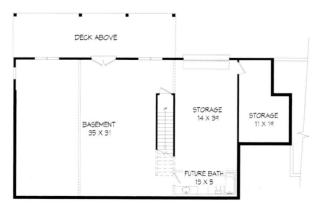

Optional Lower Level
1,787 sq. ft.

Plan #F11-141D-0061

Dimensions: 46' W x 46' D
Heated Sq. Ft.: 1,273
Bedrooms: 2 **Bathrooms:** 2
Foundation: Crawl space standard; slab, basement or walk-out basement for an additional fee

See index for more information

Special Features

- Quite possibly the perfect layout for a vacation getaway, or an empty nester home with private space for guests and the homeowners
- The vaulted country kitchen merges completely with the great room to form the core of this open and airy layout
- The master bedroom has plenty of space to relax in private and enjoys direct deck access, a posh bath and a huge walk-in closet
- Bedroom 2 has direct screen porch access and is right across the hall from a full bath and the laundry room
- So much outdoor living space surrounds this home it's easy to see why it would be the ideal home for a lake or mountain setting

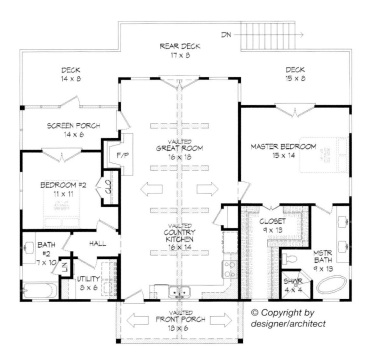

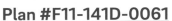

Images provided by designer/architect

Plan #F11-055D-0342

Dimensions: 60' W x 77'6" D
Heated Sq. Ft.: 2,445
Bonus Sq. Ft.: 758
Bedrooms: 4 **Bathrooms:** 3½
Foundation: Crawl space or slab standard; basement or daylight basement for an additional fee

See index for more information

Special Features

- Great dormers and a covered porch decorate the front facade of this home and offer extra charm and curb appeal
- The cheerful breakfast room also has a functional computer desk
- The private bedroom #4 enjoys its own bath and the nearby TV/media room
- There's plenty of much appreciated storage space throughout this plan
- The optional future space on the second floor has an additional 758 square feet of living area
- 2-car side entry garage

© Copyright by designer/architect

First Floor
2,129 sq. ft.

Second Floor
316 sq. ft.

Images provided by designer/architect

Plan #F11-123D-0222

Dimensions: 58' W x 59' D
Heated Sq. Ft.: 2,499
Bedrooms: 4   **Bathrooms:** 2½
Foundation: Basement standard; crawl space, slab or walk-out basement for an additional fee

See index for more information

Special Features

- Offering second floor outdoor living space, this home could be the perfect option if you have distant views of the shore
- The beautiful staircase to the left greets you as you enter the home
- A flex space can be found on the right of the entry and offers a spot for a home office if needed
- The kitchen island is angled in such a way that it can capture all the fun in the great room and nearby dining area
- The large mud room has a half bath, bench/lockers for great organization, and a laundry room
- The second floor loft has a sink and refrigerator and attaches to a large open deck outdoors - this is sure to be the place to party
- 2-car front entry garage

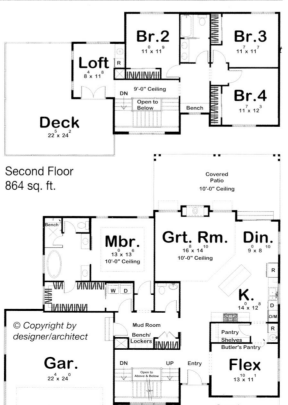

Second Floor
864 sq. ft.

First Floor
1,635 sq. ft.

Images provided by designer/architect

Plan #F11-084D-0085

Dimensions: 85' W x 64' D
Heated Sq. Ft.: 2,252
Bonus Sq. Ft.: 1,341
Bedrooms: 3   **Bathrooms:** 2
Exterior Walls: 2" x 6"
Foundation: Slab standard; crawl space for an additional fee

See index for more information

Special Features

- This special home is both timeless and fresh inside and out
- Step into the great room and discover a beautiful 12' coffered ceiling, and beyond a dining area with a beamed ceiling creating distinction between the spaces as well as great style
- The kitchen enjoys tall ceilings, a walk-in pantry and a centered island overlooking the main gathering space on the first floor
- Extra storage can be found accessible from the outdoors near the garage
- The optional second floor has an additional 1,341 square feet of living area
- 2-car side entry garage

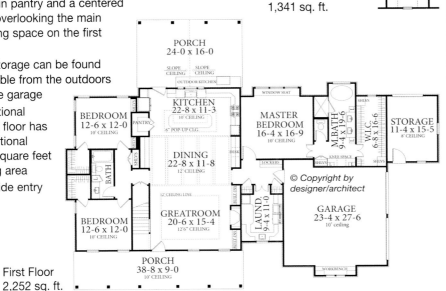

Optional Second Floor 1,341 sq. ft.

First Floor 2,252 sq. ft.

© Copyright by designer/architect

Images provided by designer/architect

Plan #F11-011D-0686

Dimensions: 40' W x 70' D
Heated Sq. Ft.: 2,009
Bedrooms: 4   **Bathrooms:** 2½
Exterior Walls: 2" x 6"
Foundation: Crawl space or slab standard; basement for an additional fee

See index for more information

Special Features

- Designed with a narrow lot in mind, yet the interior is so comfortable you will never be reminded of its more narrow footprint
- As you enter, you are greeted by the three secondary bedrooms, a full bath, and a half bath for guests
- The wide open kitchen faces the vaulted living/dining area that is accentuated with three sets of sliding glass doors that lead to a large covered outdoor living space
- Built-in shelves are exquisite extras in the kitchen and living/dining area
- The vaulted master bedroom enjoys a bath with an oversized shower and walk-in closet with direct access to the laundry room
- 2-car front entry garage

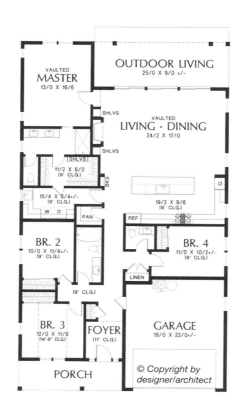

Images provided by designer/architect

Plan #F11-084D-0090

Dimensions:	73'6" W x 61' D
Heated Sq. Ft.:	2,221
Bonus Sq. Ft.:	403
Bedrooms: 4	**Bathrooms:** 2

Foundation: Slab standard; crawl space or basement for an additional fee

See index for more information

Special Features

- If you're longing for today's hottest style home, then look no further, this is the home for you
- Step into the foyer and find a vaulted living/dining area open to the kitchen
- On the left side of the home are three bedrooms and a full bath
- On the right side of the home you'll discover a private master bedroom and bath, a laundry room, and a mudroom for keeping everything organized
- The optional second floor has an additional 403 square feet of living area
- 2-car side entry garage

Optional Second Floor 403 sq. ft.

FUTURE
11-8 x 27-2
8' CEILING
SLOPED TO
5' SIDE WALLS

PORCH
30-10 x 11-8
9' CEILING

MASTER BEDROOM
14-0 x 16-3
CATHEDRAL CLG.

M.BATH
11-0 x 16-3
CLG.9'-9"x10' Pop-up

BEDROOM
11-4 x 13-0
9' CEILING

BATH
5-0 x 13-0

LIVING/DINING
30-0 x 17-4
CATHEDRAL CLG.

LAUND.
7-7 x 10-4

CLOSET
9-1 x 10-4
9' CLG.

MUDROOM
9-0 x 7-4
9' CEILING

STORAGE
14-0 x 7-4

BEDROOM
11-4 x 12-8
9' CEILING

BEDROOM
12-3 x 11-4
9' CEILING

FOYER
5-4 x 11-2
9' CEILING

KITCHEN
14-9 x 11-3
9' CLG.

© Copyright by designer/architect

GARAGE
23-4 x 23-3
9' CEILING

PORCH
27-0 x 5-8
9' CEILING

First Floor
2,221 sq. ft.

Images provided by designer/architect

First Floor
2,136 sq. ft.

Images provided by designer/architect

Second Floor
1,028 sq. ft.

Plan #F11-032D-1034

Dimensions: 70' W x 54' D
Heated Sq. Ft.: 3,164
Bedrooms: 4   **Bathrooms:** 3½
Exterior Walls: 2" x 6"
Foundation: Crawl space standard; floating slab, monolithic slab or basement for an additional fee

See index for more information

Images provided by designer/architect

Plan #F11-026D-2099

Dimensions: 54' W x 54' D
Heated Sq. Ft.: 1,936
Bedrooms: 3   **Bathrooms:** 3
Exterior Walls: 2" x 6"
Foundation: Basement standard; crawl space, slab or walk-out basement for an additional fee

See index for more information

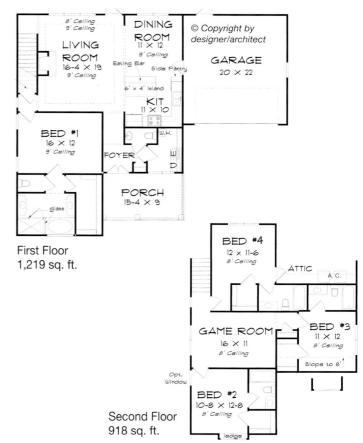

Images provided by designer/architect

First Floor
1,219 sq. ft.

Second Floor
918 sq. ft.

Plan #F11-130D-0389

Dimensions: 52' W x 44' D
Heated Sq. Ft.: 2,137
Bedrooms: 4   **Bathrooms:** 4½
Foundation: Slab standard; crawl space or basement for an additional fee

See index for more information

Images provided by designer/architect

Plan #F11-148D-0398

Dimensions: 48'6" W x 56' D
Heated Sq. Ft.: 1,390
Bedrooms: 3   **Bathrooms:** 2
Exterior Walls: 2" x 6"
Foundation: Basement

See index for more information

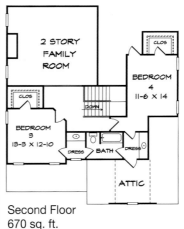

Second Floor
670 sq. ft.

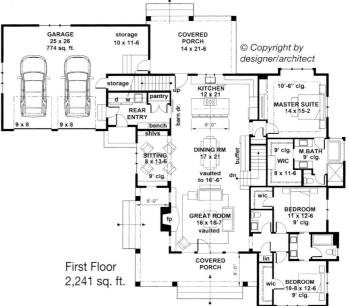

First Floor
1,760 sq. ft.

© Copyright by
designer/architect

Images provided by designer/architect

Plan #F11-076D-0286

Dimensions: 39'6" W x 70' D
Heated Sq. Ft.: 2,430
Bedrooms: 4   **Bathrooms:** 3
Foundation: Slab

See index for more information

Images provided by designer/architect

Plan #F11-091D-0506

Dimensions: 82' W x 71' D
Heated Sq. Ft.: 2,241
Bonus Sq. Ft.: 591
Bedrooms: 3   **Bathrooms:** 2½
Exterior Walls: 2" x 6"
Foundation: Crawl space standard;
slab, basement or walk-out
basement for an additional fee

See index for more information

Optional
Second Floor
591 sq. ft.

© Copyright by
designer/architect

First Floor
2,241 sq. ft.

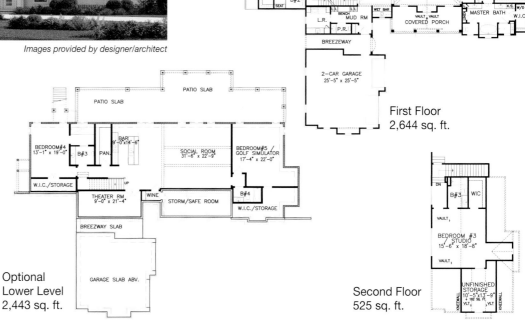

Plan #F11-056D-0128

Dimensions: 92' W x 87'8" D
Heated Sq. Ft.: 3,169
Bonus Sq. Ft.: 2,752
Bedrooms: 3   **Bathrooms:** 3½
Foundation: Basement standard;
crawl space or slab for an additional
fee

See index for more information

Images provided by designer/architect

First Floor
2,644 sq. ft.

Optional
Lower Level
2,443 sq. ft.

Second Floor
525 sq. ft.

Plan #F11-123D-0037

Dimensions: 50' W x 63' D
Heated Sq. Ft.: 2,122
Bedrooms: 3   **Bathrooms:** 2½
Foundation: Basement standard;
crawl space, slab or walk-out
basement for an additional fee

See index for more information

Images provided by designer/architect

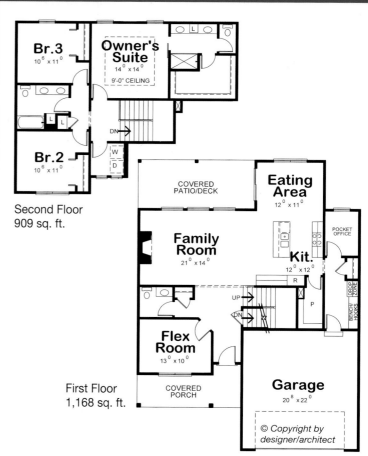

Second Floor
909 sq. ft.

First Floor
1,168 sq. ft.

© Copyright by designer/architect

Images provided by designer/architect

Plan #F11-026D-2046

Dimensions: 40' W x 54' D
Heated Sq. Ft.: 2,077
Bedrooms: 3   **Bathrooms:** 2½
Foundation: Basement standard; crawl space, slab or walk-out basement for an additional fee

See index for more information

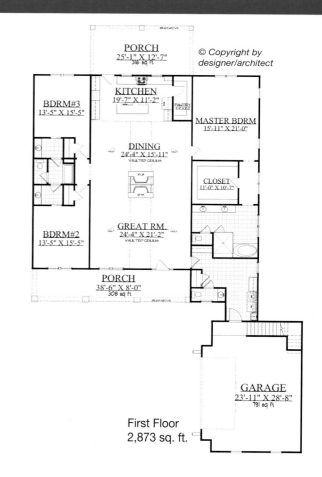

© Copyright by designer/architect

Images provided by designer/architect

Plan #F11-157D-0023

Dimensions: 65'11" W x 107' D
Heated Sq. Ft.: 2,873
Bonus Sq. Ft.: 552
Bedrooms: 3   **Bathrooms:** 2½
Foundation: Crawl space standard; slab for an additional fee

See index for more information

Optional
Second Floor
552 sq. ft.

First Floor
2,873 sq. ft.

Second Floor
1,715 sq. ft.

© Copyright by
designer/architect

Plan #F11-032D-1141

Dimensions:	60'11" W x 48' D
Heated Sq. Ft.:	3,313
Bonus Sq. Ft.:	1,435
Bedrooms: 3	**Bathrooms:** 2½
Exterior Walls:	2" x 6"

Foundation: Walk-out basement
standard; basement, crawl space,
floating slab or monolithic slab for an
additional fee

See index for more information

First Floor
1,598 sq. ft.

Images provided by designer/architect

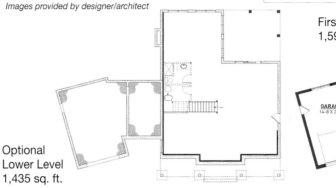

**Optional
Lower Level
1,435 sq. ft.**

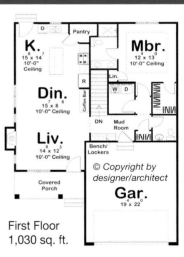

© Copyright by
designer/architect

**Optional
Lower Level
815 sq. ft.**

**First Floor
1,030 sq. ft.**

Images provided by designer/architect

Plan #F11-123D-0171

Dimensions:	37' W x 49' D
Heated Sq. Ft.:	1,030
Bonus Sq. Ft.:	815
Bedrooms: 1	**Bathrooms:** 1½

Foundation: Basement standard;
crawl space, slab or walk-out
basement for an additional fee

See index for more information

Plan #F11-167D-0008

Dimensions: 62'4" W x 50'7" D
Heated Sq. Ft.: 3,328
Bedrooms: 4   **Bathrooms:** 3½
Exterior Walls: 2" x 6"
Foundation: Crawl space standard;
slab for an additional fee
See index for more information

Special Features

- Classic American Farmhouse style with a Modern Farmhouse twist makes this a perfect home with a simple, yet stylish feel for today
- The first floor plan has a living room, large dining area, and kitchen all completely open to one another
- The handy laundry and mud rooms offer the opportunity for great organizing possibilities
- Two doors off the living area lead to a private home office
- The owner's suite has a vaulted ceiling, access to an open deck, two walk-in closets, and a private bath with a huge walk-in shower and a free-standing tub
- The second floor has another living area with access onto a covered deck
- 2-car detached garage

Detached
Garage

Images provided by designer/architect

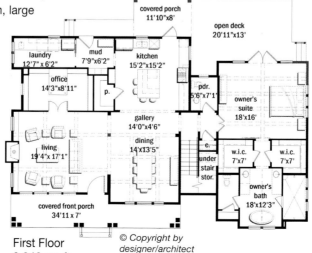

First Floor
2,046 sq. ft.

© Copyright by
designer/architect

Second Floor
1,282 sq. ft.

Plan #F11-123S-0053

Dimensions: 78' W x 52' D
Heated Sq. Ft.: 3,880
Bedrooms: 5 **Bathrooms:** 4½
Foundation: Basement standard; crawl space, slab or walk-out basement for an additional fee
See index for more information

Special Features

- This luxury Modern Farmhouse design features an apartment above the garage which is ideal for a live-in parent, or even an adult child
- The main home offers a first floor with both formal and informal open spaces in the back of the home
- The second floor of the main home houses all of the bedrooms, perfect if children are still small and need to be close
- The apartment features direct access to the outdoors down a staircase from a second floor deck, a kitchen with an island, a laundry closet, a living area, and a bedroom with a full bath
- 3-car side entry garage

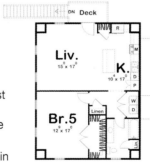

Second Floor
2,260 sq. ft.

First Floor
1,620 sq. ft.

© Copyright by designer/architect

Images provided by designer/architect

Plan #F11-020D-0397

Dimensions: 59' W x 50' D
Heated Sq. Ft.: 1,608
Bedrooms: 3 **Bathrooms:** 2
Exterior Walls: 2" x 6"
Foundation: Crawl space standard;
slab for an additional fee

See index for more information

Special Features

- The perfect sized one-story home with both covered front porch and back porches adding extra outdoor living space that's always appreciated
- The split bedroom floor plan promises privacy for the homeowners and guests
- The open kitchen layout overlooks the large living area and has a convenient bayed breakfast nook nearby
- The large master suite has access to a bath that connects to the utility room directly for added convenience
- A formal dining area is open thanks to the columns on the corner instead of walls closing it in
- Optional 2-car side entry garage

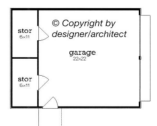

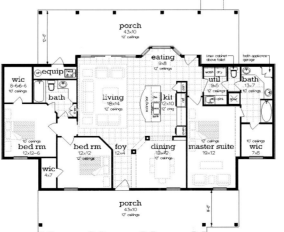

Images provided by designer/architect

Plan #F11-056D-0100

Dimensions:	50' W x 100'9" D
Heated Sq. Ft.:	2,147
Bonus Sq. Ft.:	2,547
Bedrooms: 2	**Bathrooms:** 2

Foundation: Basement standard; crawl space or slab for an additional fee

See index for more information

Special Features

- This home combines Craftsman, Modern Farmhouse and even Country French architecture styles to form an inviting dwelling that transcends time
- The vaulted lodge room is cozy and inviting and will be a family favorite after dinner
- The covered porch has a outdoor fireplace allowing the outdoors to be enjoyed well into the Fall
- The optional lower level has an additional 2,009 square feet of living area with extra space for guests and entertaining
- The optional second floor has an additional 538 square feet of living area
- 3-car side entry garage

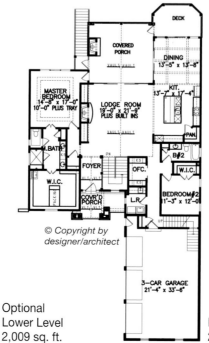

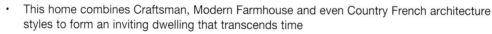

© Copyright by designer/architect

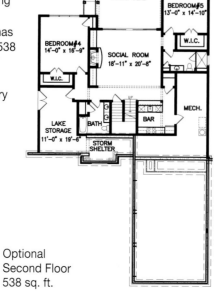

Optional
Second Floor
538 sq. ft.

Optional
Lower Level
2,009 sq. ft.

First Floor
2,147 sq. ft.

Images provided by designer/architect

Plan #F11-101D-0113

Dimensions:	89' W x 77'9" D
Heated Sq. Ft.:	3,082
Bonus Sq. Ft.:	2,250
Bedrooms: 2	**Bathrooms:** 2½
Exterior Walls:	2" x 6"

Foundation: Basement, daylight basement or walk-out basement, please specify when ordering

See index for more information

Special Features

- This one-story beauty has an inviting, yet private enclosed courtyard entrance
- Once inside, the great room draws you in with its openness and views of the backyard
- The kitchen has a huge island facing into the sunny dining area
- The private master bedroom enjoys a posh bath with a huge walk-in closet
- An office can be found behind the kitchen
- The optional lower level has an additional 2,250 square feet of living area and includes a rec room with a wet bar, an exercise room, two additional bedrooms, two full baths and one half bath
- 3-car front entry garage

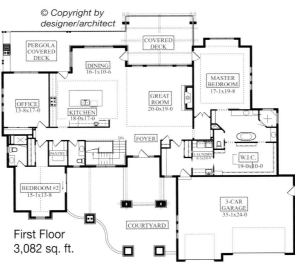

First Floor
3,082 sq. ft.

Optional
Lower Level
2,250 sq. ft.

Images provided by designer/architect

Plan #F11-032D-1134

Dimensions:	40' W x 34'4" D
Heated Sq. Ft.:	2,652
Bedrooms: 4	**Bathrooms:** 2
Exterior Walls:	2" x 6"
Foundation:	Basement

See index for more information

Special Features

- This stylish Craftsman home has Modern Farmhouse influence thanks to its black window panes, white vertical siding and light fixture choices
- Right off the foyer is a handy enclosed mud room for keeping the rest of the house neat and tidy
- The living and dining rooms are open to one another and are topped with a cathedral ceiling
- The kitchen features a huge corner walk-in pantry, an oversized island with seating and is open to the dining room
- The lower level has a spacious recreation area, two additional bedrooms, a full bath and the laundry room

© Copyright by designer/architect

First Floor
1,326 sq. ft.

Lower Level
1,326 sq. ft.

Images provided by designer/architect

Plan #F11-101D-0131

Dimensions:	99' W x 87' D
Heated Sq. Ft.:	2,889
Bonus Sq. Ft.:	2,561
Bedrooms: 2	**Bathrooms:** 2½
Exterior Walls:	2" x 6"
Foundation:	Walk-out basement

See index for more information

Special Features

- This charming Craftsman combines casual rustic style and beautiful architectural details creating tons of personality
- The beamed living and dining rooms surround the huge T-shaped kitchen island
- The private master suite bath enjoys a huge walk-in shower and walk-in closet
- The enormous mud room includes plenty of closetspace
- The optional lower level has an additional 2,561 square feet and a media area, a billiards area, an exercise room, a wet bar, a laundry room, a bunk room, a bedroom and a full bath
- 3-car side entry garage

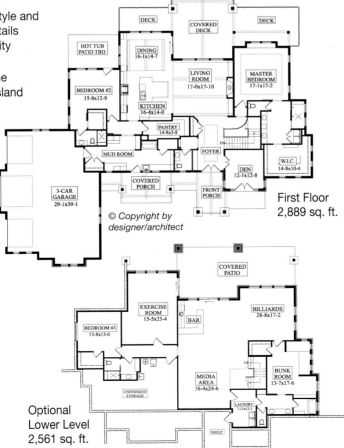

© Copyright by designer/architect

First Floor 2,889 sq. ft.

Optional Lower Level 2,561 sq. ft.

Images provided by designer/architect

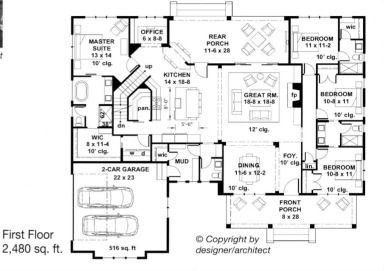

Images provided by designer/architect

Plan #F11-091D-0524

Dimensions: 69' W x 59'6" D
Heated Sq. Ft.: 2,480
Bonus Sq. Ft.: 361
Bedrooms: 4　　**Bathrooms:** 3½
Exterior Walls: 2" x 6"
Foundation: Crawl space standard; slab, basement or walk-out basement for an additional fee

See index for more information

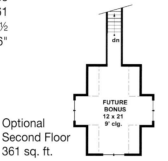

Optional
Second Floor
361 sq. ft.

First Floor
2,480 sq. ft.

© Copyright by
designer/architect

Images provided by designer/architect

Plan #F11-019S-0009

Dimensions: 97'8" W x 84'7" D
Heated Sq. Ft.: 3,220
Bonus Sq. Ft.: 292
Bedrooms: 4　　**Bathrooms:** 4
Foundation: Slab standard; crawl space or basement for an additional fee

See index for more information

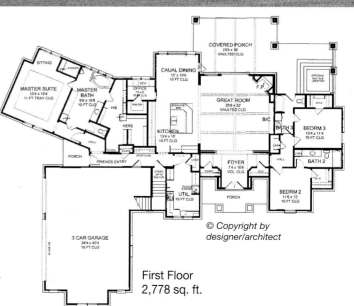

Second Floor
442 sq. ft.

First Floor
2,778 sq. ft.

© Copyright by
designer/architect

Second Floor
1,092 sq. ft.

© Copyright by designer/architect

First Floor
1,356 sq. ft.

Plan #F11-011D-0652

Dimensions: 40' W x 60' D
Heated Sq. Ft.: 2,448
Bedrooms: 3 **Bathrooms:** 2½
Exterior Walls: 2" x 6"
Foundation: Crawl space or slab standard; basement for an additional fee

See index for more information

Images provided by designer/architect

© Copyright by designer/architect

Images provided by designer/architect

Plan #F11-011D-0666

Dimensions: 93' W x 64' D
Heated Sq. Ft.: 2,798
Bedrooms: 3 **Bathrooms:** 2½
Exterior Walls: 2" x 6"
Foundation: Crawl space or slab standard; basement for an additional fee

See index for more information

Second Floor
868 sq. ft.

© Copyright by designer/architect

First Floor
885 sq. ft.

Plan #F11-123D-0118

Dimensions: 46' W x 41'8" D
Heated Sq. Ft.: 1,753
Bonus Sq. Ft.: 260
Bedrooms: 3   **Bathrooms:** 2½
Foundation: Basement standard; crawl space, slab or walk-out basement for an additional fee

See index for more information

Images provided by designer/architect

Plan #F11-139D-0080

Dimensions: 70'3" W x 78'6" D
Heated Sq. Ft.: 3,263
Bonus Sq. Ft.: 490
Bedrooms: 4   **Bathrooms:** 4½
Exterior Walls: 2" x 6"
Foundation: Crawl space standard; slab, basement, daylight basement or walk-out basement for an additional fee

See index for more information

Images provided by designer/architect

Second Floor
567 sq. ft.

Optional
Second Floor
490 sq. ft.

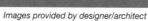

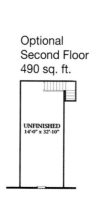

© Copyright by designer/architect

First Floor
2,696 sq. ft.

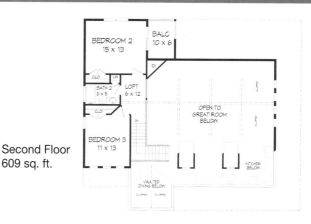

Second Floor
609 sq. ft.

Plan #F11-141D-0397

Dimensions: 53'2" W x 48'6" D
Heated Sq. Ft.: 2,366
Bonus Sq. Ft.: 1,691
Bedrooms: 3   **Bathrooms:** 2½
Exterior Walls: 2" x 6"
Foundation: Basement standard; crawl space, slab or walk-out basement for an additional fee

See index for more information

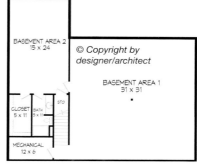

Optional
Lower Level
1,691 sq. ft.

© Copyright by designer/architect

First Floor
1,757 sq. ft.

Images provided by designer/architect

Plan #F11-155D-0165

Dimensions: 50'4" W x 63'2" D
Heated Sq. Ft.: 1,998
Bonus Sq. Ft.: 485
Bedrooms: 3   **Bathrooms:** 2
Foundation: Crawl space or slab standard; basement or daylight basement for an additional fee

See index for more information

Images provided by designer/architect

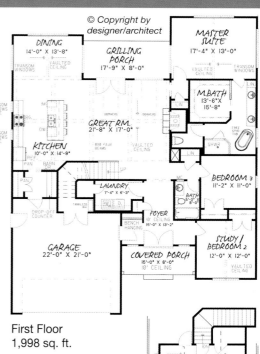

© Copyright by designer/architect

First Floor
1,998 sq. ft.

Optional
Second Floor
485 sq. ft.

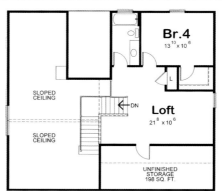

Second Floor
548 sq. ft.

First Floor
1,324 sq. ft.

© Copyright by
designer/architect

Plan #F11-026D-2162

Images provided by designer/architect

Dimensions: 40' W x 48'8" D
Heated Sq. Ft.: 1,872
Bonus Sq. Ft.: 198
Bedrooms: 4   **Bathrooms:** 3
Foundation: Slab standard; crawl space, basement or walk-out basement for an additional fee

See index for more information

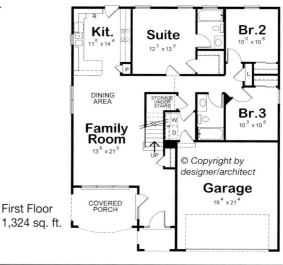

First Floor
1,263 sq. ft.

Plan #F11-123D-0239

Images provided by designer/architect

Dimensions: 45' W x 34' D
Heated Sq. Ft.: 1,507
Bedrooms: 3   **Bathrooms:** 2
Foundation: Basement standard; crawl space, slab or walk-out basement for an additional fee

See index for more information

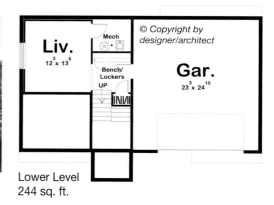

© Copyright by
designer/architect

Lower Level
244 sq. ft.

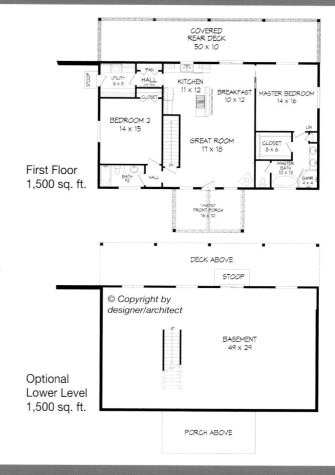

First Floor
1,500 sq. ft.

Optional
Lower Level
1,500 sq. ft.

Plan #F11-141D-0292

Dimensions: 60' W x 50' D
Heated Sq. Ft.:   1,500
Bonus Sq. Ft.:   1,500
Bedrooms: 2   **Bathrooms:** 2
Exterior Walls: 2" x 6"
Foundation: Basement standard;
crawl space or slab for an additional
fee

See index for more information

Images provided by designer/architect

Plan #F11-155D-0148

Dimensions: 72'6" W x 64'8" D
Heated Sq. Ft.:   1,897
Bonus Sq. Ft.:   395
Bedrooms: 4   **Bathrooms:** 2
Foundation: Crawl space or slab
standard; basement or daylight
basement for an additional fee

See index for more information

Images provided by designer/architect

Optional
Second Floor
395 sq. ft.

First Floor
1,897 sq. ft.

© Copyright by designer/architect

Images provided by designer/architect

Plan #F11-155D-0213

Dimensions: 107'8" W x 55'4" D
Heated Sq. Ft.: 3,246
Bedrooms: 5   **Bathrooms:** 3½
Foundation: Crawl space or slab
standard; basement or daylight
basement for an additional fee

See index for more information

First Floor
1,955 sq. ft.

© Copyright by
designer/architect

Second Floor
796 sq. ft.

Plan #F11-091D-0520

Dimensions: 64' W x 52' D
Heated Sq. Ft.: 2,751
Bedrooms: 4   **Bathrooms:** 3½
Exterior Walls: 2" x 6"
Foundation: Crawl space standard;
slab, basement or walk-out
basement for an additional fee

See index for more information

Images provided by designer/architect

© Copyright by designer/architect

Plan #F11-051D-0982

Dimensions: 79'11" W x 69'6" D
Heated Sq. Ft.: 2,150
Bedrooms: 3 **Bathrooms:** 2½
Exterior Walls: 2" x 6"
Foundation: Basement standard; crawl space or slab for an additional fee

See index for more information

Images provided by designer/architect

Images provided by designer/architect

Plan #F11-144D-0024

Dimensions: 32' W x 32' D
Heated Sq. Ft.: 1,024
Bedrooms: 1 **Bathrooms:** 1½
Exterior Walls: 2" x 6"
Foundation: Basement or daylight basement standard; crawl space, slab or walk-out basement for an additional fee

See index for more information

Plan #F11-123D-0056

Dimensions: 55' W x 55' D
Heated Sq. Ft.: 1,701
Bedrooms: 3   **Bathrooms:** 2
Foundation: Basement standard; crawl space, slab or walk-out basement for an additional fee

See index for more information

Special Features

- A perfect split bedroom ranch home designed with today's popular Modern Farmhouse design in mind
- The great room is topped with a 10' ceiling and enjoys views of the dining area and kitchen featuring a large island
- The private master bedroom has its own private bath and a walk-in closet
- Enter the mud room from the garage and drop belongings here to keep them out of the main gathering spaces
- The large covered front porch is an inviting way to relax and enjoy the outdoors in the shade
- 3-car front entry garage

Images provided by designer/architect

© Copyright by designer/architect

Plan #F11-028D-0064

Dimensions: 38' W x 52' D
Heated Sq. Ft.: 1,292
Bedrooms: 2   **Bathrooms:** 2
Exterior Walls: 2" x 6"
Foundation: Basement, crawl space or monolithic slab, please specify when ordering

See index for more information

Images provided by designer/architect

Special Features

- Two large covered porches in the front and back offer plenty of desirable outdoor living space with their wide design

- The combined kitchen/dining area is open to the sunny great room making this the main gathering place in this home

- A large laundry room provides plenty of space for household chores and has direct access to the outdoors

- Each of the two bedrooms includes ample walk-in closet space for keeping things organized

PORCH 2
8' DEEP

KITCHEN/DINING
14' X 13'

GREAT ROOM
20' X 17'

LAUNDRY

BATH

BEDROOM 1
14' X 12'

FOYER
6' WIDE

BEDROOM 2
14' X 12'

BATH

LINEN

PORCH 1

© Copyright by designer/architect

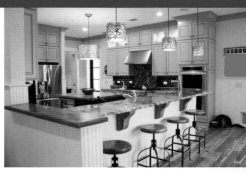

Plan #F11-024S-0024

Dimensions:	52' W x 62' D
Heated Sq. Ft.:	3,610
Bedrooms: 5	**Bathrooms:** 4
Foundation:	Slab

See index for more information

Images provided by designer/architect

Special Features

- The oversized rear covered porch enjoys a built-in sink and grill space for cooking outdoors

- The second floor sitting room makes a great spot for a computer area

- Two sets of double doors lead from the dining area to the covered porch creating a great set-up when entertaining

- The second floor bonus/bedroom 5 is included in the square footage

- 2-car detached garage

© Copyright by designer/architect

Second Floor
1,286 sq. ft.

First Floor
2,324 sq. ft.

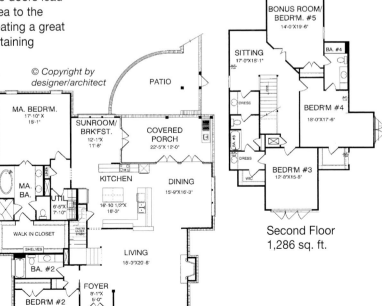

Plan #F11-028D-0103

Dimensions:	40' W x 46' D
Heated Sq. Ft.:	1,520
Bedrooms: 2	**Bathrooms:** 1
Exterior Walls:	2" x 6"
Foundation:	Crawl space

See index for more information

Special Features

- No wasted space is found in this popular Modern Farmhouse design
- Step inside from the deep covered front porch and enjoy the comfort of the great room with fireplace
- A breakfast bar counter from the kitchen overlooks into the great room
- There is also a small dining area near the kitchen with island
- A bath/laundry area provides great function and is centrally located for added convenience
- Two bedrooms, each with oversized closets enjoy a quiet place in the back of the home

© Copyright by designer/architect

Images provided by designer/architect

Call toll-free 1-800-373-2646   houseplansandmore.com

Plan #F11-056D-0096

Dimensions: 91'6" W x 70' D
Heated Sq. Ft.: 2,510
Bonus Sq. Ft.: 2,510
Bedrooms: 3   **Bathrooms:** 2½
Foundation: Basement standard;
crawl space or slab for an additional
fee

See index for more information

Special Features

- This wonderful home is designed in the popular Modern Farmhouse style
- A vaulted lodge room is connected to the kitchen and breakfast area
- Both laundry and mud rooms make this home highly efficient
- The split bedroom floor plan has the master suite separated from the other bedrooms for privacy
- The optional lower level has an additional 2,510 square feet of living area and includes a future social room, card area, wet bar, theater, three bedrooms, a wine cellar and three full baths
- 2-car side entry garage

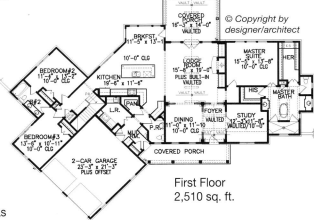

First Floor
2,510 sq. ft.

Optional
Lower Level
2,510 sq. ft.

Images provided by designer/architect

Plan #F11-032D-1124

Dimensions: 66' W x 50' D
Heated Sq. Ft.: 2,117
Bonus Sq. Ft.: 360
Bedrooms: 3   **Bathrooms:** 2
Exterior Walls: 2" x 6"
Foundation: Crawl space standard; floating slab, monolithic slab, basement or walk-out basement for an additional fee

See index for more information

Special Features

- This Modern Farmhouse inspired one-story home has an open and split bedroom layout families love today
- Step into the foyer and be greeted by the formal dining room on the left side and straight ahead the vaulted living room and open kitchen
- The master suite and bath enjoy two walk-in closets, a double vanity, a walk-in oversized shower and a freestanding tub as the focal point
- Two secondary bedrooms on the opposite side of the home from the master bedroom share a full bath
- 2-car front entry garage

Optional
Second Floor
360 sq. ft.

BONUS ROOM
12-4 X 15-6

© Copyright by
designer/architect

First Floor
2,117 sq. ft.

Images provided by designer/architect

Plan #F11-123D-0160

Dimensions:	38' W x 60' D
Heated Sq. Ft.:	3,042
Bedrooms: 4	**Bathrooms:** 2½

Foundation: Basement standard; crawl space, slab or walk-out basement for an additional fee

See index for more information

Special Features

- Sleek and modern, this home merges nicely with the outdoors thanks to its large floor-to-ceiling windows and second floor outdoor deck off the master bedroom
- Enter and find a two-story living area with a fireplace, perfect as a home office space right at the front entrance of the home
- The dining area, kitchen and great room join forces to create an airy gathering space with covered patio views
- The master bedroom is topped with a cathedral ceiling and has triple sliding glass doors onto a spacious sunny outdoor deck
- 2-car front entry garage

Second Floor
1,636 sq. ft.

© Copyright by designer/architect

First Floor
1,406 sq. ft.

Images provided by designer/architect

Plan #F11-123S-0043

Dimensions: 62' W x 79' D
Heated Sq. Ft.: 3,371
Bonus Sq. Ft.: 2,489
Bedrooms: 4   **Bathrooms:** 3½
Foundation: Basement standard; crawl space, slab or walk-out basement for an additional fee

See index for more information

Special Features

- Create your homestead life in this classic rustic barn style home complete with three levels of spaces designed for both relaxing and entertaining
- The kitchen shares views of the see-through fireplace with the two-story great room
- The quiet master bedroom enjoys a sunny reading room and a private bath with a freestanding tub, an oversized shower and a double bowl vanity
- The optional lower level has an additional 1,519 square feet of living area and is filled with many great extras including a wet bar, a recreation room and family room that share a see-through fireplace, an exercise room, and a fifth bedroom with a full bath nearby
- The bonus room on the second floor has an additional 970 square feet of living area
- 3-car side entry garage, and a 1-car side entry garage

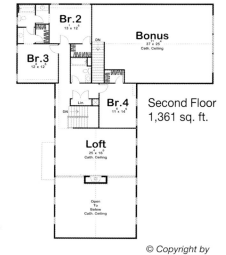

Br.2
13' x 12'

Bonus
37' x 25'
Cath. Ceiling

Br.3
12' x 12'

Br.4
11' x 14'

Second Floor
1,361 sq. ft.

Loft
25' x 16'
Cath. Ceiling

Open To Below
Cath. Ceiling

© Copyright by designer/architect

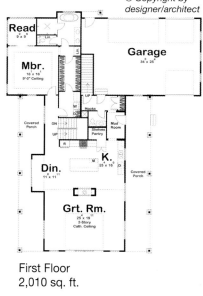

Read
9' x 9'

Garage
34' x 25'

Mbr.
16' x 16'
9'-0" Ceiling

Covered Porch

Mud Room

Shelves Pantry

Din.
11' x 14'

K.
25' x 16'

Covered Porch

Grt. Rm.
25' x 19'
2-Story
Cath. Ceiling

First Floor
2,010 sq. ft.

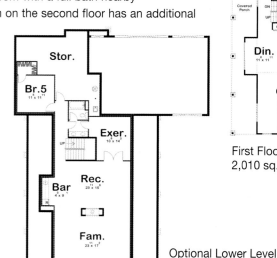

Stor.

Br.5
11' x 11'

Exer.
10' x 14'

Rec.
23' x 15'

Bar
4' x 9'

Fam.
23' x 17'

Optional Lower Level
1,519 sq. ft.

Plan #F11-123D-0107

Dimensions: 74' W x 59' D
Heated Sq. Ft.: 2,337
Bedrooms: 3 **Bathrooms:** 2½
Foundation: Basement standard;
crawl space, slab or walk-out
basement for an additional fee
See index for more information

Special Features

- Uncomplicated Farmhouse exterior offers tremendous curb appeal and intrigue
- Enter to find a cozy den to the right and a formal coffered dining room to the left
- The open great room is topped with a cathedral ceiling that focuses on the fireplace
- The secondary bedrooms enjoy a private location, walk-in closets, and a Jack and Jill bath
- The master bedroom has covered patio access and a bath with a double vanity, linen closet, spa tub, separate shower, a toilet room, and a walk-in closet similar to a dressing room
- 3-car side entry garage

Images provided by designer/architect

Plan #F11-056D-0139

Dimensions: 82'3" W x 58'3" D
Heated Sq. Ft.: 3,830
Bonus Sq. Ft.: 2,839
Bedrooms: 3   **Bathrooms:** 2½
Exterior Walls: 2" x 6"
Foundation: Basement standard; crawl space or slab for an additional fee

See index for more information

Optional Second Floor 1,802 sq. ft.

Special Features

- Enchanting simplicity resonates with this Modern Farmhouse design
- The great room with fireplace has surrounding built-ins and is a lovely place to gather when entertaining
- The master suite has a lavish bath with a freestanding tub, a separate shower, and a dressing area style walk-in closet with a center island style dresser
- The optional second floor has an additional 1,802 square feet of living area; while the optional lower level has an additional 1,037 square feet of living area
- 2-car side entry garage

Lower Level 1,037 sq. ft.

First Floor 2,793 sq. ft.

Images provided by designer/architect

Plan #F11-011D-0664

Dimensions: 64' W x 67'6" D
Heated Sq. Ft.: 2,576
Bonus Sq. Ft.: 374
Bedrooms: 3   **Bathrooms:** 2½
Exterior Walls: 2" x 6"
Foundation: Crawl space or slab standard; basement for an additional fee

See index for more information

Special Features

- This one-story home has all of the curb appeal and style a homeowner wants plus great interior features
- The open living area merges with the kitchen featuring a large island with dining space
- The vaulted dining area has porch access and a cheerful atmosphere
- A quiet home office is found behind the kitchen near the laundry room
- Three bedrooms can be found on the opposite side of the home from the office
- The optional second floor has an additional 374 square feet of living area
- 3-car front entry garage

Optional Second Floor
374 sq. ft.

GAME RM
14/0 X 24/0
(9' CLG.)

First Floor
2,576 sq. ft.

© Copyright by designer/architect

Plan #F11-123D-0242

Dimensions: 78' W x 52' D
Heated Sq. Ft.: 2,970
Bedrooms: 4   **Bathrooms:** 3½
Foundation: Basement standard;
crawl space, slab or walk-out
basement for an additional fee
See index for more information

Special Features

- This Modern Farmhouse design has a purposefully placed barn style door on the exterior of the garage that truly enhances the farmhouse theme to the fullest
- The wrap-around porch further takes you to a rural setting that feels tranquil and relaxing
- Enter the foyer and find the more formal spaces at the front of the home and the more casual gathering spaces at the back of the home
- The great room has two sets of double doors that act as design elements while increasing the amount of sunlight coming into the space
- The kitchen faces the spacious great room merging the spaces together naturally
- A bench and lockers greet you as you enter from the garage
- All of the bedrooms are located on the second floor for privacy and ease when caring for smaller children
- 3-car side entry garage

Second Floor
1,350 sq. ft.

First Floor
1,620 sq. ft.

Images provided by designer/architect

Plan #F11-076D-0220

Dimensions: 97'2" W x 87'7" D
Heated Sq. Ft.: 3,061
Bonus Sq. Ft.: 3,644
Bedrooms: 3   **Bathrooms:** 3½
Foundation: Basement, crawl space or slab, please specify when ordering
See index for more information

Special Features

- This home is loaded with curb appeal thanks to multiple gables, and a covered front porch
- The first floor is open and airy with the main gathering spaces combining perfectly maximizing the square footage
- The kitchen is open to the family room with a covered terrace
- The optional lower level has an additional 2,975 square feet of living area with a hobby room, theater, office, and a recreation area with a bar
- The optional second floor has an additional 669 square feet of living area with 277 square feet in the bedroom and 392 square feet in the recreation area
- 3-car front entry garage

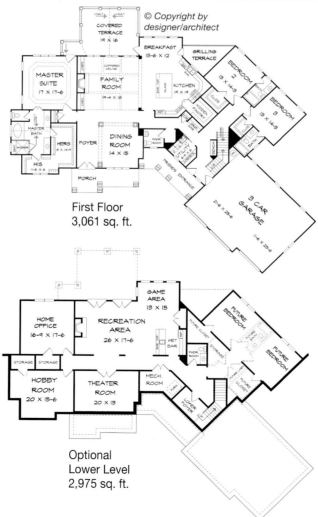

© Copyright by designer/architect

First Floor
3,061 sq. ft.

Optional
Lower Level
2,975 sq. ft.

Optional
Second Floor
669 sq. ft.

Images provided by designer/architect

Plan #F11-123D-0150

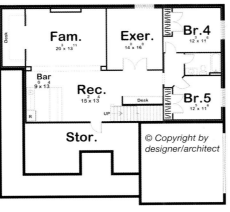

Dimensions: 57' W x 64'8" D
Heated Sq. Ft.: 2,076
Bonus Sq. Ft.: 1,984
Bedrooms: 3   **Bathrooms:** 2½
Foundation: Basement standard; crawl space, slab or walk-out basement for an additional fee

See index for more information

Images provided by designer/architect

Special Features

- Classic Farmhouse style reigns in this wrap-around porch design
- Follow the entrance hall to the great room, dining area and kitchen in the back of the home
- The kitchen has a large square island, great when entertaining and the corner walk-in pantry will be your favorite place to stow extra appliances out of sight
- The master bedroom is split from the other bedrooms for privacy
- The optional second floor has an additional 389 square feet of living area
- The optional lower level has an additional 1,595 square feet of living area and has a rec area, family room, a wet bar, an exercise room, two built-in desk spaces, two bedrooms, and a full bath
- 2-car side entry garage

Optional Second Floor 389 sq. ft.

First Floor 2,076 sq. ft.

© Copyright by designer/architect

Optional Lower Level 1,595 sq. ft.

Plan #F11-028D-0118

Dimensions: 50' W x 44' D
Heated Sq. Ft.: 1,500
Bedrooms: 3 **Bathrooms:** 2
Exterior Walls: 2" x 6"
Foundation: Crawl space or monolithic slab, please specify when ordering

See index for more information

Images provided by designer/architect

Special Features

- A wonderful home with a split bedroom layout for privacy
- The master bedroom is large, has easy access to a walk-in closet and a spa-style private bath
- The master bath has dual sinks, a free-standing tub, a custom shower, and a large window for added sunlight
- Access the huge master walk-in closet from the master bath which makes getting dressed easier with lots of storage
- The kitchen has a large island with a counter height snack bar, and French doors leading out onto the covered rear porch
- The kitchen has a large walk-in pantry, and close proximity to the nice sized laundry room

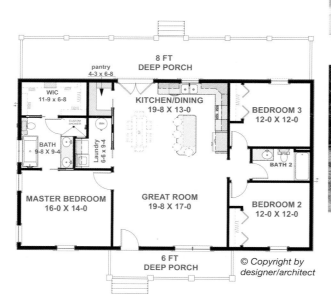

© Copyright by designer/architect

Plan #F11-032D-1158

Dimensions: 54' W x 52'4" D
Heated Sq. Ft.: 2,885
Bedrooms: 3 **Bathrooms:** 3
Exterior Walls: 2" x 6"
Foundation: Floating slab standard; crawl space or basement for an additional fee

See index for more information

Special Features

- This Modern masterpiece uses two story ceilings to create an environment so pleasing it will be hard to leave
- The kitchen features a huge island with enough seating for five, a walk-in pantry, and a built-in desk perfect for a computer
- There's an office with closetspace and covered porch views in a quiet location
- The second floor has a long balcony in the mezzanine for taking in views of the living and dining rooms below
- The second floor also has a casual family room, the laundry room, and all of the bedrooms
- 2-car front entry garage

First Floor
1,285 sq. ft.

© Copyright by designer/architect

Second Floor
1,600 sq. ft.

Images provided by designer/architect

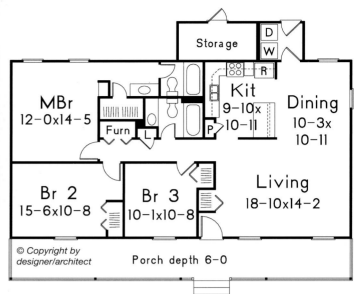

Images provided by designer/architect

Plan #F11-001D-0067

Dimensions: 48' W x 37'8" D
Heated Sq. Ft.: 1,285
Bedrooms: 3   **Bathrooms:** 2
Foundation: Crawl space standard; basement or slab for an additional fee

See index for more information

Images provided by designer/architect

Plan #F11-155D-0211

Dimensions: 115'6" W x 61'8" D
Heated Sq. Ft.: 3,777
Bedrooms: 4   **Bathrooms:** 4
Foundation: Crawl space or slab standard; basement or daylight basement for an additional fee

See index for more information

Plan #F11-123D-0154

Dimensions: 22' W x 100' D
Heated Sq. Ft.: 1,848
Bedrooms: 3   **Bathrooms:** 2
Foundation: Slab standard; crawl space or walk-out basement for an additional fee

See index for more information

Images provided by designer/architect

© Copyright by designer/architect

© Copyright by designer/architect

First Floor
2,895 sq. ft.

Second Floor
1,245 sq. ft.

Images provided by designer/architect

Plan #F11-155D-0131

Dimensions: 108'2" W x 92'4" D
Heated Sq. Ft.: 4,140
Bedrooms: 5   **Bathrooms:** 5½
Foundation: Crawl space or slab standard; basement or daylight basement for an additional fee

See index for more information

Images provided by designer/architect

Plan #F11-091D-0522

Dimensions: 64' W x 60'4" D
Heated Sq. Ft.: 2,148
Bonus Sq. Ft.: 387
Bedrooms: 3   **Bathrooms:** 2½
Exterior Walls: 2" x 6"
Foundation: Crawl space standard; slab, basement or walk-out basement for an additional fee

See index for more information

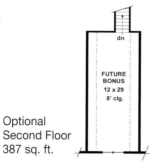

Optional
Second Floor
387 sq. ft.

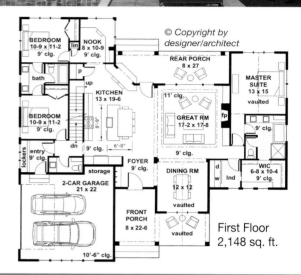

First Floor
2,148 sq. ft.

Images provided by designer/architect

Plan #F11-028D-0104

Dimensions: 60' W x 72' D
Heated Sq. Ft.: 2,160
Bedrooms: 3   **Bathrooms:** 2
Exterior Walls: 2" x 6"
Foundation: Basement or slab, please specify when ordering

See index for more information

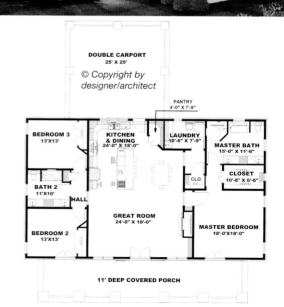

Second Floor
878 sq. ft.

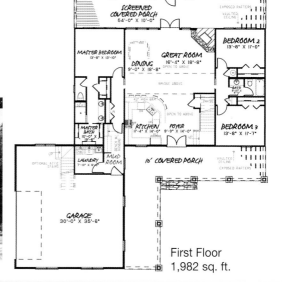

© Copyright by designer/architect

Plan #F11-155D-0108

Dimensions: 70'8" W x 80'7" D
Heated Sq. Ft.: 2,860
Bedrooms: 5   **Bathrooms:** 3
Foundation: Crawl space or slab standard; basement or daylight basement for an additional fee

See index for more information

Images provided by designer/architect

First Floor
1,982 sq. ft.

Images provided by designer/architect

Plan #F11-084D-0092

Dimensions: 58' W x 80'2" D
Heated Sq. Ft.: 2,366
Bonus Sq. Ft.: 809
Bedrooms: 3   **Bathrooms:** 2
Foundation: Slab standard; crawl space or basement for an additional fee

See index for more information

Optional Second Floor
809 sq. ft.

First Floor
2,366 sq. ft.

First Floor
1,178 sq. ft.

Images provided by designer/architect

Optional
Lower Level
1,178 sq. ft.

Plan #F11-032D-1121

Dimensions:	52' W x 36' D
Heated Sq. Ft.:	1,178
Bonus Sq. Ft.:	1,178
Bedrooms: 2	**Bathrooms:** 1
Exterior Walls:	2" x 6"

Foundation: Basement standard;
crawl space for an additional fee

See index for more information

Images provided by designer/architect

Plan #F11-123D-0247

Dimensions:	65' W x 70' D
Heated Sq. Ft.:	2,719
Bedrooms: 3	**Bathrooms:** 3½

Foundation: Basement standard;
crawl space, slab or walk-out
basement for an additional fee

See index for more information

First Floor
1,259 sq. ft.

Second Floor
1,460 sq. ft.

Images provided by designer/architect

Plan #F11-148D-0396

Dimensions:	32' W x 32' D
Heated Sq. Ft.:	1,258
Bonus Sq. Ft.:	778
Bedrooms: 2	**Bathrooms:** 1½
Exterior Walls:	2" x 6"
Foundation:	Basement

See index for more information

Second Floor
480 sq. ft.

Optional
Lower Level
778 sq. ft.

© *Copyright by designer/architect*

First Floor
778 sq. ft.

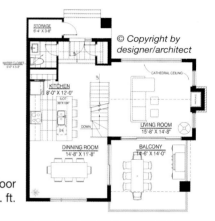

Optional
Lower Level
1,672 sq. ft.

Images provided by designer/architect

Plan #F11-056S-0021

Dimensions:	64'4" W x 67'10" D
Heated Sq. Ft.:	3,314
Bonus Sq. Ft.:	1,956
Bedrooms: 5	**Bathrooms:** 4

Foundation: Basement standard;
crawl space or slab for an additional
fee

See index for more information

Second Floor
1,642 sq. ft.

© *Copyright by designer/architect*

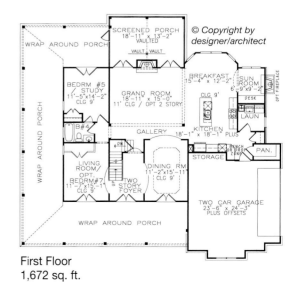

First Floor
1,672 sq. ft.

Plan #F11-155D-0178

Dimensions: 81' W x 50'3" D
Heated Sq. Ft.: 2,540
Bedrooms: 3   **Bathrooms:** 3
Exterior Walls: 2" x 6"
Foundation: Crawl space or slab
standard; basement or daylight
basement for an additional fee

See index for more information

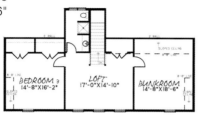

Second Floor
955 sq. ft.

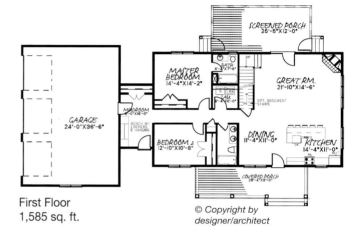

First Floor
1,585 sq. ft.

Plan #F11-123D-0254

Dimensions: 46' W x 38' D
Heated Sq. Ft.: 2,056
Bedrooms: 3   **Bathrooms:** 2½
Foundation: Basement standard;
crawl space, slab or walk-out
basement for an additional fee

See index for more information

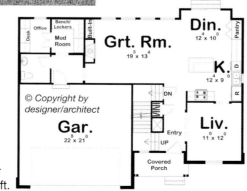

First Floor
1,002 sq. ft.

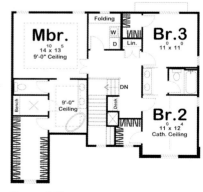

Second Floor
1,054 sq. ft.

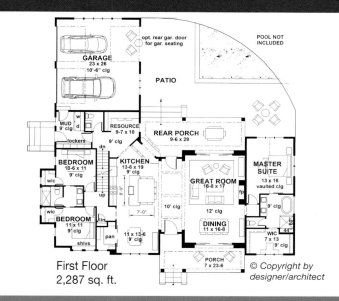

Plan #F11-091D-0516

Dimensions:	71' W x 73'2" D
Heated Sq. Ft.:	2,287
Bonus Sq. Ft.:	535
Bedrooms: 3	**Bathrooms:** 2½
Exterior Walls:	2" x 6"

Foundation: Crawl space standard; slab, basement or walk-out basement for an additional fee

See index for more information

Optional
Second Floor
535 sq. ft.

First Floor
2,287 sq. ft.

© Copyright by
designer/architect

Plan #F11-028D-0119

Dimensions:	56' W x 52' D
Heated Sq. Ft.:	2,096
Bedrooms: 4	**Bathrooms:** 3
Exterior Walls:	2" x 6"
Foundation:	Slab

See index for more information

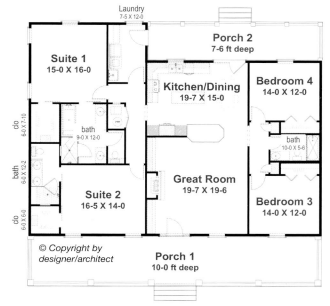

© Copyright by
designer/architect

Owner's Suite
16⁰ x 14⁰
9'-0" CEILING

Loft
11⁶ x 9⁸

Br.2
10⁶ x 14⁴

Br.3
10⁶ x 12⁰

Second Floor
1,126 sq. ft.

OPTIONAL PATIO

Family Room
16⁴ x 14⁰

Dining Area
12⁰ x 9⁰

Kit.
12⁰ x 9⁸

DROP ZONE

UP

Garage
21⁴ x 20⁸

First Floor
696 sq. ft.

© Copyright by designer/architect

Images provided by designer/architect

Plan #F11-026D-2094

Dimensions: 29' W x 45' D
Heated Sq. Ft.:   1,822
Bedrooms: 3   **Bathrooms:** 2½
Foundation: Slab standard; crawl space, basement or walk-out basement for an additional fee

See index for more information

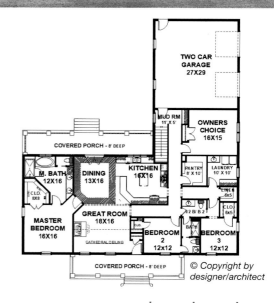

Images provided by designer/architect

Plan #F11-028D-0113

Dimensions: 68' W x 84' D
Heated Sq. Ft.:   2,582
Bedrooms: 3   **Bathrooms:** 2½
Exterior Walls: 2" x 6"
Foundation: Basement

See index for more information

TWO CAR GARAGE
27X29

MUD RM
11' X 5'

OWNERS CHOICE
16X15

COVERED PORCH - 8' DEEP

M. BATH
12X16

DINING
13X16

KITCHEN
16X16

PANTRY
8' X 10'

LAUNDRY
10' X 10'

CLO.
8X8

GREAT ROOM
18X16

MASTER BEDROOM
16X16

CATHEDRAL CEILING

BEDROOM 2
12X12

BEDROOM 3
12X12

COVERED PORCH - 8' DEEP

© Copyright by designer/architect

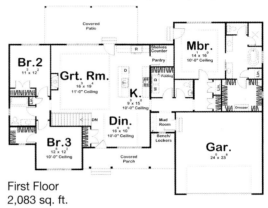
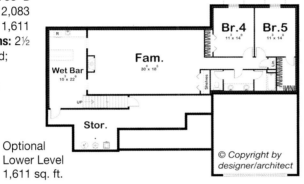

Images provided by designer/architect

Plan #F11-123D-0203

Dimensions: 77' W x 55' D
Heated Sq. Ft.: 2,083
Bonus Sq. Ft.: 1,611
Bedrooms: 3 **Bathrooms:** 2½
Foundation: Basement standard; crawl space, slab or walk-out basement for an additional fee

See index for more information

Optional Lower Level 1,611 sq. ft.

© Copyright by designer/architect

First Floor 2,083 sq. ft.

Images provided by designer/architect

Lower Level 1,443 sq. ft.

© Copyright by designer/architect

First Floor 1,443 sq. ft.

Plan #F11-032D-1161

Dimensions: 42' W x 38'4" D
Heated Sq. Ft.: 2,886
Bedrooms: 4 **Bathrooms:** 1½
Exterior Walls: 2" x 6"
Foundation: Basement standard; crawl space, floating slab or monolithic slab for an additional fee

See index for more information

Plan #F11-128D-0306

Dimensions: 31'7" W x 64' D
Heated Sq. Ft.: 1,643
Bedrooms: 3   **Bathrooms:** 2
Foundation: Basement or crawl space, please specify when ordering

See index for more information

Images provided by designer/architect

OPTIONAL 2 CAR GARAGE
25'-7" X 22'-0"

MASTER BEDROOM
15'-6" X 13'-8"

© Copyright by designer/architect

Plan #F11-155D-0104

Dimensions: 79'10" W x 53'4" D
Heated Sq. Ft.: 3,421
Bonus Sq. Ft.: 845
Bedrooms: 6   **Bathrooms:** 4
Foundation: Crawl space or slab standard; basement or daylight basement for an additional fee

See index for more information

Images provided by designer/architect

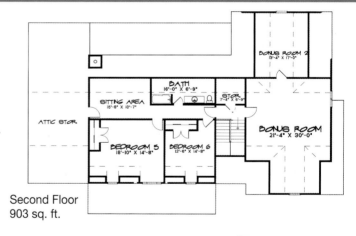

Second Floor
903 sq. ft.

First Floor
2,518 sq. ft.

© Copyright by designer/architect

First Floor
2,213 sq. ft.

Plan #F11-011D-0650

Dimensions:	60' W x 53' D
Heated Sq. Ft.:	2,213
Bonus Sq. Ft.:	442
Bedrooms: 3	**Bathrooms:** 2
Exterior Walls:	2" x 6"

Foundation: Crawl space or slab standard; basement for an additional fee

See index for more information

Optional
Second Floor
442 sq. ft.

Images provided by designer/architect

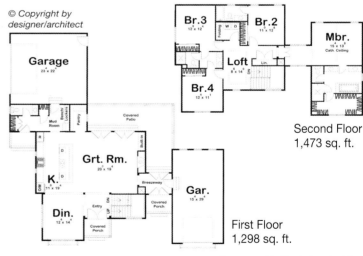

Second Floor
1,473 sq. ft.

First Floor
1,298 sq. ft.

Images provided by designer/architect

Plan #F11-123D-0245

Dimensions:	66' W x 68' D
Heated Sq. Ft.:	2,771
Bedrooms: 4	**Bathrooms:** 3½

Foundation: Basement standard; crawl space, slab or walk-out basement for an additional fee

See index for more information

Plan #F11-084D-0091

Dimensions: 59' W x 68'2" D
Heated Sq. Ft.: 1,936
Bedrooms: 3   **Bathrooms:** 2
Foundation: Slab standard; crawl space for an additional fee

See index for more information

Special Features

- The perfect stylish ranch home with a split bedroom layout
- Enter the dining/foyer and find a beamed ceiling for added interest and it opens to the vaulted living area with a centered fireplace
- The kitchen enjoys an open feel and has an island and a mud room entrance from the garage
- The vaulted master bedroom has a built-in bench for added character plus a walk-in closet, and a private bath with an oversized tub and a walk-in shower with seat
- Two additional bedrooms share a full bath
- 2-car side entry garage

Images provided by designer/architect

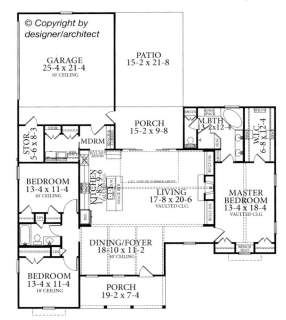

7 outdoor trends
you need in your life now

1 front porches are in fashion

Today's popular floor plans are including plentiful front porches that have enough space to create an outdoor living space. Helping to create a sense of community in a neighborhood, these porches offer an opportunity to enjoy the outdoors and have face-to-face contact with people in their neighborhood. With many homes now featuring oversized living spaces in the front of the home, outdoor living has extended not just to the backyard, but to the front, too. Providing curb appeal and a welcoming feel to the front exterior, these covered porches are now offering cozy seating, soft lighting, and maybe even a water element for a tranquil feel. If a home doesn't have a front porch, then often a courtyard is created providing a front patio space that welcomes people in. Other fun focal points include a statement front door. Whether it's a door with a unique window, a trendy Dutch-Style door, or a door painted in a bold unexpected color, a statement door might as well say, "Come on in!"

2 it's all black & white

It's no secret with the popularity of Modern Farmhouse style homes, that black and white color schemes are the top choice in interior design right now. Well, that color palette has extended itself to the outdoors, too. Using a similar color palette to your interior spaces not only looks attractive, but it creates a visual extension that is seamless inside and out. Plus, classic black and white palettes are timeless, classy, clean and tend to look great with many types of architecture whether your home is industrial modern or a modern farmhouse. If you need a little color in your life, then go with the calm, cool hues like the blues, and the greens you would see in nature, or stick with a completely neutral palette void of any color at all and let nature itself add the color to your outdoor surroundings.

3 minimalist, clean spaces

Think Scandinavian style chic! Part Utilitarian and part Ikea®-inspired, homeowners are craving good function and clean un-cluttered dwellings. Perfect for escaping the clutter of work, and the outside world, these types of spaces are calming and tranquil and it should come as no surprise that our outdoor spaces are quickly turning to this minimalist style of living with sleeker furniture styles that have far less ornamentation than we've seen previously. Solid plastic pieces or sleek metal styles all have a place on today's patio, too.

4 mixed materials aren't a mixed message

Say goodbye to matching your patio furniture and look for several types of materials to create your outdoor space. Wooden benches sit alongside metal end tables and a rope swing may be a fun add-in. Mix glass accessories, metal, wrought iron, and wood and create a casual space with thoughtful choices. To soften up all of those hard surfaces look to oversized pillows you can throw down on the patio floor, outdoor rugs, or take a cozy throw blanket outside when the weather becomes chilly.

5 the kitchen is closed, but the bar is open

Outdoor kitchens still remain popular, and so do any fire elements such as a cozy fireplace or fire pit, but if you're adding a social spot outdoors, think more happy hour and less dinnertime. Outdoor bar spaces are quickly becoming a popular, fun choice that are playful and much more affordable than adding an outdoor kitchen. Find a neat rolling cart and recycle into an outdoor bar for something inexpensive and portable, or invest in a built-in area with a refrigerator and high-top tables. The ideas are endless and this addition to your outdoor space may have you saying, "last call" much more frequently.

6 eco-friendly exteriors

Homeowners are reducing their carbon footprint by creating living walls composed of plants, and herbs that can be utilized easily in an indoor or outdoor kitchen. Add some LED lighting that relies on the sun for its power and you've created a eco-fun and friendly outdoor oasis. If you choose to add a deck, then look to sustainable choices or composite decking. Many stylish rugs, and furniture are made from recycled products giving these things a new useful life on your very own sustainable and responsible patio.

7 bright lighting

Continuing with the theme of carrying the indoors outside, lighting is an important element in making your outdoor space shine. From candles made with essential oils to LED illuminated umbrellas, or even nostalgic tiki torches, there are countless choices for lighting your backyard space and creating that inviting ambiance that draws people in to relax and stay awhile. The ever-popular fire pits and fireplaces are also great illumination choices especially in the cooler months.

Whether you choose a couple of these trends, or find a way to implement all of them, your outdoor living area will become a place that rivals, or even surpasses your favorite indoor space. Creating a space that uses subtle colors, modern lines and an abundance of texture will keep your outdoor space interesting and relevant.

Images provided by designer/architect

Plan #F11-144D-0039

Dimensions: 71' W x 49' D
Heated Sq. Ft.: 2,148
Bonus Sq. Ft.: 707
Bedrooms: 3 **Bathrooms:** 2½
Exterior Walls: 2" x 6"
Foundation: Crawl space standard; slab or basement for an additional fee

See index for more information

Special Features

- The classic country style home has a thoughtful exterior and great interior updates making it the ideal choice for today's homeowners
- Enter to find a coveted open concept floor plan with a large great room topped with a tall ceiling
- The kitchen and dining area overlook the great room and its centered fireplace
- A quiet study has French doors leading to the outdoors
- The optional second floor has an additional 707 square feet of living area
- 2-car side entry garage

BONUS ROOM
14-0 x 28-0

Optional
Second Floor
707 sq. ft.

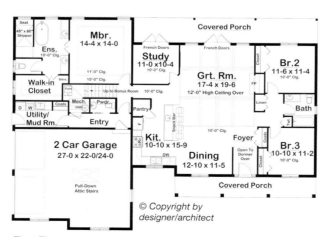
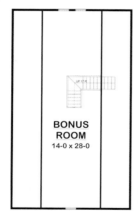

© Copyright by designer/architect

First Floor
2,148 sq. ft.

Plan #F11-101D-0062

Dimensions: 87' W x 79'6" D
Heated Sq. Ft.: 2,648
Bonus Sq. Ft.: 1,799
Bedrooms: 3   **Bathrooms:** 3½
Exterior Walls: 2" x 6"
Foundation: Basement, daylight basement or walk-out basement, please specify when ordering

See index for more information

Special Features

- A touch of rustic charm enhances the curb appeal of this inviting home
- Once inside, the great room, kitchen and dining area form the main gathering space
- The first floor has a variety of formal and informal spaces that are comfortable and spacious for entertaining, or everyday living
- A private office is hidden off the landing of the staircase
- The optional lower level has an additional 1,799 square feet of living area and includes a gym, a large rec area with a half bath, and two additional bedrooms that share a bath
- 2-car side entry garage, and a 1-car front entry garage

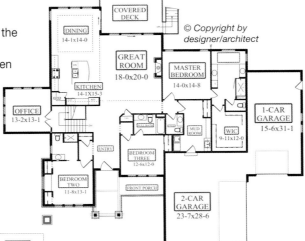

© Copyright by designer/architect

First Floor
2,648 sq. ft.

Optional Lower Level
1,799 sq. ft.

Images provided by designer/architect

Plan #F11-101D-0142

Dimensions:	72' W x 82'6" D
Heated Sq. Ft.:	2,700
Bonus Sq. Ft.:	1,991
Bedrooms: 2	**Bathrooms:** 2½
Exterior Walls:	2" x 6"
Foundation:	Walk-out basement

See index for more information

Special Features

- Slightly leaning a bit more toward Modern than Modern Farmhouse, this home does feature the color scheme and details those who love Modern Farmhouse plans appreciate in a home design

- The remarkable great room has a towering fireplace, a beamed ceiling and is completely open to the kitchen and dining area

- The luxury master bedroom has covered deck access, a bathroom that feels like a sanctuary, and a dressing room-sized walk-in closet

- The mud room is uncommon in size with tons of storage and cubbies

- The optional lower level has an additional 1,991 square feet of living area and has a rec room with a wet bar, a home theater, two bedrooms, two baths, and a half bath

- 3-car front entry garage

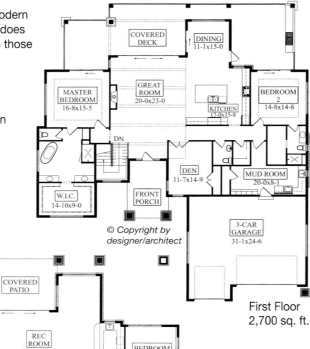

© Copyright by designer/architect

First Floor
2,700 sq. ft.

Optional Lower Level
1,991 sq. ft.

Images provided by designer/architect

Plan #F11-032D-1107

Dimensions: 35' W x 33' D
Heated Sq. Ft.: 1,050
Bonus Sq. Ft.: 1,050
Bedrooms: 2   **Bathrooms:** 1
Foundation: Basement standard; crawl space or monolithic slab for an additional fee

See index for more information

Special Features

- If you're longing for today's hottest style home but in a more manageable size, then look no further, this is the home for you
- Step inside and find a living room open to the kitchen and dining room straight ahead
- On the left side of the home are two bedrooms and a full bath
- The optional lower level has an additional 1,050 square feet of living area

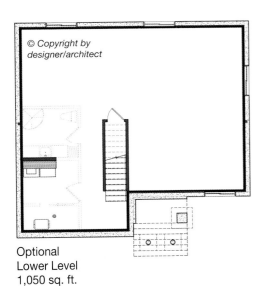

Optional
Lower Level
1,050 sq. ft.

First Floor
1,050 sq. ft.

Images provided by designer/architect

Images provided by designer/architect

Plan #F11-055D-0990

Dimensions: 113' W x 95'8" D
Heated Sq. Ft.: 2,555
Bonus Sq. Ft.: 509
Bedrooms: 4   **Bathrooms:** 3
Foundation: Crawl space or slab standard; basement or daylight basement for an additional fee

See index for more information

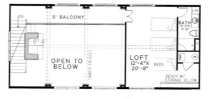

Second Floor
506 sq. ft.

Optional
Second Floor
509 sq. ft.

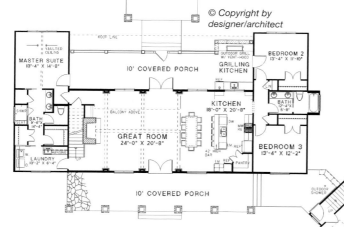

© Copyright by designer/architect

First Floor
2,049 sq. ft.

Special Features

- Lodge-like living is perfectly achieved in this modern farmhouse with a split bedroom floor plan
- The rear covered porch has a 10' ceiling, an outdoor kitchen, and leads to a remote outdoor living porch with a fireplace
- The master suite has direct access to the laundry room making this chore a lot easier to tackle
- Above the garage is a guest suite with an additional 509 square feet of living area featuring a bath and privacy that will be appreciated when people visit
- 2-car front entry garage

Plan #F11-020D-0399

Dimensions: 66' W x 72' D
Heated Sq. Ft.: 1,932
Bonus Sq. Ft.: 1,162
Bedrooms: 3   **Bathrooms:** 2
Exterior Walls: 2" x 6"
Foundation: Slab

See index for more information

Special Features

- Relaxed and refined, this Modern Farmhouse's use of symmetry is clearly striking
- Become enveloped in the living space the moment you enter and marvel in the beauty of the living room fireplace towering two stories above
- The kitchen is angled for character and has great views of the large deck out the bay window
- The master suite is private and has easy access to the utility room through its private bath
- The two secondary bedrooms are located on the opposite side of the home and share a bath
- The optional second floor has an additional 1,162 square feet of living area
- 3-car side entry garage

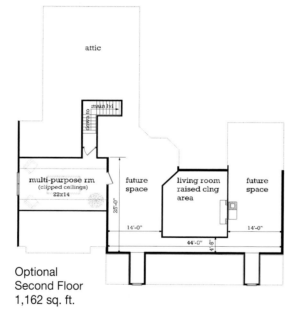

Optional
Second Floor
1,162 sq. ft.

© Copyright by designer/architect

First Floor
1,932 sq. ft.

Images provided by designer/architect

Plan #F11-144D-0023

Dimensions: 58' W x 32' D
Heated Sq. Ft.: 928
Bedrooms: 2 **Bathrooms:** 2
Exterior Walls: 2" x 6"
Foundation: Crawl space or slab standard; basement, daylight basement or walk-out basement for an additional fee

See index for more information

Special Features

- Stylish and charming, this small Craftsman Modern Farmhouse home has an inviting entry with space for outdoor relaxation
- Enter the home and discover an open living room with a kitchen behind it
- The kitchen features a large breakfast bar with space for up to four people to casually dine
- To the left of the entry is an office/guest room with direct access to a full bath and beyond into a mud room
- To the right of the entry is the master bedroom with a large bath and walk-in closet
- 2-car front entry garage

© Copyright by designer/architect

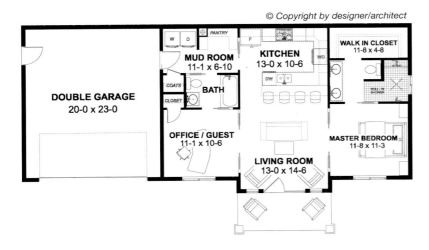

Images provided by designer/architect

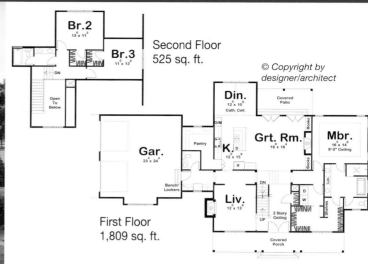

Second Floor
525 sq. ft.

© Copyright by designer/architect

Br.2
13' x 11'

Br.3
11' x 12'

Open To Below

DN

Din.
12' x 10⁶
Cath. Ceil.

Covered Patio

Gar.
23' x 24'

Pantry

K.
12' x 15

Grt. Rm.
16' x 16'

Mbr.
16' x 14'
9'-0" Ceiling

Bench/Lockers

Liv.
12' x 13'

2 Story Ceiling

UP

DN

First Floor
1,809 sq. ft.

Covered Porch

Images provided by designer/architect

Plan #F11-123D-0237

Dimensions: 84' W x 51' D
Heated Sq. Ft.: 2,334
Bedrooms: 3 **Bathrooms:** 2½
Foundation: Basement standard; crawl space, slab or walk-out basement for an additional fee

See index for more information

© Copyright by designer/architect

CARPORT
22'-0" X 22'-0"

BRZ-WAY

Images provided by designer/architect

Plan #F11-055D-0196

Dimensions: 60'6" W x 91'4" D
Heated Sq. Ft.: 2,039
Bonus Sq. Ft.: 1,155
Bedrooms: 4 **Bathrooms:** 3
Foundation: Crawl space or slab standard; basement or daylight basement

See index for more information

PROPOSED GAME ROOM.
33'-2" X 33'-7"

DN

Optional
Second Floor
1,155 sq. ft.

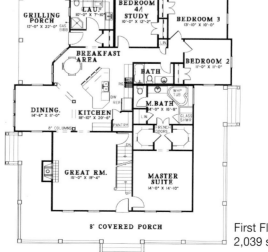

GRILLING PORCH
12'-0" X 22'-0"

LAU.
10'-0" X 7'-10"

BEDROOM 4/STUDY
10'-0" X 12'-2"

BEDROOM 3
13'-10" X 10'-0"

BREAKFAST AREA

BATH

BEDROOM 2
11'-0" X 11'-0"

DINING.
14'-6" X 11'-0"

KITCHEN
18'-10" X 20'-6"

M.BATH
14'-0" X 16'-8"

PANTRY

GREAT RM.
15'-0" X 19'-4"

MASTER SUITE
14'-0" X 14'-10"

8' COVERED PORCH

First Floor
2,039 sq. ft.

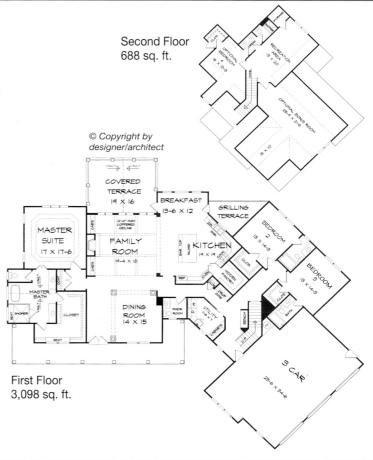

Second Floor
688 sq. ft.

© Copyright by
designer/architect

First Floor
3,098 sq. ft.

Plan #F11-076D-0311

Dimensions: 105'8" W x 80'8" D
Heated Sq. Ft.: 3,786
Bedrooms: 4   **Bathrooms:** 4½
Foundation: Slab

See index for more information

Images provided by designer/architect

© Copyright by
designer/architect

Plan #F11-091D-0528

Dimensions: 68'4" W x 76'2" D
Heated Sq. Ft.: 2,743
Bonus Sq. Ft.: 470
Bedrooms: 4   **Bathrooms:** 4½
Exterior Walls: 2" x 6"
Foundation: Crawl space standard;
slab, basement or walk-out
basement for an additional fee

See index for more information

Images provided by designer/architect

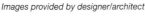

Second Floor
715 sq. ft.

First Floor
2,028 sq. ft.

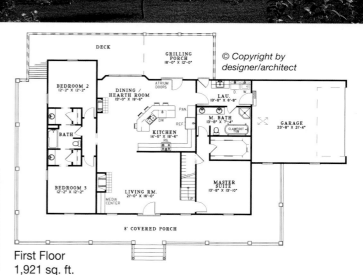

Plan #F11-055D-0162

Dimensions: 84' W x 55'6" D
Heated Sq. Ft.: 1,921
Bonus Sq. Ft.: 812
Bedrooms: 3 **Bathrooms:** 2
Foundation: Crawl space or slab standard; basement or daylight basement for an additional fee

See index for more information

Optional
Second Floor
812 sq. ft.

First Floor
1,921 sq. ft.

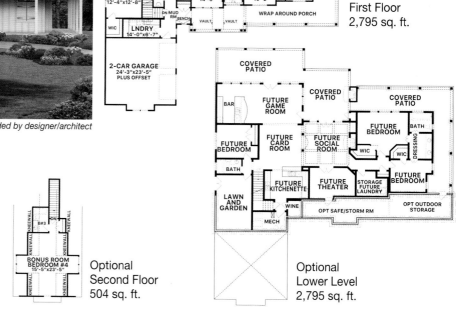

First Floor
2,795 sq. ft.

Plan #F11-056S-0012

Dimensions: 81'6 W x 93'5" D
Heated Sq. Ft.: 2,795
Bonus Sq. Ft.: 3,299
Bedrooms: 3 **Bathrooms:** 3½
Foundation: Basement standard; crawl space or slab for an additional fee

See index for more information

Optional
Second Floor
504 sq. ft.

Optional
Lower Level
2,795 sq. ft.

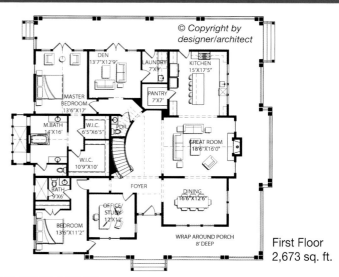

First Floor
2,673 sq. ft.

Plan #F11-167D-0009

Dimensions: 67'11" W x 65'10" D
Heated Sq. Ft.: 3,363
Bedrooms: 4   **Bathrooms:** 3½
Exterior Walls: 2" x 6"
Foundation: Crawl space standard; slab for an additional fee

See index for more information

Images provided by designer/architect

Second Floor
690 sq. ft.

2-Car Detached Garage

Second Floor
1,394 sq. ft.

Plan #F11-123D-0246

Dimensions: 42' W x 63'8" D
Heated Sq. Ft.: 2,417
Bedrooms: 4   **Bathrooms:** 2½
Foundation: Basement standard; crawl space, slab or walk-out basement for an additional fee

See index for more information

Images provided by designer/architect

© Copyright by designer/architect

First Floor
1,023 sq. ft.

First Floor
1,464 sq. ft.

© Copyright by
designer/architect

Plan #F11-141D-0393

Dimensions: 68'5" W x 52' D
Heated Sq. Ft.: 2,569
Bonus Sq. Ft.: 1,464
Bedrooms: 3 **Bathrooms:** 2½
Foundation: Walk-out basement
standard; crawl space, slab or
basement for an additional fee

See index for more information

Images provided by designer/architect

Second Floor
1,105 sq. ft.

Optional
Lower Level
1,464 sq. ft.

Lower Level
1,040 sq. ft.

First Floor
1,040 sq. ft.

© Copyright by
designer/architect

Images provided by designer/architect

Plan #F11-032D-1156

Dimensions: 36'2" W x 50'2" D
Heated Sq. Ft.: 2,080
Bedrooms: 3 **Bathrooms:** 2
Exterior Walls: 2" x 6"
Foundation: Basement

See index for more information

houseplansandmore.com

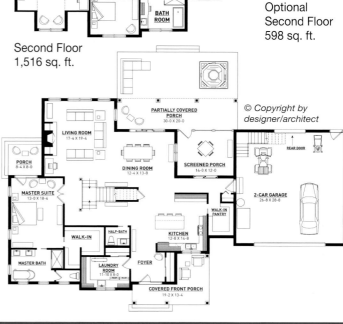

GUEST SUITE
17-6 X 11-8

BATH ROOM

WALK-IN

BEDROOM 3
17-4 X 13-4

BEDROOM 2
13-0 X 12-4

BATH ROOM

READING NOOK / LIBRARY / DEN
13-0 X 18-8

BUILT-INS

BANQUET

Second Floor
1,516 sq. ft.

BONUS SPACE
18-0 X 28-8

Optional
Second Floor
598 sq. ft.

© Copyright by
designer/architect

PARTIALLY COVERED PORCH
30-0 X 20-0

LIVING ROOM
17-4 X 19-4

PORCH
8-4 X 8-0

DINING ROOM
12-4 X 13-8

SCREENED PORCH
14-0 X 12-0

REAR DOOR

MASTER SUITE
13-0 X 18-4

2-CAR GARAGE
26-8 X 28-8

WALK-IN PANTRY

WALK-IN

HALF-BATH

KITCHEN
12-8 X 14-8

MASTER BATH

LAUNDRY ROOM
11-10 X 8-0

FOYER

COVERED FRONT PORCH
19-2 X 13-4

First Floor
2,016 sq. ft.

Images provided by designer/architect

Plan #F11-032D-1069

Dimensions:	84' W x 49'6" D
Heated Sq. Ft.:	3,532
Bonus Sq. Ft.:	598
Bedrooms: 4	**Bathrooms:** 3½
Exterior Walls:	2" x 6"

Foundation: Crawl space or walk-out basement standard; floating slab or monolithic slab for an additional fee

See index for more information

ATTIC STORAGE

BR.2
10/0 X 12/2 +

BONUS
21/2 X 11/6

LINEN

OPEN TO BELOW

MECH CHASE

Second Floor
941 sq. ft.

BR.4
11/0 X 17/0

BR.3
10/6 X 14/10 +

OPEN TO BELOW

DN.

ATTIC STORAGE

© Copyright by
designer/architect

PATIO

VAULTED MASTER
15/6 X 17/2

NOOK
10/2 X 12/6
(9' CLG.)

PORCH
18/0 X 12/0 +/-

TILE SHWR

PAN

LIN

VAULTED GREAT RM.
17/6 X 17/10

SEAT

W D

REF

UP

GARAGE
29/0 X 22/6 +/-

STOR UNDER LANDING

BUILT-IN

(2 STORY)

DINING
10/6 X 14/0 +/-
(9' CLG.)

FOYER

DEN
11/0 X 10/6
(9' CLG.)

PORCH

First Floor
2,003 sq. ft.

Plan #F11-011D-0663

Dimensions:	59' W x 61' D
Heated Sq. Ft.:	2,944
Bonus Sq. Ft.:	260
Bedrooms: 4	**Bathrooms:** 3½
Exterior Walls:	2" x 6"

Foundation: Crawl space or slab standard; basement for an additional fee

See index for more information

Images provided by designer/architect

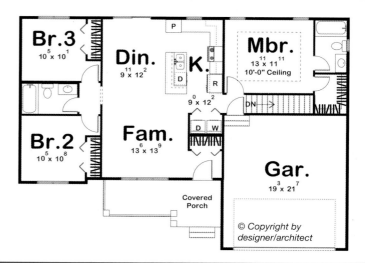

Floor plan labels: Br.3 10⁵ x 10¹ · Din. 9¹¹ x 12² · K. 9⁰ x 12² · Mbr. 13¹¹ x 11¹¹ 10'-0" Ceiling · P · D · R · DN · Br.2 10⁵ x 10⁸ · Fam. 13⁶ x 13⁹ · D · W · Gar. 19³ x 21⁷ · Covered Porch · © Copyright by designer/architect

Plan #F11-123D-0060

Dimensions: 52' W x 38' D
Heated Sq. Ft.:   1,185
Bedrooms: 3   **Bathrooms:** 2
Foundation: Basement standard; crawl space, slab or walk-out basement for an additional fee

See index for more information

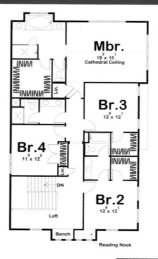

Second Floor
1,616 sq. ft.

Floor plan labels: Mbr. 19³ x 15⁰ Cathedral Ceiling · Lin. · Br.3 12⁹ x 12¹ · Br.4 11⁰ x 12⁵ · Lin. · DN · Br.2 12⁹ x 12⁹ · Loft · Bench · Reading Nook

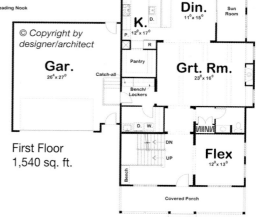

Floor plan labels: Covered Patio · K. 12⁰ x 17⁰ · D. · Din. 11⁶ x 15⁰ · Sun Room · P. · R · Pantry · Grt. Rm. 23³ x 16⁶ · © Copyright by designer/architect · Gar. 26⁴ x 27⁰ · Catch-all · Bench/Lockers · D. W. · DN · UP · Flex 12⁰ x 13⁰ · Bench · Covered Porch

First Floor
1,540 sq. ft.

Plan #F11-123D-0235

Dimensions: 60' W x 72' D
Heated Sq. Ft.:   3,156
Bedrooms: 4   **Bathrooms:** 3½
Foundation: Basement standard; crawl space, slab or walk-out basement for an additional fee

See index for more information

Images provided by designer/architect

Plan #F11-026D-2167

Dimensions: 40' W x 50' D
Heated Sq. Ft.: 1,176
Bedrooms: 3   **Bathrooms:** 2
Foundation: Basement standard; crawl space, slab or walk-out basement for an additional fee

See index for more information

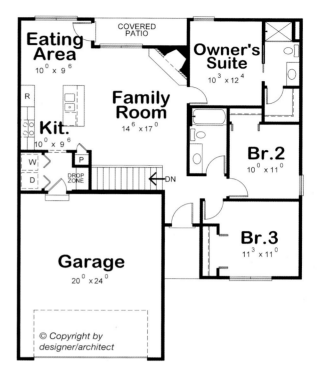

Images provided by designer/architect

Plan #F11-056S-0006

Dimensions: 107' W x 84'8" D
Heated Sq. Ft.: 3,171
Heated Sq. Ft.: 797
Bedrooms: 3   **Bathrooms:** 2½
Foundation: Slab standard; crawl space or basement for an additional fee

See index for more information

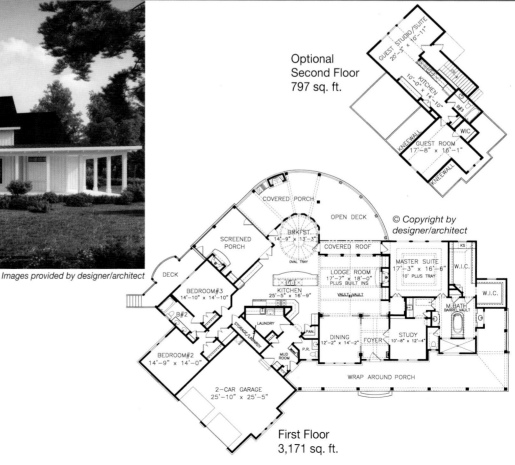

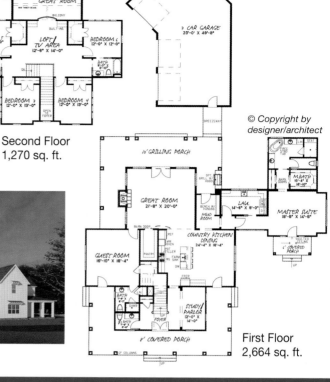

Second Floor
1,270 sq. ft.

Plan #F11-155D-0142

Dimensions: 77' W x 132'11" D
Heated Sq. Ft.: 3,934
Bedrooms: 6   **Bathrooms:** 4½
Foundation: Crawl space or slab standard; basement or daylight basement for an additional fee

See index for more information

Images provided by designer/architect

© Copyright by designer/architect

First Floor
2,664 sq. ft.

Plan #F11-091D-0508

Dimensions: 72' W x 65'2" D
Heated Sq. Ft.: 2,528
Bonus Sq. Ft.: 430
Bedrooms: 4   **Bathrooms:** 3½
Exterior Walls: 2" x 6"
Foundation: Crawl space standard; slab, basement, daylight basement or walk-out basement for an additional fee

See index for more information

Images provided by designer/architect

First Floor
1,732 sq. ft.

Second Floor
796 sq. ft.

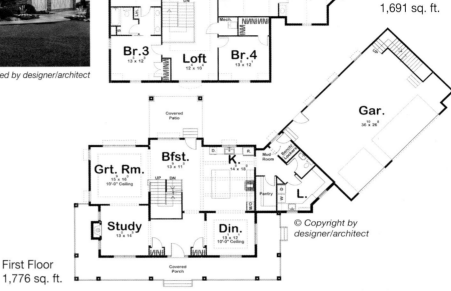

Second Floor
1,691 sq. ft.

First Floor
1,776 sq. ft.

© Copyright by
designer/architect

Plan #F11-123S-0029

Dimensions: 103'9" W x 71'6" D
Heated Sq. Ft.: 3,467
Bonus Sq. Ft.: 409
Bedrooms: 4   **Bathrooms:** 3½
Foundation: Basement standard;
crawl space, slab or walk-out
basement for an additional fee

See index for more information

First Floor
1,953 sq. ft.

© Copyright by
designer/architect

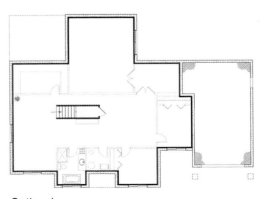

Optional
Lower Level
1,953 sq. ft.

Plan #F11-032D-1146

Dimensions: 68' W x 50' D
Heated Sq. Ft.: 1,953
Bonus Sq. Ft.: 1,953
Bedrooms: 3   **Bathrooms:** 2
Exterior Walls: 2" x 6"
Foundation: Basement standard;
crawl space, floating slab or
monolithic slab for an additional fee

See index for more information

Images provided by designer/architect

Second Floor
1,614 sq. ft.

First Floor
1,647 sq. ft.

Plan #F11-056S-0005

Dimensions:	67' W x 62'1" D
Heated Sq. Ft.:	3,261
Bonus Sq. Ft.:	1,647
Bedrooms: 6	**Bathrooms:** 4

Foundation: Basement standard; crawl space or slab for an additional fee

See index for more information

© Copyright by designer/architect

Optional
Lower Level
1,647 sq. ft.

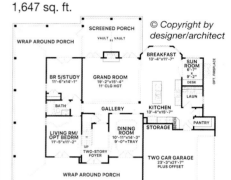

© Copyright by designer/architect

First Floor
1,112 sq. ft.

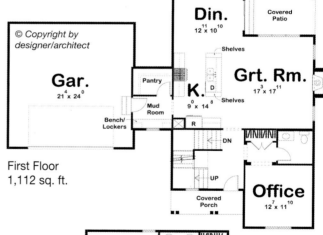

Plan #F11-123D-0236

Dimensions:	60' W x 45'4" D
Heated Sq. Ft.:	1,994
Bedrooms: 3	**Bathrooms:** 2½

Foundation: Basement standard; crawl space, slab or walk-out basement for an additional fee

See index for more information

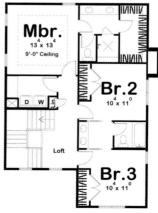

Second Floor
882 sq. ft.

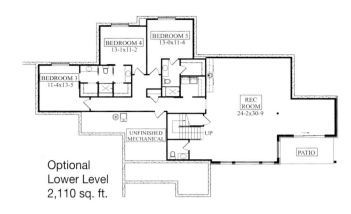

Optional Lower Level
2,110 sq. ft.

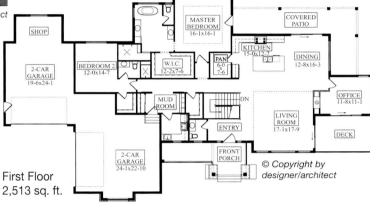

Plan #F11-101D-0143

Dimensions:	105'6" W x 60'6" D
Heated Sq. Ft.:	2,513
Bonus Sq. Ft.:	2,110
Bedrooms: 2	**Bathrooms:** 2½
Exterior Walls:	2" x 6"
Foundation:	Walk-out basement

See index for more information

Images provided by designer/architect

First Floor
2,513 sq. ft.

© Copyright by designer/architect

© Copyright by designer/architect

First Floor
1,120 sq. ft.

Plan #F11-141D-0391

Images provided by designer/architect

Dimensions:	45' W x 38' D
Heated Sq. Ft.:	1,610
Bonus Sq. Ft.:	952
Bedrooms: 3	**Bathrooms:** 2½
Exterior Walls:	2" x 6"

Foundation: Basement standard; crawl space, slab or walk-out basement for an additional fee

See index for more information

Second Floor
490 sq. ft.

Optional Lower Level
952 sq. ft.

Plan #F11-101D-0144

Dimensions: 98' W x 63' D
Heated Sq. Ft.: 2,344
Bonus Sq. Ft.: 882
Bedrooms: 2   **Bathrooms:** 2½
Exterior Walls: 2" x 6"
Foundation: Daylight basement

See index for more information

Images provided by designer/architect

Special Features

- Epic Modern aesthetics form this truly original refuge that is just waiting to be explored
- Step into an entirely open floor plan featuring only a see-through fireplace as a partition between the entrance and the rest of the home
- The TV room offers a spot to relax more casually in a private location is the home office when it's time to get some work completed
- The master bedroom has a private patio, a large walk-in closet and a simple, yet serene bath
- The optional lower level has an additional 882 square feet of living area including two additional bedrooms with walk-in closets that share a full bath
- 3-car side entry garage

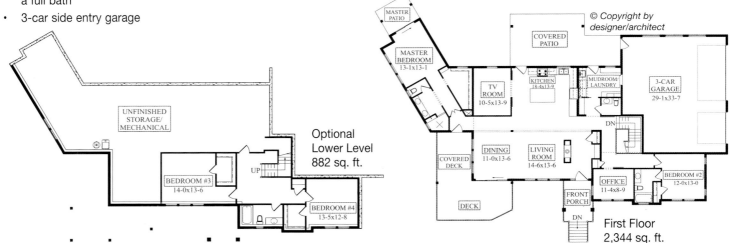

Optional
Lower Level
882 sq. ft.

First Floor
2,344 sq. ft.

Plan #F11-051D-0960

Dimensions: 117' W x 50'8" D
Heated Sq. Ft.: 2,784
Bedrooms: 3   **Bathrooms:** 2
Exterior Walls: 2" x 6"
Foundation: Basement standard; crawl space or slab for an additional fee

See index for more information

Special Features

- This Traditional ranch home with Modern Farmhouse influences is sure to win you over with its very classy exterior
- You are welcomed into the home with high ceilings that top both the great room and the kitchen
- All three bedrooms, including the master bedroom, are located to the right as you enter the home
- The master bedroom includes a spa style bath with a freestanding tub, dual sinks, as well as a spacious walk-in closet
- Two other bedrooms share a full bath nearby
- The three-stall garage is located on the left side of the house with a large screened-in porch behind it
- 3-car front entry garage

Images provided by designer/architect

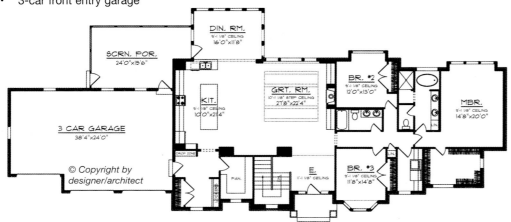

Plan #F11-123D-0253

Dimensions: 29' W x 77' D
Heated Sq. Ft.: 1,963
Bonus Sq. Ft.: 761
Bedrooms: 3 **Bathrooms:** 2½
Foundation: Basement standard; crawl space, slab or walk-out basement for an additional fee

See index for more information

Special Features

- This two-story has lots of extras packed into its small footprint
- An office greets you as you enter the foyer from the covered front porch
- Ahead is an open great room, dining area and kitchen with island facing the fireplace
- The second floor has the master bedroom, two additional bedrooms, a centrally located laundry closet and a loft space
- The optional lower level has an additional 761 square feet of living area and includes a family room, extra storage, bedroom and a full bath
- 2-car rear entry detached garage

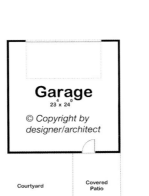

Garage
23'4 x 24'0

© Copyright by designer/architect

First Floor
1,023 sq. ft.

Mbr.
13'4 x 15'8
9'-0" Ceiling

Br.2
10'3 x 10'0

Br.3
10'3 x 10'0

Second Floor
940 sq. ft.

Br.4
11'3 x 11'0

Stor.

Fam.
16'8 x 20'4

Optional
Lower Level
761 sq. ft.

Images provided by designer/architect

Plan #F11-172D-0026

Dimensions: 78'8" W x 43'6" D
Heated Sq. Ft.: 3,223
Heated Sq. Ft.: 2,010
Bedrooms: 4   **Bathrooms:** 3
Exterior Walls: 2" x 6"
Foundation: Walk-out basement standard; monolithic slab, stem wall slab, crawl space or daylight basement for an additional fee

See index for more information

Images provided by designer/architect

Special Features

- This stylish home has many great features including a first floor with an office as well as a secluded living room
- The casual family room is located near the dining area and kitchen
- There's a first floor bedroom, perfect when guests stay over
- The second floor features four bedrooms and a laundry room for convenience
- The optional lower level has an additional 2,010 square feet of living area and offers an additional kitchen, two additional bedrooms, a bath, a family room and dining area creating a separate apartment accessible directly from the outdoors
- 2-car front entry garage

Second Floor
1,633 sq. ft.

© Copyright by designer/architect

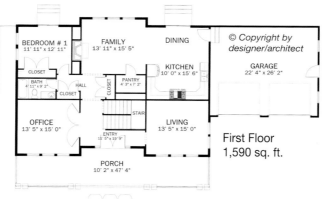

First Floor
1,590 sq. ft.

Optional
Lower Level
2,010 sq. ft.

Plan #F11-056D-0140

Dimensions:	61'8" W x 72'6" D
Heated Sq. Ft.:	2,449
Bonus Sq. Ft.:	649
Bedrooms: 3	**Bathrooms:** 2½

Foundation: Basement standard; crawl space or slab for an additional fee

See index for more information

Images provided by designer/architect

Special Features

- This home channels cottage style living and Modern Farmhouse appeal to create a dwelling that's extremely inviting to come home to
- Enter to a find a cheerful lodge room open to the kitchen with an island and the breakfast area
- The vaulted covered porch will be a wonderful sanctuary anytime of the year thanks to its cozy outdoor fireplace for the colder months
- The remote vaulted master suite will be an oasis for the homeowners with its large pampering bath and tranquil location
- The lower level includes a social room, a card area, an impressive wet bar, a wine pantry, a covered patio with an outdoor fireplace, a lawn and garden garage, a safe room, and optional bedrooms and a bath that can be finished as needed with an additional 649 square feet of living area
- 2-car side entry garage, and a 1-car drive under rear entry lawn and garden garage

Lower Level
649 sq. ft.

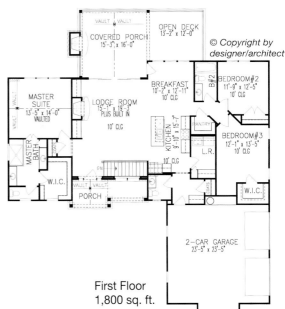

First Floor
1,800 sq. ft.

© Copyright by designer/architect

8' WIDE DECK

| BEDROOM 3 12-0 X 11-6 | KITCHEN/DINING 17-8 X 12-6 | LAUNDRY 14-0 X 6-8 |

CLO

| BEDROOM 2 12-0 X 11-6 | GREAT ROOM 17-8 X 16-0 | MASTER BEDROOM 14-0 X 12-6 |

COVERED PORCH

© Copyright by designer/architect

Plan #F11-028D-0100

Dimensions: 46' W x 42'6" D
Heated Sq. Ft.: 1,311
Bedrooms: 3   **Bathrooms:** 2
Exterior Walls: 2" x 6"
Foundation: Crawl space or slab, please specify when ordering

See index for more information

Images provided by designer/architect

Images provided by designer/architect

Plan #F11-123D-0162

Dimensions: 76' W x 57'4" D
Heated Sq. Ft.: 1,781
Bedrooms: 3   **Bathrooms:** 2½
Exterior Walls: 2" x 6"
Foundation: Slab standard; crawl space, basement or walk-out basement for an additional fee

See index for more information

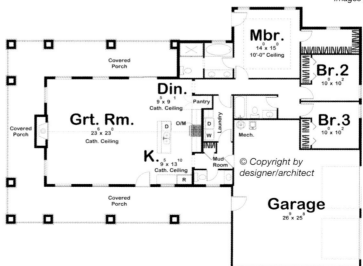

Covered Porch

Mbr. 14 x 15 10'-0" Ceiling

Br.2 10 x 10

Din. 5 x 9 Cath. Ceiling

Pantry

Grt. Rm. 23 x 23 Cath. Ceiling

Laundry

Br.3 10 x 10

Mech.

K. 9 x 13 Cath. Ceiling

Mud Room

© Copyright by designer/architect

Covered Porch

Garage 26 x 25

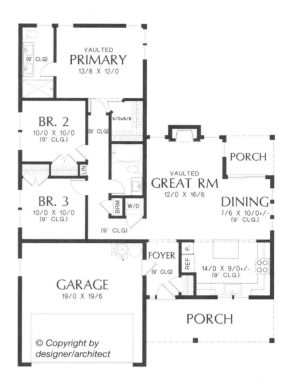

Plan #F11-011D-0676

Dimensions: 40' W x 55'6" D
Heated Sq. Ft.: 1,196
Bedrooms: 3 **Bathrooms:** 2
Exterior Walls: 2" x 6"
Foundation: Crawl space or slab
standard; basement for an additional
fee

See index for more information

Images provided by designer/architect

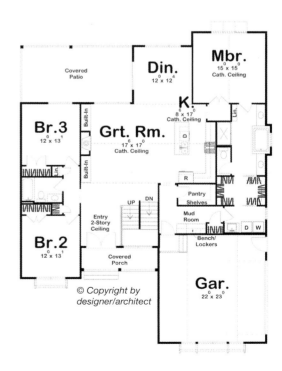

Plan #F11-123D-0156

Dimensions: 53' W x 67' D
Heated Sq. Ft.: 2,015
Bedrooms: 3 **Bathrooms:** 2
Foundation: Basement standard;
crawl space, slab or walk-out
basement for an additional fee

See index for more information

Images provided by designer/architect

Images provided by designer/architect

© Copyright by designer/architect

Deck

Master Bedroom
13'-4" x 12'-6"
8' CLG HGT

Clos

Pan.

Dining/Kitchen
18'-1" x 13'-7"

Bath
CLG HGT

Lin.

Great Room
18'-1" x 15'-4"

Bedroom
12'-4" x 10'-8"
8' CLG HGT

Raised Floor

Closet

First Floor
1,029 sq. ft.

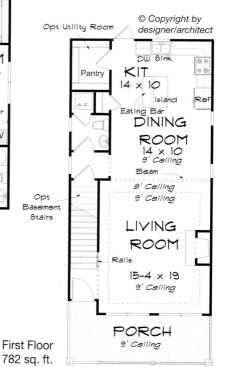

Basement

Optional
Lower Level
1,029 sq. ft.

Unex.

Plan #F11-065D-0457

Dimensions:	35' W x 49'8" D
Heated Sq. Ft.:	1,029
Bonus Sq. Ft.:	1,029
Bedrooms: 2	**Bathrooms:** 1
Foundation:	Walk-out basement

See index for more information

Images provided by designer/architect

BED #1
12 x 15-4
8' Ceiling

GAME ROOM
Opt Bedroom #3
15-4 x 11
8' Ceiling

Rails

Sliding Barn Door

D W

BED #2
10 x 12
8' Ceiling

Second Floor
782 sq. ft.

Opt Utility Room

© Copyright by designer/architect

Pantry

A.C.

DW Sink

KIT
14 x 10

Island

Ref

Eating Bar

DINING
ROOM
14 x 10
9' Ceiling

Beam

8' Ceiling

9' Ceiling

Opt Basement Stairs

LIVING
ROOM
15-4 x 19
9' Ceiling

Rails

PORCH
9' Ceiling

First Floor
782 sq. ft.

Plan #F11-130D-0381

Dimensions:	20' W x 46'6" D
Heated Sq. Ft.:	1,564
Bedrooms: 2	**Bathrooms:** 2½

Foundation: Slab standard; crawl space or basement for an additional fee

See index for more information

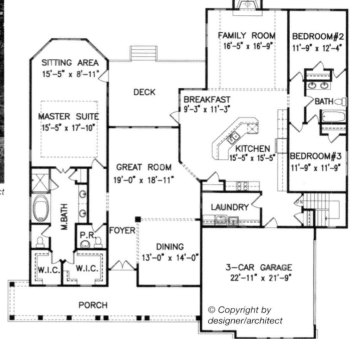

Plan #F11-056D-0049

Dimensions: 69' W x 69'6" D
Heated Sq. Ft.: 2,830
Bedrooms: 3 **Bathrooms:** 2½
Foundation: Basement standard;
crawl space or slab for an additional
fee

See index for more information

Images provided by designer/architect

© Copyright by designer/architect

Second Floor
1,114 sq. ft.

© Copyright by designer/architect

Plan #F11-032D-1053

Dimensions: 56' W x 67'4" D
Heated Sq. Ft.: 3,354
Bedrooms: 4 **Bathrooms:** 3½
Exterior Walls: 2" x 6"
Foundation: Crawl space standard;
basement, floating slab or monolithic
slab for an additional fee

See index for more information

Images provided by designer/architect

First Floor
2,240 sq. ft.

First Floor
1,706 sq. ft.

© Copyright by
designer/architect

Images provided by designer/architect

Plan #F11-065D-0460

Dimensions: 68'3" W x 45'9" D
Heated Sq. Ft.: 1,706
Bonus Sq. Ft.: 1,706
Bedrooms: 3   **Bathrooms:** 2
Foundation: Walk-out basement

See index for more information

Optional
Lower Level
1,706 sq. ft.

Images provided by designer/architect

Plan #F11-056D-0091

Dimensions: 82'7" W x 60'6" D
Heated Sq. Ft.: 2,708
Bedrooms: 3   **Bathrooms:** 2½
Foundation: Basement standard;
crawl space or slab for an additional
fee

See index for more information

© Copyright by
designer/architect

Second Floor
712 sq. ft.

First Floor
1,996 sq. ft.

© Copyright by designer/architect

First Floor
1,667 sq. ft.

Optional Lower Level
1,667 sq. ft.

Images provided by designer/architect

Plan #F11-065D-0462

Dimensions:	55' W x 55' D
Heated Sq. Ft.:	1,667
Bonus Sq. Ft.:	1,667
Bedrooms: 3	**Bathrooms:** 2
Foundation:	Basement

See index for more information

Images provided by designer/architect

Plan #F11-019D-0047

Dimensions:	70' W x 64' D
Heated Sq. Ft.:	2,066
Bedrooms: 3	**Bathrooms:** 2

Foundation: Slab standard; crawl space or basement for an additional fee

See index for more information

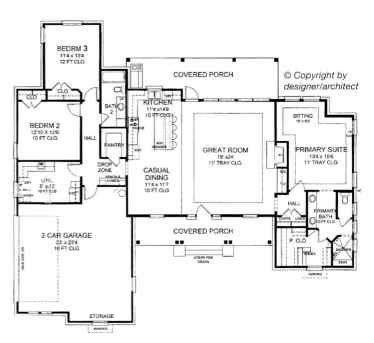

© Copyright by designer/architect

Optional
Second Floor
645 sq. ft.

Bonus
10' x 40'
Cathedral Ceiling

First Floor
2,301 sq. ft.

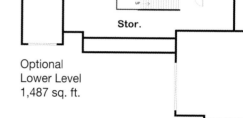

Optional
Lower Level
1,487 sq. ft.

Plan #F11-123D-0148

Dimensions: 76' W x 76' D
Heated Sq. Ft.: 2,301
Bonus Sq. Ft.: 2,132
Bedrooms: 3   **Bathrooms:** 2½
Foundation: Basement standard; crawl space, slab or walk-out basement for an additional fee

See index for more information

Images provided by designer/architect

Second Floor
1,133 sq. ft.

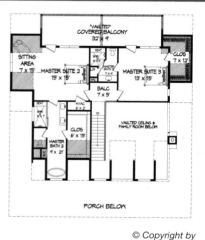

Plan #F11-141D-0415

Dimensions: 49' W x 56'6" D
Heated Sq. Ft.: 2,718
Bonus Sq. Ft.: 1,585
Bedrooms: 3   **Bathrooms:** 3½
Exterior Walls: 2" x 6"
Foundation: Basement standard; crawl space, slab or walk-out basement for an additional fee

See index for more information

Images provided by designer/architect

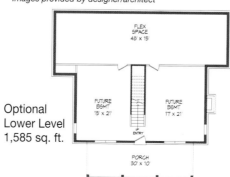

Optional
Lower Level
1,585 sq. ft.

First Floor
1,585 sq. ft.

Optional
Second Floor
856 sq. ft.

Second Floor
1,133 sq. ft.

Plan #F11-139D-0094

Dimensions: 67'7" W x 65'5" D
Heated Sq. Ft.: 2,915
Bonus Sq. Ft.: 856
Bedrooms: 3   **Bathrooms:** 3½
Exterior Walls: 2" x 6"
Foundation: Crawl space standard;
slab, basement, daylight basement
or walk-out basement for an
additional fee

See index for more information

Images provided by designer/architect

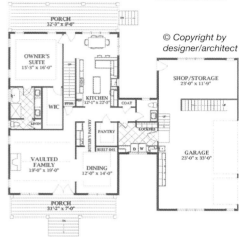

*© Copyright by
designer/architect*

First Floor
1,782 sq. ft.

Images provided by designer/architect

Plan #F11-056D-0129

Dimensions: 80'10" W x 59' D
Heated Sq. Ft.: 2,389
Bonus Sq. Ft.: 1,034
Bedrooms: 3   **Bathrooms:** 2½
Foundation: Slab standard; crawl
space or basement for an additional
fee

See index for more information

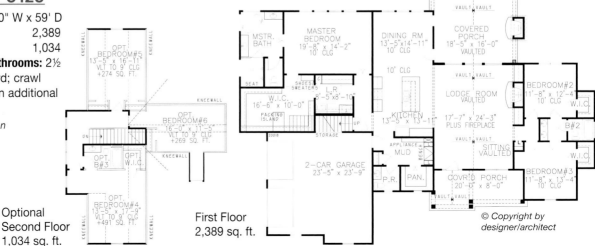

Optional
Second Floor
1,034 sq. ft.

First Floor
2,389 sq. ft.

*© Copyright by
designer/architect*

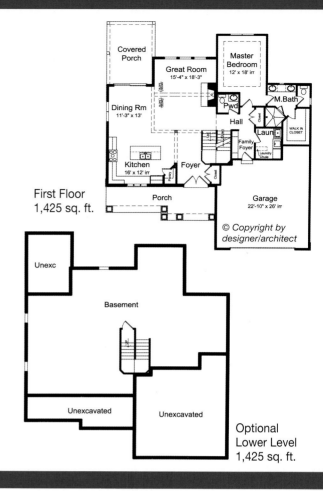

First Floor
1,425 sq. ft.

© Copyright by
designer/architect

Plan #F11-065D-0446

Images provided by designer/architect

Dimensions:	50'6" W x 58' D
Heated Sq. Ft.:	2,094
Bonus Sq. Ft.:	1,425
Bedrooms: 4	**Bathrooms:** 2½
Foundation:	Basement

See index for more information

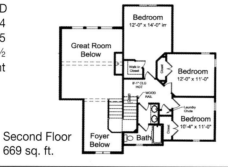

Second Floor
669 sq. ft.

Basement

Optional
Lower Level
1,425 sq. ft.

Plan #F11-087D-1774

Images provided by designer/architect

Dimensions:	52' W x 64' D
Heated Sq. Ft.:	3,187
Bedrooms: 2	**Bathrooms:** 2
Foundation:	Slab

See index for more information

© Copyright by
designer/architect

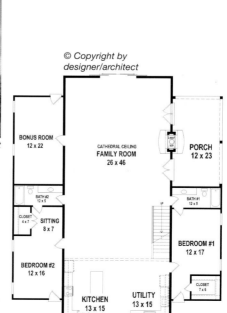

First Floor
2,692 sq. ft.

Second Floor
495 sq. ft.

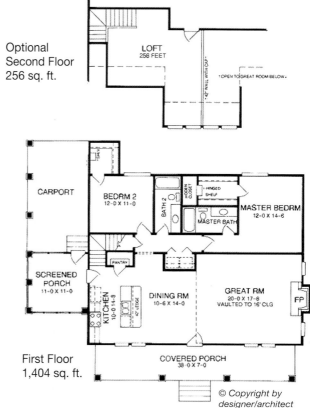

Images provided by designer/architect

Plan #F11-019D-0035

Dimensions: 54'7" W x 46'6" D
Heated Sq. Ft.:   1,404
Bonus Sq. Ft.:   256
Bedrooms: 2   **Bathrooms:** 2
Foundation: Slab standard; crawl space or basement for an additional fee

See index for more information

Optional Second Floor 256 sq. ft.

First Floor 1,404 sq. ft.

© Copyright by designer/architect

Images provided by designer/architect

Plan #F11-065D-0459

Dimensions: 55'4" W x 42' D
Heated Sq. Ft.:   2,700
Bonus Sq. Ft.:   1,400
Bedrooms: 4   **Bathrooms:** 2½
Foundation: Basement

See index for more information

Second Floor 1,300 sq. ft.

© Copyright by designer/architect

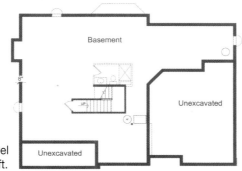

Optional Lower Level 1,400 sq. ft.

First Floor 1,400 sq. ft.

Home Plan Index

Plan Number	Square Feet	PDF File	5-Sets	CAD File	Material List	Page	Plan Number	Square Feet	PDF File	5-Sets	CAD File	Material List	Page
F11-001D-0067	1,285	$889	$889	$1,389	$125	218	F11-026D-2079	1,600	$1,055	-	$1,740	$175	69
F11-007D-0113	2,547	$1,189	$1,189	$1,989	$125	69	F11-026D-2091	1,603	$1,055	-	$1,740	$175	70
F11-007D-0140	1,591	$989	$989	$1,589	$125	118	F11-026D-2092	2,448	$1,105	-	$1,830	-	149
F11-007D-5060	1,344	$889	$889	$1,389	$125	109	F11-026D-2094	1,822	$1,055	-	$1,740	-	226
F11-011D-0579	2,292	$1,452	$1,652	$2,904	$275	94	F11-026D-2099	1,936	$1,055	-	$1,740	$175	178
F11-011D-0617	2,104	$1,495	$1,695	$2,990	$275	131	F11-026D-2134	1,387	$955	-	$1,580	$175	100
F11-011D-0627	1,878	$1,331	$1,531	$2,662	$275	49	F11-026D-2143	1,642	$1,055	-	$1,740	-	89
F11-011D-0630	2,495	$1,525	$1,725	$3,050	$275	118	F11-026D-2149	1,603	$1,055	-	$1,740	$175	57
F11-011D-0650	2,213	$1,574	$1,774	$3,148	$275	229	F11-026D-2158	2,077	$1,105	-	$1,830	-	74
F11-011D-0651	2,492	$1,712	$1,912	$3,424	$275	150	F11-026D-2161	2,437	$1,105	-	$1,830	-	135
F11-011D-0652	2,448	$1,504	$1,704	$3,008	$275	193	F11-026D-2162	1,872	$1,005	-	$1,650	-	196
F11-011D-0653	3,032	$1,709	$1,909	$3,418	$275	169	F11-026D-2167	1,176	$1,005	-	$1,650	$175	255
F11-011D-0657	1,394	$1,143	$1,343	$2,286	$275	15	F11-028D-0064	1,292	$795	$910	-	-	202
F11-011D-0658	2,618	$1,565	$1,765	$3,130	$275	103	F11-028D-0097	1,908	$920	$1,020	-	-	18
F11-011D-0660	1,704	$1,288	$1,488	$2,576	$275	127	F11-028D-0099	1,320	$795	$910	-	-	84
F11-011D-0662	2,460	$1,528	$1,728	$3,056	$275	22	F11-028D-0100	1,311	$795	$910	-	$100	266
F11-011D-0663	2,944	$1,777	$1,977	$3,554	$275	253	F11-028D-0103	1,520	$920	$1,020	-	-	204
F11-011D-0664	2,576	$1,691	$1,891	$3,382	$275	212	F11-028D-0104	2,160	$1,000	$1,110	-	-	220
F11-011D-0666	2,798	$1,652	$1,852	$3,304	$275	193	F11-028D-0108	890	$745	$810	-	-	67
F11-011D-0674	1,552	$1,194	$1,394	$2,388	$275	72	F11-028D-0112	1,611	$920	$1,020	-	-	23
F11-011D-0676	1,196	$1,074	$1,274	$2,148	$275	267	F11-028D-0113	2,582	$1,060	$1,200	-	-	226
F11-011D-0678	2,055	$1,440	$1,640	$2,880	$275	148	F11-028D-0115	1,035	$795	$910	-	-	39
F11-011D-0681	2,577	$1,509	$1,709	$3,018	$275	160	F11-028D-0116	1,120	$795	$910	-	-	145
F11-011D-0682	2,451	$1,465	$1,665	$2,930	$275	143	F11-028D-0117	1,425	$795	$910	-	-	130
F11-011D-0683	944	$958	$1,158	$1,916	$275	123	F11-028D-0118	1,500	$920	$1,020	-	-	216
F11-011D-0684	1,373	$1,132	$1,332	$2,264	$275	144	F11-028D-0119	2,096	$1,000	$1,110	-	-	225
F11-011D-0686	2,009	$1,322	$1,522	$2,644	$275	176	F11-032D-0887	1,212	$1,110	$1,235	$1,710	-	86
F11-011D-0687	1,975	$1,352	$1,552	$2,704	$275	78	F11-032D-0963	1,178	$1,020	$1,145	$1,620	-	156
F11-011D-0692	1,855	$1,261	$1,461	$2,522	$275	58	F11-032D-1032	1,824	$1,255	$1,380	$1,855	-	149
F11-013D-0253	2,943	$1,395	$1,445	$1,895	$195	66	F11-032D-1034	3,164	$1,650	$1,775	$2,250	-	178
F11-013D-0255	2,156	$1,295	$1,345	$1,795	$195	105	F11-032D-1053	3,354	$1,735	$1,860	$2,335	-	269
F11-019D-0035	1,404	$935	-	-	$85	275	F11-032D-1060	3,249	$1,735	$1,860	$2,335	-	133
F11-019D-0047	2,066	$1,895	-	$2,995	-	271	F11-032D-1067	3,599	$1,860	$1,985	$2,460	-	12
F11-019D-0048	2,248	$1,895	-	$2,995	-	142	F11-032D-1069	3,532	$1,860	$1,985	$2,460	-	253
F11-019D-0049	2,766	$1,895	-	$2,995	-	134	F11-032D-1081	1,604	$1,190	$1,315	$1,790	-	34
F11-019S-0009	3,220	$1,995	-	$2,995	-	192	F11-032D-1083	1,617	$1,190	$1,315	$1,790	-	120
F11-020D-0386	2,754	$1,100	$1,230	$2,100	-	165	F11-032D-1107	1,050	$1,020	$1,145	$1,620	-	243
F11-020D-0397	1,608	$900	$1,030	$1,700	-	187	F11-032D-1121	1,178	$1,020	$1,145	$1,620	-	222
F11-020D-0399	1,932	$1,000	-	$1,900	-	246	F11-032D-1123	2,496	$1,325	$1,450	$1,925	-	20
F11-024S-0024	3,610	$3,025	-	$3,025	-	203	F11-032D-1124	2,117	$1,255	$1,380	$1,855	-	206
F11-026D-2013	1,925	$1,055	-	$1,740	-	168	F11-032D-1127	1,512	$1,190	$1,315	$1,790	-	166
F11-026D-2046	2,077	$1,105	-	$1,830	$175	182	F11-032D-1134	2,652	$1,390	$1,515	$1,990	-	190
F11-026D-2072	1,619	$1,055	-	$1,740	$175	77	F11-032D-1135	1,788	$1,190	$1,315	$1,790	-	113
							F11-032D-1137	1,840	$1,255	$1,380	$1,855	-	36

Home Plan Index

Plan Number	Square Feet	PDF File	5-Sets	CAD File	Material List	Page	Plan Number	Square Feet	PDF File	5-Sets	CAD File	Material List	Page
F11-032D-1140	2,965	$1,650	$1,775	$2,250	-	147	F11-056D-0138	2,795	$2,495	-	$3,445	-	134
F11-032D-1141	3,313	$1,735	$1,860	$2,335	-	183	F11-056D-0139	3,830	$1,795	-	$2,845	-	210
F11-032D-1143	1,891	$1,255	$1,380	$1,855	-	24	F11-056D-0140	2,449	$1,495	-	$2,445	-	265
F11-032D-1145	2,814	$1,650	$1,775	$2,250	-	63	F11-056S-0005	3,261	$1,289	-	$2,339	-	258
F11-032D-1146	1,953	$1,255	$1,380	$1,855	-	257	F11-056S-0006	3,171	$1,894	-	$2,944	-	255
F11-032D-1151	2,113	$1,255	$1,380	$1,855	-	128	F11-056S-0008	3,818	$1,295	-	$2,245	-	26
F11-032D-1156	2,080	$1,255	$1,380	$1,855	-	252	F11-056S-0009	3,818	$1,295	-	$2,245	-	152
F11-032D-1158	2,885	$1,650	$1,775	$2,250	-	217	F11-056S-0010	3,795	$2,495	-	$3,545	-	97
F11-032D-1161	2,886	$1,650	$1,775	$2,250	-	227	F11-056S-0012	3,299	$2,495	-	$3,545	-	250
F11-032D-1164	2,041	$1,255	$1,380	$1,855	-	102	F11-056S-0021	3,314	$1,443	-	$2,339	-	223
F11-032D-1165	1,810	$1,255	$1,380	$1,855	-	99	F11-058D-0266	2,176	$625	$560	$725	$80	121
F11-032D-1167	1,914	$1,255	$1,380	$1,855	-	106	F11-065D-0446	2,094	$995	$1,050	$1,650	-	274
F11-032D-1169	1,487	$1,110	$1,235	$1,710	-	140	F11-065D-0457	1,029	$695	$750	$1,000	-	268
F11-032D-1170	1,487	$1,110	$1,235	$1,710	-	55	F11-065D-0459	2,700	$995	$1,050	$1,650	-	275
F11-036D-0242	3,341	$1,685	$1,395	-	-	29	F11-065D-0460	1,706	$895	$950	$1,350	-	270
F11-051D-0926	2,025	$1,234	$979	$1,953	-	26	F11-065D-0462	1,667	$895	$950	$1,350	-	271
F11-051D-0947	1,495	$1,107	$882	$1,744	-	106	F11-076D-0220	3,061	$1,950	$1,200	$2,600	-	214
F11-051D-0956	2,178	$1,234	$979	$1,953	-	163	F11-076D-0286	2,430	$1,600	$995	$2,100	-	180
F11-051D-0960	2,784	$1,352	$1,081	$2,162	-	262	F11-076D-0311	3,786	$1,950	$1,200	$2,600	-	249
F11-051D-0962	3,205	$1,397	$1,112	$2,224	-	130	F11-077D-0019	1,400	$1,300	$1,200	$1,725	$150	104
F11-051D-0977	1,837	$1,188	$949	$1,887	-	141	F11-077D-0288	2,107	$1,465	$1,365	$1,990	$150	121
F11-051D-0978	1,871	$1,188	$949	$1,887	-	90	F11-077D-0293	1,800	$1,465	$1,365	$1,990	$150	29
F11-051D-0979	1,921	$1,188	$949	$1,887	-	30	F11-077D-0294	1,600	$1,425	$1,325	$1,850	$150	132
F11-051D-0982	2,150	$1,234	$979	$1,953	-	199	F11-084D-0085	2,252	$1,195	$1,290	$2,145	-	175
F11-052D-0157	2,067	$989	$989	$1,589	-	165	F11-084D-0090	2,221	$1,195	$1,290	$2,145	-	177
F11-052D-0170	3,290	$1,289	$1,289	$2,189	-	71	F11-084D-0091	1,936	$1,095	$1,190	$1,995	-	230
F11-052D-0171	3,562	$1,289	$1,289	$2,189	-	131	F11-084D-0092	2,366	$1,195	$1,290	$2,145	-	221
F11-055D-0162	1,921	$1,100	$1,200	$2,200	-	250	F11-087D-1682	740	$1,010	$830	$1,090	-	56
F11-055D-0196	2,039	$1,100	$1,200	$2,200	-	248	F11-087D-1774	3,187	$2,016	$1,516	$2,516	-	274
F11-055D-0342	2,445	$1,200	$1,300	$2,400	-	173	F11-091D-0506	2,241	$2,050	$2,250	$2,700	$450	180
F11-055D-0990	2,555	$2,050	$2,150	$4,100	-	244	F11-091D-0508	2,528	$2,050	$2,250	$2,700	$450	256
F11-055S-0115	4,501	$2,050	$2,150	$4,100	-	65	F11-091D-0509	2,886	$2,050	$2,250	$2,700	$450	38
F11-056D-0049	2,830	$895	-	-	-	269	F11-091D-0515	2,837	$2,050	$2,250	$2,700	$450	71
F11-056D-0091	2,708	$1,924	-	$2,874	-	270	F11-091D-0516	2,287	$2,050	$2,250	$2,700	$450	225
F11-056D-0092	3,152	$1,495	-	$2,545	-	133	F11-091D-0518	3,011	$2,050	$2,250	$2,700	$450	27
F11-056D-0095	2,510	$2,295	-	$3,245	-	151	F11-091D-0520	2,751	$2,050	$2,250	$2,700	$450	198
F11-056D-0096	2,510	$2,295	-	$3,245	-	205	F11-091D-0521	2,332	$2,050	$2,250	$2,700	$450	79
F11-056D-0100	2,147	$2,195	-	$3,145	-	188	F11-091D-0522	2,148	$2,050	$2,250	$2,700	$450	220
F11-056D-0104	1,925	$1,245	-	$2,095	-	90	F11-091D-0523	2,514	$2,050	$2,250	$2,700	$450	93
F11-056D-0106	2,407	$1,795	-	$2,745	-	120	F11-091D-0524	2,480	$2,050	$2,250	$2,700	$450	192
F11-056D-0107	2,407	$1,795	-	$2,745	-	100	F11-091D-0525	2,453	$2,050	$2,250	$2,700	$450	148
F11-056D-0128	3,169	$2,195	-	$3,245	-	181	F11-091D-0528	2,743	$2,050	$2,250	$2,700	$450	249
F11-056D-0129	2,389	$1,245	-	$2,095	-	273	F11-091D-0534	3,952	$2,050	$2,250	$2,700	$450	52
F11-056D-0137	2,342	$1,495	-	$2,445	-	161							

Home Plan Index

Plan Number	Square Feet	PDF File	5-Sets	CAD File	Material List	Page	Plan Number	Square Feet	PDF File	5-Sets	CAD File	Material List	Page
F11-091D-0535	3,879	$2,050	$2,250	$2,700	$450	19	F11-123D-0149	2,296	$1,400	-	$1,900	$150	43
F11-101D-0050	4,784	$3,300	-	$5,000	-	98	F11-123D-0150	2,076	$1,400	-	$1,900	$150	215
F11-101D-0062	2,648	$1,650	-	$2,950	-	241	F11-123D-0151	2,461	$1,500	-	$2,000	$150	31
F11-101D-0068	3,231	$2,100	-	$3,600	-	92	F11-123D-0154	1,848	$1,300	-	$1,800	$150	219
F11-101D-0080	2,682	$1,650	-	$2,950	-	45	F11-123D-0156	2,015	$1,400	-	$1,900	$150	267
F11-101D-0089	2,509	$1,650	-	$2,950	-	21	F11-123D-0160	3,042	$1,700	-	$2,200	-	207
F11-101D-0090	2,875	$1,850	-	$3,350	-	167	F11-123D-0162	1,781	$1,300	-	$1,800	$150	266
F11-101D-0093	2,615	$1,650	-	$2,950	-	17	F11-123D-0166	2,075	$1,400	-	$1,900	-	150
F11-101D-0097	2,526	$1,650	-	$2,950	-	87	F11-123D-0171	1,030	$1,000	-	$1,500	$150	183
F11-101D-0113	3,082	$1,850	-	$3,350	-	189	F11-123D-0176	1,797	$1,300	-	$1,800	$150	122
F11-101D-0115	2,251	$1,450	-	$2,750	-	25	F11-123D-0200	3,205	$1,700	-	$2,200	$150	96
F11-101D-0117	2,925	$1,850	-	$3,350	-	83	F11-123D-0202	1,856	$1,300	-	$1,800	$150	152
F11-101D-0121	3,380	$2,100	-	$3,600	-	157	F11-123D-0203	2,083	$1,400	-	$1,900	$150	227
F11-101D-0122	4,966	$3,750	-	$5,450	-	153	F11-123D-0212	3,124	$1,700	-	$2,200	$150	159
F11-101D-0125	2,970	$1,850	-	$3,350	-	129	F11-123D-0222	2,499	$1,500	-	$2,000	$150	174
F11-101D-0126	3,907	$2,550	-	$4,050	-	41	F11-123D-0234	1,589	$1,200	-	$1,700	$150	164
F11-101D-0131	2,889	$1,850	-	$3,350	-	191	F11-123D-0235	3,156	$1,700	-	$2,200	$150	254
F11-101D-0132	3,717	$2,300	-	$3,800	-	32	F11-123D-0236	1,994	$1,300	-	$1,800	-	258
F11-101D-0140	4,626	$3,300	-	$5,000	-	60	F11-123D-0237	2,334	$1,500	-	$2,000	$150	248
F11-101D-0142	2,700	$1,650	-	$2,950	-	242	F11-123D-0239	1,507	$1,200	-	$1,700	$150	196
F11-101D-0143	2,513	$1,650	-	$2,950	-	259	F11-123D-0241	2,835	$1,600	-	$2,100	-	80
F11-101D-0144	2,344	$1,450	-	$2,750	-	260	F11-123D-0242	2,970	$1,600	-	$2,100	$150	213
F11-101D-0145	2,413	$1,650	-	$2,950	-	110	F11-123D-0244	2,627	$1,600	-	$2,100	$150	56
F11-101D-0146	2,346	$1,450	-	$2,750	-	35	F11-123D-0245	2,771	$1,600	-	$2,100	$150	229
F11-101D-0149	2,105	$1,450	-	$2,750	-	37	F11-123D-0246	2,417	$1,500	-	$2,000	$150	251
F11-101D-0150	2,290	$1,450	-	$2,750	-	108	F11-123D-0247	2,719	$1,600	-	$2,100	$150	222
F11-111D-0042	1,074	$995	-	$1,995	-	88	F11-123D-0250	2,318	$1,500	-	$2,000	$150	48
F11-111D-0081	2,137	$1,445	-	$2,445	-	107	F11-123D-0251	2,572	$1,500	-	$2,000	$150	167
F11-111D-0084	2,169	$1,445	-	$2,445	-	123	F11-123D-0253	1,963	$1,300	-	$1,800	-	263
F11-111D-0095	2,458	$1,445	-	$2,445	-	68	F11-123D-0254	2,056	$1,400	-	$1,900	$150	224
F11-121D-0025	1,368	$889	$889	$1,389	$125	169	F11-123D-0255	807	$1,000	-	$1,500	$150	31
F11-123D-0037	2,122	$1,400	-	$1,900	$150	181	F11-123D-0256	2,637	$1,600	-	$2,100	$150	54
F11-123D-0056	1,701	$1,300	-	$1,800	$150	200	F11-123D-0257	2,155	$1,400	-	$1,900	$150	85
F11-123D-0060	1,185	$1,100	-	$1,600	$150	254	F11-123S-0027	4,332	$2,000	-	$2,500	$150	166
F11-123D-0107	2,337	$1,500	-	$2,000	$150	209	F11-123S-0029	3,467	$1,700	-	$2,200	$150	257
F11-123D-0109	2,810	$1,600	-	$2,100	$150	14	F11-123S-0039	3,319	$1,700	-	$2,200	$150	146
F11-123D-0112	1,797	$1,300	-	$1,800	$150	74	F11-123S-0043	3,371	$1,700	-	$2,200	$150	208
F11-123D-0118	1,753	$1,300	-	$1,800	$150	194	F11-123S-0051	3,958	$1,800	-	$2,300	$150	44
F11-123D-0139	1,777	$1,300	-	$1,800	$150	76	F11-123S-0053	3,880	$1,800	-	$2,300	$150	186
F11-123D-0141	2,278	$1,400	-	$1,900	$150	104	F11-128D-0306	1,643	$1,000	$700	-	-	228
F11-123D-0144	2,025	$1,400	-	$1,900	$150	62	F11-130D-0381	1,564	$965	-	$1,260	-	268
F11-123D-0146	2,309	$1,500	-	$2,000	$150	46	F11-130D-0387	1,878	$1,005	-	$1,300	-	109
F11-123D-0147	2,388	$1,500	-	$2,000	$150	112	F11-130D-0389	2,137	$1,025	-	$1,320	-	179
F11-123D-0148	2,301	$1,500	-	$2,000	$150	272	F11-139D-0080	3,263	$1,495	$1,620	$2,995	-	194

Home Plan Index

Plan Number	Square Feet	PDF File	5-Sets	CAD File	Material List	Page	Plan Number	Square Feet	PDF File	5-Sets	CAD File	Material List	Page
F11-139D-0086	4,357	$1,495	$1,620	$2,995	-	154	F11-155D-0142	3,934	$1,650	$1,750	$3,300	-	256
F11-139D-0087	3,409	$1,495	$1,620	$2,995	-	75	F11-155D-0143	2,269	$1,100	$1,200	$2,200	-	160
F11-139D-0088	3,121	$1,495	$1,620	$2,995	-	119	F11-155D-0145	2,031	$1,550	$1,650	$3,100	-	132
F11-139D-0090	2,337	$1,495	$1,620	$2,995	-	28	F11-155D-0147	2,073	$1,350	$1,450	$2,700	-	66
F11-139D-0091	3,163	$1,495	$1,620	$2,995	-	91	F11-155D-0148	1,897	$1,200	$1,300	$2,400	-	197
F11-139D-0093	3,556	$1,495	$1,620	$2,995	-	151	F11-155D-0157	2,112	$1,200	$1,300	$2,400	-	168
F11-139D-0094	2,915	$1,495	$1,620	$2,995	-	273	F11-155D-0159	2,073	$1,350	$1,450	$2,700	-	75
F11-139D-0104	2,716	$1,495	$1,620	$2,995	-	164	F11-155D-0165	1,998	$1,200	$1,300	$2,400	-	195
F11-139D-0106	2,402	$1,495	$1,620	$2,995	-	16	F11-155D-0170	1,897	$1,200	$1,300	$2,400	-	102
F11-141D-0061	1,273	$1,323	$1,554	$2,023	$295	172	F11-155D-0178	2,540	$1,200	$1,300	$2,400	-	224
F11-141D-0202	5,317	$3,073	$3,423	$3,843	-	50	F11-155D-0186	2,113	$1,100	$1,200	$2,200	-	27
F11-141D-0223	2,095	$1,673	$1,904	$2,443	-	89	F11-155D-0210	2,191	$1,100	$1,200	$2,200	-	107
F11-141D-0290	2,227	$1,673	$1,904	$2,443	-	40	F11-155D-0211	3,777	$1,550	$1,650	$3,100	-	218
F11-141D-0292	1,500	$1,323	$1,554	$2,023	-	197	F11-155D-0213	3,246	$1,850	$1,950	$3,700	-	198
F11-141D-0314	5,400	$3,493	$3,843	$4,263	-	82	F11-155D-0232	3,014	$1,650	$1,750	$3,300	-	92
F11-141D-0323	1,787	$1,533	$1,764	$2,303	-	170	F11-157D-0006	2,883	$1,029	$1,134	$2,058	-	70
F11-141D-0326	2,835	$2,093	$2,324	$2,863	-	68	F11-157D-0010	3,287	$1,029	$1,134	$2,058	-	103
F11-141D-0340	1,586	$1,393	$1,624	$2,093	-	153	F11-157D-0023	2,873	$1,029	$1,134	$2,058	-	182
F11-141D-0345	1,972	$1,533	$1,764	$2,303	-	58	F11-159D-0014	2,340	$1,350	$1,200	$2,000	-	73
F11-141D-0349	2,806	$2,793	$3,024	$3,563	-	162	F11-161D-0016	3,275	$1,995	$2,095	$2,795	-	64
F11-141D-0391	1,610	$1,953	$2,184	$2,723	-	259	F11-163D-0018	2,760	$2,450	-	$2,850	-	101
F11-141D-0393	2,569	$1,953	$2,184	$2,723	-	252	F11-163D-0019	2,689	$2,450	-	$2,850	-	91
F11-141D-0397	2,366	$1,813	$2,044	$2,583	-	195	F11-163D-0020	3,306	$2,700	-	$3,500	-	163
F11-141D-0403	3,403	$2,653	$2,884	$3,423	-	161	F11-164D-0044	3,287	$2,137	-	$3,123	-	72
F11-141D-0405	2,365	$1,813	$2,044	$2,583	-	73	F11-167D-0001	2,017	$1,089	$1,089	$1,789	-	119
F11-141D-0415	2,718	$3,213	$3,563	$3,983	-	272	F11-167D-0002	2,063	$1,089	$1,089	$1,789	-	79
F11-144D-0017	1,043	$1,090	$1,215	$1,585	-	78	F11-167D-0003	2,569	$1,189	$1,189	$1,989	-	122
F11-144D-0023	928	$1,040	$1,165	$1,535	$85	247	F11-167D-0005	2,753	$1,189	$1,189	$1,989	-	162
F11-144D-0024	1,024	$1,090	$1,215	$1,585	$95	199	F11-167D-0006	2,939	$1,189	$1,189	$1,989	-	77
F11-144D-0039	2,148	$1,270	$1,520	$1,765	$105	240	F11-167D-0008	3,328	$1,289	$1,289	$2,189	-	184
F11-148D-0396	1,258	$1,273	$892	$1,897	-	223	F11-167D-0009	3,363	$1,289	$1,289	$2,189	-	251
F11-148D-0398	1,390	$1,273	$892	$1,897	-	179	F11-167D-0010	3,409	$1,289	$1,289	$2,189	-	101
F11-148D-0404	1,282	$1,273	$892	$1,897	-	88	F11-169D-0001	1,400	$889	$889	$1,389	-	30
F11-148D-0406	1,512	$1,531	$1,132	$2,346	-	24	F11-169D-0002	1,762	$989	$989	$1,589	-	108
F11-155D-0052	4,072	$2,250	$2,350	$4,500	-	93	F11-169D-0003	1,762	$989	$989	$1,589	-	67
F11-155D-0070	2,464	$1,550	$1,650	$3,100	-	124	F11-170D-0003	2,672	$945	$995	$1,795	-	25
F11-155D-0104	3,421	$1,850	$1,950	$3,700	-	228	F11-170D-0005	1,422	$745	$795	$1,350	-	59
F11-155D-0108	2,860	$1,550	$1,650	$3,100	-	221	F11-170D-0012	2,605	$945	$995	$1,795	-	57
F11-155D-0114	3,414	$2,050	$2,150	$4,100	-	76	F11-170D-0016	3,013	$1,045	$1,095	$1,895	-	28
F11-155D-0116	3,277	$1,850	$1,950	$3,700	-	126	F11-170D-0020	3,626	$1,045	$1,095	$1,895	-	59
F11-155D-0118	3,310	$2,650	$2,750	$5,300	-	105	F11-172D-0008	3,016	$1,350	$1,200	$2,200	-	158
F11-155D-0121	6,301	$2,050	$2,150	$4,100	-	42	F11-172D-0026	3,223	$1,350	$1,200	$2,200	-	264
F11-155D-0129	2,220	$1,350	$1,450	$2,700	-	135	F11-172D-0041	2,313	$1,050	$995	$1,850	-	47
F11-155D-0131	4,140	$1,850	$1,950	$3,700	-	219	F11-172S-0003	4,658	$1,500	$1,300	$2,300	-	51

why buy
stock plans?

Building a home yourself presents many opportunities to showcase your creativity, individuality, and dreams turned into reality. With these opportunities, many challenges and questions will crop up. Location, size, and budget are all important to consider, as well as special features and amenities. When you begin to examine everything, it can become overwhelming to search for your dream home. But, before you get too anxious, start the search process an easier way and choose a home design that's a stock home plan.

Custom home plans, as well as stock home plans, offer positives and negatives; what is "best" can only be determined by your lifestyle, budget, and time. A customized home plan is one that a homeowner and designer or architect work together to develop from scratch, taking ideas and putting them down on paper. These plans require extra patience, as it may be months before the architect has them drawn and ready. A stock plan is a pre-developed plan that fits the needs and desires of a group of people, or the general population. These are often available within days of purchasing and typically cost up to one-tenth of the price of customized home plans. They still have all of the amenities you were looking for in a home, and usually at a much more affordable price than having custom plans drawn for you.

When compared to a customized plan, some homeowners fear that a stock home will be a carbon copy home, taking away the opportunity for individualism and creating a unique design. This is a common misconception that can waste a lot of money and time!

As you can see from the home designs throughout this book, the variety of stock plans available is truly impressive, encompassing the most up-to-date features and amenities. With a little patience, browse the numerous available stock plans available throughout this book, and easily purchase a plan and be ready to build almost immediately.

Plus, stock plans can be customized. For example, perhaps you see a stock plan that is just about perfect, but you wish the mud room was a tad larger. Rather than go through the cost and time of having a custom home design drawn, you could have our customizing service modify the stock home plan and have your new dream plan ready to go in no time. Also, stock home plans often have a material list available, helping to eliminate unknown costs from developing during construction.

It's often a good idea to speak with someone who has recently built. Did they use stock or custom plans? What would they recommend you do, or do not undertake? Can they recommend professionals that will help you narrow down your options? As you take a look at plans throughout this publication, don't hesitate to take notes, or write down questions. Also, take advantage of our website, houseplansandmore.com. This website is very user-friendly, allowing you to search for the perfect house design by style, size, budget, and a home's features. With all of these tools readily available to you, you'll find the home design of your dreams in no time at all, thanks to the innovative stock plans readily available today that take into account your wishes in a floor plan as well as your wallet.

how can I find out if I can **afford** to build a home?

The most important question for someone wanting to build a new home is, "How much is it going to cost?" Obviously, you must have an accurate budget set before ordering house plans and beginning construction, or your dream home will quickly turn into a nightmare. We make building your dream home a much simpler reality thanks to the estimated cost-to-build report available for all of the home plans in this book and on our website, houseplansandmore. com.

Price is always the number one factor when choosing a new home. Price dictates the size and the quality of materials you will use. So, it comes as no surprise that having an accurate building estimate prior to making your final decision on a home plan quite possibly is the most important step.

If you feel you've found "the" home, then before buying the plans, order a cost-to-build report for the zip code where you want to build. This report is created specifically for you when ordered, and it will educate you on all costs associated with building the home. Simply order the cost-to-build report on houseplansandmore.com for the home design you want to build and gain knowledge of the material and labor cost. Not only does the report allow you to choose the quality of the materials, you can also select from various options from lot condition to contractor fees. Successfully manage your construction budget in all areas, clearly see where the majority of the costs lie, and save money from start to finish.

Listed to the right are the categories included in a cost-to-build report. Each category breaks down labor cost, material cost, funds needed, and the report offers the ability to manipulate over/under adjustments if necessary.

Basic information includes your contact information, the state and zip code where you intend to build and material class. This section also includes: square footage, number of windows, fireplaces, balconies, baths, garage location and size, decks, foundation type, and bonus room square footage.

General soft costs include cost for plans, customizing (if applicable), building permits, pre-construction services, and planning expenses.

Site work & utilities include water, sewer, electric, and gas. Choose the type of site work and if you'll need a driveway.

Foundation includes a menu that lists the most common types.

Framing rough shell calculates rough framing costs including framing for fireplaces, balconies, decks, porches, basements and bonus rooms.

Roofing includes several common options.

Dry out shell allows you to select doors, windows, and siding.

Electrical includes wiring and the quality of the light fixtures.

Plumbing includes labor costs, plumbing materials, plumbing fixtures, and fire proofing materials.

HVAC includes costs for both labor and materials.

Insulation includes costs for both labor and materials.

Finish shell includes drywall, interior doors and trim, stairs, shower doors, mirrors, bath accessories, and labor costs.

Cabinets & vanities select the grade of your cabinets, vanities, kitchen countertops, and bathroom vanity materials, as well as appliances.

Painting includes all painting materials, paint quality, and labor.

Flooring includes over a dozen flooring material options.

Special equipment needs calculate cost for unforeseen expenses.

Contractor fee / project manager includes the cost of your cost-to-build report, project manager and/or general contractor fees. If you're doing the managing yourself, your costs will be tremendously lower in this section.

Land payoff includes the cost of your land.

Reserves / closing costs includes interest, contingency reserves, and closing costs.

We've taken the guesswork out of figuring out what your new home is going to cost. Take control of construction, determine the major expenses, and save money. Supervise all costs, from labor to materials and manage construction with confidence, which allows you to avoid costly mistakes and unforeseen expenses. To order a Cost-To-Build Report, visit houseplansandmore.com and search for the specific plan. Then, look for the button that says, "Request Your Report" and get started.

what kind of **plan package** do I need?

5-Set plan package

Includes five complete sets of construction drawings. Besides one set for yourself, additional sets of blueprints will be required for your lender, your local building department, your contractor, and any other tradespeople working on your project. Please note: These 5 sets of plans are copyrighted, so they can't be altered or copied.

8-Set plan package

Includes eight complete sets of construction drawings. Besides one set for yourself, additional sets of blueprints will be required for your lender, your local building department, your contractor, and any other tradespeople working on your project. Please note: These 8 sets of plans are copyrighted, so they can't be altered or copied.

Reproducible masters

One complete paper set of construction drawings that can be modified. They include a one-time build copyright release that allows you to draw changes on the plans. This allows you, your builder, or local design professional to make the necessary drawing changes without the major expense of entirely redrawing the plans. Easily make minor drawing changes by using correction fluid to cover up small areas of the existing drawing, then draw in your modifications. Once the plan has been altered to fit your needs, you have the right to copy, or reproduce the modified plans as needed for building your home. Please note: The right of building only one home from these plans is licensed exclusively to the buyer. You may not use this design to build a second or multiple dwelling(s) without purchasing a multi-build license (see page 287 for more information).

PDF file format

Our most popular plan package option because of how fast you can receive your blueprints (usually within 24 to 48 hours Monday through Friday), and their ability to be easily shared via email with your contractor, subcontractors, and local building officials. The PDF file format is a complete set of construction drawings in an electronic file format. It includes a one-time build copyright release that allows you to make changes and copies of the plans. Typically you will receive a PDF file via email within 24-48 hours (Mon-Fri, 7:30am-4:30pm CST) allowing you to save money on shipping. Upon receiving, visit a local copy or print shop and print the number of plans you need to build your home, or print one and alter the plan by using correction fluid and drawing in your modifications. Please note: These are flat image files and cannot be altered electronically. PDF files are non-refundable and not returnable.

CAD file format

The actual computer files for a plan directly from AutoCAD, or another computer aided design program. CAD files are the best option if you have a significant amount of changes to make to the plan, or if you need to make the plan fit your local codes. If you purchase a CAD File, it allows you, or a local design professional the ability to modify the plans electronically in a CAD program, so making changes to the plan is easier and less expensive than using a paper set of plans when modifying. A CAD package also includes a one-time build copyright release that allows you to legally make your changes, and print multiple copies of the plan. See the specific plan page for availability and pricing. Please note: CAD files are non-refundable and not returnable.

Mirror reverse sets

Sometimes a home fits a site better if it is flipped left to right. A mirror reverse set of plans is simply a mirror image of the original drawings causing the lettering and dimensions to read backwards. Therefore, when ordering a mirror reverse set of plans, you must purchase at least one set of the original plans to read from, and use the mirror reverse set for construction. Some plans offer right reading reverse for an additional fee. This means the plan has been redrawn by the designer as the mirrored version and can easily be read.

Additional sets

You can order extra plan sets of a plan for an additional fee. A 5-set, 8-set, or reproducible master must have been previously purchased. Please note: Only available within 90 days after purchase of a plan package.

2" x 6" exterior walls

2" x 6" exterior walls can be purchased for some plans for an additional fee (see houseplansandmore.com for availability and pricing).

Please note: Not all plan packages listed are available for every plan. There may be additional plan options available. Please visit houseplansandmore.com for a plan's options and pricing, or call 1-800-373-2646 for all current options. The plan pricing shown in this book is subject to change without notice.

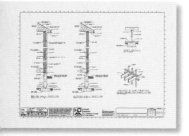

our **plan packages** include...

Quality plans for building your future, with extras that provide unsurpassed value, ensure good construction and long-term enjoyment. A quality home - one that looks good, functions well, and provides years of enjoyment - is a product of many things - design, materials, and craftsmanship. But it's also the result of outstanding blueprints - the actual plans and specifications that tell the builder exactly how to build your home.

And with our BLUEPRINT PACKAGES you get the absolute best. A complete set of blueprints is available for every design in this book. These "working drawings" are highly detailed, resulting in two key benefits:

- **BETTER UNDERSTANDING BY THE CONTRACTOR OF HOW TO BUILD YOUR HOME AND...**

- **MORE ACCURATE CONSTRUCTION ESTIMATES THAT WILL SAVE YOU TIME AND MONEY.**

Below is a sample of the plan information included for most of the designs in this book. Specific details may vary with each designer's plan. While this information is typical for most plans, we cannot assure the inclusion of all the following referenced items. Please contact us at 1-800-373-2646 for a plan's specific information, including which of the following items are included.

1 cover sheet is included with many of the plans, the cover sheet is the artist's rendering of the exterior of the home. It will give you an idea of how your home will look when completed and landscaped.

2 foundation plan shows the layout of the basement, walk-out basement, crawl space, slab or pier foundation. All necessary notations and dimensions are included. See plan page for the foundation types included. If the home plan you choose does not have your desired foundation type, our Customer Service Representatives can advise you on how to customize your foundation to suit your specific needs or site conditions.

3 floor plans show the placement of walls, doors, closets, plumbing fixtures, electrical outlets, columns, and beams for each level of the home.

4 interior elevations provide views of special interior elements such as fireplaces, kitchen cabinets, built-in units and other features of the home.

5 exterior elevations illustrate the front, rear and both sides of the house, with all details of exterior materials and the required dimensions.

6 sections show detail views of the home or portions of the home as if it were sliced from the roof to the foundation. This sheet shows important areas such as load-bearing walls, stairs, joists, trusses and other structural elements, which are critical for proper construction.

7 details show how to construct components such as the roof system, stairs, deck, etc.

do you want to make
changes to your plan?

We understand that sometimes it is difficult to find blueprints that meet all of your specific needs.
That is why we offer home plan modification services so you can build a home exactly the way you want it!

Are you thinking about customizing a plan?

If you're like many customers, you may want to make changes to your home plan to make it the dream home you've always wanted. That's where our expert design and modification partners come in. You won't find a more efficient and economic way to get your changes done than by using our home plan customizing services.

Whether it's enlarging a kitchen, adding a porch, or converting a crawl space to a basement, we can customize any plan and make it perfect for your needs. Simply create your wish list and let us go to work. Soon you'll have the blueprints for your new home, and at a fraction of the cost of hiring a local architect!

It's easy!

- We can customize any of the plans in this book, or on houseplansandmore.com.
- We provide a FREE cost estimate for your home plan modifications within 24-48 hours (Monday-Friday, 7:30am-4:30pm CST).
- Average turn-around time to complete the modifications is typically 4-5 weeks.
- You will receive one-on-one design consultations.

Customizing facts

- The average cost to have a house plan customized is typically less than 1 percent of the building costs — compare that to the national average of 7 percent of building costs.
- The average modification cost for a home is typically $800 to $1,500. This does not include the cost of purchasing the PDF file format of the blueprints, which is required to legally make plan changes.

Other helpful information

- Sketch, or make a specific list of changes you'd like to make on the Home Plan Modification Request Form.
- A home plan modification specialist will contact you within 24-48 hours with your free estimate.
- Upon accepting the estimate, you will need to purchase the PDF or CAD file format.
- A contract, which includes a specific list of changes and fees will be sent to you prior for your approval.
- Upon approving the contract, our design partners will keep you up to date by emailing sketches throughout the project.
- Plans can be converted to metric, or to a Barrier-free layout (also referred to as a universal home design, which allows easy mobility for an individual with limitations of any kind).

2 Easy steps!

1 Visit
houseplansandmore. com and click on the Resource tab at the top of the home page, then click, "How to Customize Your House Plan," or scan the QR code here to download the Home Plan Modification Request Form.

2 Email
your completed form to: customizehpm@designamerica.com, or fax it to: 651-602-5050.

If you are not able to access the Internet, please call 1-800-373-2646 (Monday - Friday, 7:30am - 4:30 pm CST).

helpful **building aids**

Your Blueprint Package will contain all of the necessary construction information you need to build your home. But, we also offer the following products and services to save you time and money during the building process.

Material list

Many of the home plans in this book have a material list available for purchase that gives you the quantity, dimensions, and description of the building materials needed to construct the home (see the index on pages 276-279 for availability and pricing). Keep in mind, due to variations in local building code requirements, exact material quantities cannot be guaranteed. Note: Material lists are created with the standard foundation type only. Please review the material list and the construction drawings with your material supplier to verify measurements and quantities of the materials listed before ordering supplies.

The legal kit

Avoid many legal pitfalls and build your home with confidence using the forms and contracts featured in this kit. Included are request for proposal documents, various fixed price and cost plus contracts, instructions on how and when to use each form, warranty statements and more. Save time and money before you break ground on your new home or start a remodeling project. All forms are reproducible. This kit is ideal for homebuilders and contractors. Cost: $35.00

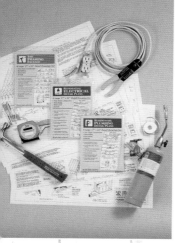

Detail plan packages - Electrical, framing & plumbing packages

Three separate packages offer homebuilders details for constructing various foundations; numerous floor, wall and roof framing techniques; simple to complex residential wiring; sump and water softener hookups; plumbing connection methods; installation of septic systems, and more. Each package includes three dimensional illustrations and a glossary of terms. Purchase one or all three. Please note: These drawings do not pertain to a specific home plan, but they include general guidelines and tips for construction in all 3 of these trades. Cost: $30.00 each or all three for $60.00

Express delivery

Most orders are processed within 24 hours of receipt. Please allow 7-10 business days for standard delivery. If you need to place a rush order, please call us by 11:00 am Monday through Friday CST and ask for express service (allow 1-2 business days). Please see page 287 for all shipping and handling charges.

Technical assistance

If you have questions about your blueprints, we offer technical assistance by calling 1-314-770-2228 between 7:30 am and 4:30 pm Monday through Friday CST. Whether it involves design modifications or field assistance, our home plans team is extremely familiar with all of our home designs and will be happy to help. We want your home to be everything you expect it to be.

before you **order**

Please note: Plan pricing is subject to change without notice. For current pricing, visit houseplansandmore.com, or call us at 1-800-373-2646.

Building code requirements

At the time the construction drawings were prepared, every effort was made to ensure that these plans and specifications met nationally recognized codes. These plans conform to most national building codes. Because building codes vary from area to area, some drawing modifications and/or the assistance of a professional designer or architect may be necessary to comply with your local codes, or to accommodate your specific building site conditions. We advise you to consult with your local building official, or a local builder for information regarding codes governing your area prior to ordering blueprints.

Copyright

Plans are protected under Copyright Law. Reproduction by any means is strictly prohibited. The right of building only one structure from all plan packages is licensed exclusively to the buyer and the plans may not be resold unless by express written authorization from the home designer, or architect. You may not use this plan to build a second or multiple structure(s) without purchasing a multi-build license. Each violation of the Copyright Law is punishable in a fine.

License to build

When you purchase a "full set of construction drawings" from Design America, Inc., you are purchasing an exclusive one-time "License to Build," not the rights to the design. Design America, Inc. is granting you permission on behalf of the plan's designer or architect to use the construction drawings one-time for the building of the home. The construction drawings (also referred to as blueprints/plans and any derivative of that plan whether extensive or minor) are still owned and protected under copyright laws by the original designer. The blueprints/plans cannot be resold, transferred, rented, loaned or used by anyone other than the original purchaser of the "License to Build" without written consent from Design America, Inc., or the plan designer. If you are interested in building the plan more than once, please call 1-800-373-2646 and inquire about purchasing a Multi-Build License that will allow you to build a home design more than one time. Please note: A multi-build license can only be purchased if a CAD file or PDF file were initially purchased.

Exchange policy

Since blueprints are printed in response to your order, we cannot honor requests for refunds.

Shipping & Handling Charges

U.S. SHIPPING

(AK and HI express only)

Regular (allow 7-10 business days)	$30.00
Priority (allow 3-5 business days)	$50.00
Express* (allow 1-2 business days)	$70.00

CANADA SHIPPING**

Regular (allow 8-12 business days)	$50.00
Express* (allow 3-5 business days)	$100.00

OVERSEAS SHIPPING/INTERNATIONAL

Call, fax, or e-mail (customerservice@designamerica.com) for shipping costs.

*　For express delivery please call us by 11:00 am Monday-Friday CST

**　Orders may be subject to custom's fees and or duties/taxes.

Note: Shipping and handling does not apply on PDF and CAD File orders. PDF and CAD File orders will be emailed within 24-48 hours (Monday - Friday, 7:30 am - 4:30 pm CST) of purchase.

Order Form

Please send me the following:

Plan Number: F11-_____

Select Foundation Type: (Select ONE - see plan page for available options).

☐ Slab ☐ Crawl space ☐ Basement

☐ Walk-out basement ☐ Pier

☐ Optional Foundation for an additional fee

   Enter foundation cost here $_____
(see houseplansandmore.com for foundation additional fee)

Choose plan package   Cost

☐ CAD File $_____

☐ PDF File Format (recommended) $_____

☐ Reproducible Masters $_____

☐ 8-Set Plan Package $_____

☐ 5-Set Plan Package $_____

See the index on pages 276-279 for the most commonly ordered plan packages, or visit houseplansandmore.com to see current pricing and all plan package options available.

Important extras

For pricing and Material List availability, see the index on pages 276-279. For the other plan options listed below, visit houseplansandmore.com, or call 1-800-373-2646.

☐ Additional plan sets*:

   _____ set(s) at $_____ per set $_____

☐ Print in right-reading reverse:

   one-time additional fee of $_____ $_____

☐ Print in mirror reverse:

   _____ set(s) at $_____ per set $_____
   (where right reading reverse is not available)

☐ Material list (see the index on pages 276-279) $_____

☐ Legal Kit (001D-9991, see page 286) $_____

Detail Plan Packages: (see page 286)

   ☐ Framing ☐ Electrical ☐ Plumbing $_____
   (001D-9992)   (001D-9993)   (001D-9994)

Shipping (see page 287) $_____

SUBTOTAL $_____

Sales Tax (MO residents only, add 8.2380%) $_____

TOTAL $_____

*Available only within 90 days after purchase of plan.

Name _____
(Please print or type)

Street _____
(Please do not use a P.O. Box)

City _____ State _____

Country _____ Zip _____

Daytime telephone (_____)_____

E-Mail _____
(For invoice and tracking information)

<u>Payment</u>   ☐ Bank check/money order. No personal checks.
   Make checks payable to Design America, Inc.

☐ MasterCard ☐ VISA ☐ DISCOVER ☐ American Express Cards

Credit card number _____

Expiration date (mm/yy) _____ CID _____

Signature _____

☐ I hereby authorize Design America, Inc. to charge this purchase to my credit card.

Please check the appropriate box:
☐ Building home for myself
☐ Building home for someone else

Order online
houseplansandmore.com

Order toll-free by phone
1-800-373-2646
Fax: 314-770-2226

Express delivery
Most orders are processed within 24 hours of receipt. If you need to place a rush order, please call us by 11:00 am CST and ask for express service.
Business Hours: Monday - Friday (7:30 am - 4:30 pm CST)

Mail your order to:
Design America, Inc.
734 West Port Plaza, Suite #208
St. Louis, MO 63146

Helpful tips

☐ You can upgrade to a different plan package within 90 days of your original plan purchase.

☐ Additional sets cannot be ordered without the purchase of a 5-Set, 8-Set, or Reproducible Masters.

Ultimate Book of Modern Farmhouse Plans

SOURCE CODE **F11**